YOUTH TO ELDERLY & ALZHEIMER'S

Sex, Intimacy, Love and Romance in Elderly & Alzheimer's Patients

S. S. Sanbar, MD, PHD, JD
3rd Edition

Publication Details

About the Author

Born in Haifa, Israel, Dr. S. S. Sanbar, is a physician, biochemist, and attorney at law. He is a past President of the American College of Legal Medicine, a past Chairman of the American Board of Legal Medicine, and an Adjunct Professor of Medical Education at the University of Oklahoma Health Sciences Center, Oklahoma City.

He has served in the U.S. Army Medical Corps, first at Fitzsimmons General Hospital, in Denver, Colorado, then in the U.S. Army Medical Corps, U.S. Army Hospital, in Danang, Vietnam. He became a Lt. Colonel and received a Bronze Star Medal Award for his efforts in Vietnam before he was honorably discharged on July 4, 1970.

He is an advocate and has a keen interest in the personal behavioral issues of young and elderly people. His service areas include issues, such as privacy, confidentiality, and the rights of nursing home residents. He also handles highly charged and sensitive matters involving sex, intimacy, love, romance, exercise, driving, gambling, marijuana, opioids, and abuse in the elderly and Alzheimer's sufferers.

He is a prolific author and editor of several books and has published over 200 articles. He is a State, National, and International Lecturer on Legal Medicine and Medical Ethics.

Dedication

For the young and elderly patients with all types of disorders, especially those with Alzheimer's disease and their loved ones, caregivers, and all health care providers.

Acknowledgment

Special thanks to the co-authors of previous editions, Judy Rector and Irene Pearson.

Thanks also to the authors and publishers of the printed materials and online stories for the essays and articles, which are compiled, referenced, and discussed in this novel.

All the character names in this book are pseudonyms.

All the pictures in this book were obtained online, and most of them are linked to their respective sources.

Foreword for 3rd Edition

The 3rd Edition presents extremely important issues about elderly people. Firstly, approximately 47 million adult Americans are probably *Pre-Alzheimer's* – they have no symptoms clinically. Fortunately, many of those *Pre-Alzheimer's* people never develop dementia, but some do. As of yet, treatments are limited.

Secondly, the MIND diet is described. The diet provides the brain with the necessary food to minimize the chances of Alzheimer's dementia.

Thirdly, exercise and physical activity is presented, which, when coupled with a healthy lifestyle, has been shown to deter Alzheimer's.

Fourthly, driving by the elderly is another significant topic. Some elderly people, particularly those who become cognitively impaired, should limit or stop driving altogether; alternatives to driving are discussed.

Finally, the elderly and Alzheimer's patients suffer greatly from excessive medications, compulsive gambling, alcohol, marijuana, and opium abuse, and most recently, from the coronavirus (CO-VID-19) Pandemic.

Foreword for 2nd Edition

Love, intimacy, romance, human relationships, and sexual behavior in the U.S. are the essences of this book, as portrayed by two ladies, Annie and Sherry, who met at a nursing home, where their parents resided. The ladies developed a wonderful, friendly, close, and personal relationship. Annie is a retired businesswoman. Sherry is a psychologist and a journalist, who writes columns for a newspaper. Both ladies are highly knowledgeable, intelligent, and curious to continue to learn and expand their wealth of practical experience and knowledge. In this book, they share their collective knowledge and experiences over the years about human love relationships and conduct.

Annie and Sherry state that love is truly a splendored thing. The words, 'I LOVE YOU' are intimate, passionate, explicit, and formidable. Putting those words in writing lasts a lifetime. Most people write love letters to their special, beloved people, as acknowledgments of endearing relationships and devotion. Others write about love in diaries, blogs, or articles. Love letters and other writings are wells of heartfelt and private memories reflecting the carvings of human emotional fingerprints, while this book is a more elaborated and treasurable version of love letters.

The two ladies expound on all types, definitions, and idioms of love, beginning with Chinese and Greek cultures. They describe romantic, passionate, companionate, unconditional, and other feelings of love. They discuss present, novel, marital, and single (unmarried) adult love relationships in the U.S., including consensual non-monogamous love relationships and polyamory.

Annie and Sherry delve into sex, intimacy, love, and romance in the ever-increasing healthy and vibrant American elderly population. They research and discuss at some length issues of privacy, security, and consent to have intimate relations at home and in nursing homes.

Contents

Page Left Blank Intentionally

Introduction

This novel depicts two ladies, Annie and Sherry. They met at Lakewood nursing home in Wichita, Kansas, where their parents resided. They developed a close friendship. Annie is a retired businesswoman and a widow. Sherry is a semi-retired psychologist and a journalist/author who writes columns for a local newspaper. Both ladies enjoyed great marriages that were joyful, happy, intimate, and loving.

The concerns of Annie and Sherry for their parents lead them to a research project of this book. They conduct research into the scientific literature and Internet sites and take the reader along with them in their venture. Their research provides the reader glimpses into the world of the elderly's intimate relationships. Annie and Sherry became alive through the authors' sensitive and skilled writing about the real-life experiences of people in seeking out their needs for intimacy and sexual expression in the process of destroying myths about such behaviors during the "golden years" of their lives. The moral, philosophical, psychological, and legal issues are addressed in their research.

Elderly couples, affected by dementia, hardly maintain physical intimacy, love, and romance. Some couples prefer non- intercourse, intimate activities over intercourse. The early treatment of sexual dysfunction in Alzheimer's and dementia sufferers may assist partners in modifying activities, behaviors, and expectations about the future of the intimate or sexual relationship. Sexual dysfunction is common in elderly patients with dementia caused by various disorders, such as Parkinson's, Alzheimer's, and Huntington's diseases. The sexual problems may be due to decreased desire, erectile dysfunction, difficulties in reaching orgasm, and sexual dissatisfaction.

Interestingly, Huntington's disease sufferers can exhibit hyper sexuality, pedophilia, promiscuity, and marital infidelity.

Behavioral problems, including inappropriate sexual behavior, are distressing for patients and their caregivers. 'Inappropriate sexual behavior' may be observed in dementia sufferers in the form of either 'intimacy-seeking' or 'sexual disinhibition,' resulting in overt sexual expression. Such inappropriate sexual behavior occurs in the moderate-to-severe stages of

Alzheimer's and dementia diseases. It is often better managed without drugs. To date, there is no well-established treatment for dementia-related inappropriate sexual behavior. Various non-drug and drug treatments may be helpful. Ironically, some patients who are receiving treatment for Parkinson's disease may develop drug-related 'hyper sexuality' and 'delusional

jealousy', which may occur independently or together.

This book demonstrates a deep sense of understanding of the complexities, pain, and emotional, social, legal, and psychological challenges that children and adults, especially patients, caregivers, families, and staff of senior citizen facilities face daily in dealing with Alzheimer's and dementia patients. All of these concerns have been addressed through the two leading women in this book; Annie and Sherry. The treatment of sex and intimacy in this book is clear and direct, but a rather sensitive subject is presented through the conversations between these two women; who experienced the needs and transformation of their loved ones from a happy, productive, and loving life to an alienated, misunderstood, and humiliating life.

Annie

Once in a lifetime, one meets a truly genuine friend, a great human being, utterly respectful of herself and others. Annie is a widow in her late 60's. She does not seek a definition from any person she is with. She does not expect her friends to read her mind. She is a strong lady, most capable of articulating her needs. Her strength of character is so powerful that it makes her friends admire her, and most of her yearnings and expectations come true. She knows love, teaches how to love, and gives love. She recognizes that her love has great value and should be reciprocated by family and close friends. She does not take love for granted. Love resides in and around her. It never disappears from her life. She is an inspiring woman. She regards her lifelong knowledge and experiences as valuable lessons in understanding herself. She is simply a phenomenal, fabulous, and fantastic woman.

Annie has impressed everyone around her with her beauty, demeanor, and intelligence. She has blue eyes, blond hair, and off-white skin that tans easily. She is extraordinarily gifted and well-rounded.

Sherry

Sherry is a witty, interesting, and dual professional lady. She has a Ph.D. in clinical psychology and a Master's degree in journalism. She retired from her full-time practice as a clinical psychologist at the age of 61, two years before the writing of this novel. She follows and treats a handful of patients with psychological problems at her home. She also works part-time as a columnist for a local newspaper in Wichita, Kansas. Her father, John, is 83. He is suffering from advanced Alzheimer's disease. He resides at Lakewood nursing home in Wichita. He rarely has visitors other than his wife and daughter. Most of his buddies have already passed away.

Sherry visits her father at the nursing home quite regularly, three times a week. Her dad seems to look forward to her visits. Her mother, Barbara, is disabled and essentially housebound. She suffers from heart disease and severe, crippling, advanced degenerative arthritis. Fortunately, her mind is intact. She has had right knee and shoulder replacements. She is tired of joint surgeries and the prolonged post-operative rehabilitation. Because of her precarious physical condition, she visits her husband infrequently, about once a month.

The Origin

In late September, Sherry had a productive day at her newspaper office. She was elated. She had completed the first of five-part columns dealing with Alzheimer's patients for the newspaper. She was concerned about her father's Alzheimer's condition and worsening dementia. That afternoon, she decided to leave work early and visit her father at the nursing home.

She collected her handbag and a copy of her new article to review at home and show it to her 'cheerleader' husband, Mortimer. He was always eager to read Sherry's columns and make encouraging remarks. He always exhibited an enthusiastic and genuine interest in her writings and gave her compliments profusely.

It was a warm and humid day. Sherry left the newspaper office building and walked to an adjacent garage where her new white Ford C-Max hybrid car was parked. The car was a surprise 63rd birthday present from Mortimer, a dream come true for her. She got into her hybrid car and began driving toward Lakewood nursing home. It was already the beginning of the rush hour. She did not mind taking her sweet time driving slowly in the lane far-right and enjoying the scenery. It was a beautiful day in late September. Her mind soon turned to an extremely important matter for her – clothing. She started thinking about her winter wardrobe, what to wear, and what she needs to shop for. It won't be too long, she thought, before she needs to wear warmer clothes in the upcoming cold months. Sherry loved the month of September for three good reasons – she was born in that month; she has a wonderful loving husband; she is a writer. Whenever an occasion arises, she reminds her friends and acquaintances that September has been designated, among many others, as "Love Note Day" and "Be Kind to Editors and Writers Month". To her, September is a "mellow month," as described by Harvey Schmidt and Tom Jones in their famous 1960s song.

Sherry arrived at Lakewood nursing home just before supper time. She parked her car and got out, shut the door, and started walking toward the entrance to the nursing home. She pressed the car lock button on the remote and strolled, admiring a variety of colorful flowers surrounding the grand entrance. The entrance was indeed grand with impressive columns supporting an enormous *porte cochere*, large enough to accommodate four large vehicles. Sherry looked across the street and noticed an ambulance picking up a lady on a gurney from the Lakewood adult care center. She was curious to see what was going on and who that person was. She paused for a moment. The gurney was lifted by two young attendants and securely placed in the back of the ambulance. The back doors were closed. Further, the ambulance was driven slowly about 500 feet and parked under the *porte cochere* (carriage porch) of the Lakewood nursing home, close to where Sherry was standing. Her curiosity increased exponentially.

The journalist inside her was fully awakened and alert. Her eyes were wide open. She was soaking everything in sight and every movement that was going on. The ambulance personnel opened the back doors, jumped into the back, untied the gurney, lifted it out of the ambulance, and placed it on the pavement. Only the lady's face was visible. She appeared to be thin and pale. Sherry noticed another lady and a gentleman walking across the street from the adult care center. The couple stopped by the side of the ambulance. The lady was stunning with gorgeous clothing – a colorful top, silk pants, and white shoes. She had golden hair, blue eyes, and mildly tanned skin. She looked fabulous and had a nice smile on her face. She held sunglasses in one hand and had an exquisite name-brand white purse on her forearm. The gentleman was tall and handsome looking, with brown hair, brown eyes, and tanned skin. He was neatly dressed in a blue shirt, dark blue pants, and black shoes. Sherry's curiosity had reached a boiling point and was overflowing. She felt compelled to slowly approach the attractive couple. When she got close to the couple, she stopped for a moment, saying nothing.

Then she managed to muster enough courage to say in a most pleasant voice, "Good afternoon."

The couple looked at her and answered almost in unison, *"Good afternoon to you."*

When the couple responded so nicely together, Sherry breathed a sigh of relief. She introduced herself, saying, *"I'm Sherry."*

"I'm Annie. It's nice to meet you, Sherry. Do you happen to work at this nursing home?" replied Annie.

"No, I'm here to visit my dad." Sherry extended her right arm toward Annie, hoping to shake hands. Annie did not hesitate to raise her arm and shake Sherry's hand. Sherry then turned to the gentleman to shake his hand.

He responded, shook hands with her, and said, *"I'm Chris. Pleased to make your acquaintance, Sherry."*

Sherry turned her head toward the lady on the gurney and asked Annie, *"I presume she is a relative of yours?"*

"Yes, she is my mother, Lucy," said Annie.

Sherry asked, *"How long has she been residing at the Lakewood adult care center?"*

Annie answered, *"A little over two years."*

Sherry asked, *"And why are you moving her to the nursing home now?"*

Annie said, *"She has very advanced Parkinson's disease and dementia. She can no longer care for herself. She needs more attention and full nursing home care."*

Sherry said, *"I'm sorry to hear that. It must be hard on you."*

Annie said, *"Thank you. Tell me about your dad. How long has he been residing at the nursing home?"*

"About six months," said Sherry. *"Why is he living here?"* asked Annie. Sherry answered, *"He has advanced Alzheimer's disease and dementia."*

Annie said, *"I'm sorry, too. It seems that we have something in common. Our parents have terrible diseases of dementia."*

Sherry said, *"My Dad was diagnosed with Alzheimer's disease about seven years ago. He has gradually gotten progressively worse. My mother took care of him for over six years at home until he became very difficult to handle. My mother is 83 years old. She is disabled. My Dad was wandering around the neighborhood and getting lost. The neighbors had to bring him back home. So, he had to be admitted to the nursing home."*

"Does he like this nursing home?" asked Annie.

Sherry said, *"Sometimes he does, but at other times, he complains that it is better to be at home with my mother."* *"I hope to meet your father,"* said Annie.

"Please do come and visit him. Which room will your

mother be in?" Sherry asked.

"It's room number 128. You're welcome to visit her whenever you want," said Annie.

Sherry said, *"Yes, I shall do so."*

Annie's mother was taken inside the nursing home to her room. Annie and Chris bid Sherry goodbye and followed Lucy. Chris carried a small bag containing some of Lucy's clothes and personal belongings. Sherry went to visit her dad. She was very excited about the new acquaintances. She felt like she had known the couple for quite some time. The three of them connected very well on their first meeting.

Chapter 1
Types of Love and Relationships

Love

Love is a truly magical emotional ecstasy. The words, *'I Love You,'* reflect sentiments of intimacy, passion, intimidation, and unequivocalness. The impression of these words on a piece of paper lasts a lifetime, for it holds unparalleled value. Love is a sensation that has been engraved in our brain right from the time of our birth. Although it is well-understood that as human beings step into the various phases of life, they tend to develop feelings of affection and intimacy. This intimacy can connect them to a sheer acquisitive thing, an animal, or another being.

True Love

True love creates attachments through passionate energy between lovers. Strong emotional, physical, and mental connections are formed through physical contact, as well as conscious and subconscious vows, agreements, and spoken and unspoken promises. Lovers experience memorable experiences and events. They connect from a place of higher level by giving love, gratitude, and compassion to complete their love relationship in the highest of ways. The love relationship evolves into a connection and union of higher love and understanding. The lovers demonstrate a true and special union because they do not expect anything back in return. Their love becomes unconditional, and the two lovers become truly whole. Neither do they tend to extract worldly means or desires from them, nor do they attempt to inflict constant changes in their lover!

Expressing Love

The human mind is so composed and concise that even today, we have not been able to interpret the love of our very creator in its precise intellect; a creator whom we have known and learned about since the time we first acquired the wisdom to think and question, yet we struggle to understand His ways and plot. Nevertheless, we expect the same understanding that we ourselves actually lack, from another individual, only because we claim to love them and expect the same kind of emotions from them. Love has to be created, developed, and rekindled all the time to keep it fresh and innovative. Some of the most common expressions of love that we expect to hear from our loved ones, or we tend to deliver to those we love, are made by communicating or offering them gift-wrapped presents that illustrate love.

The most common expression that young lovers tend to say is, 'I want to spend a lifetime with you, to grow old with you, and to cling close to you until death parts us.' However, we also have some lovers expressing themselves like, 'Love drives me on, and makes my heart flutter'; 'I love you, and I'm obsessed with you so much that every time I see you, I want to fall in love with you all over again.

'I feel that there's an intimacy between us, which allows me to be openly expressive to you regarding anything; I feel that our souls are one'; 'I feel the need to have you beside me most of the time; being with you makes me feel desirable, belonging, complete and protected'; 'I think of you every second and every minute of my life; it is as though our love continues to mature and nurture no matter what circumstances we might be exposed to. It is as profound as the sea and just as boundless.'; 'In health and in sickness, I wish to always hold you close to me; physically and emotionally too'; 'You are now a significant part of my life, and it feels absolutely great to wake up knowing that I have your presence to cherish; you brighten my mornings and pacify my nights'; or 'You are pure and simple beauty; you mean the world, you mean everything to me.'

Greek Terminology of Love

With reference to the Greek terminologies of Love, the distinguished sense of love in every phase and aspect of life becomes clear and inclusive. Ancient Greeks acknowledged four types of love, which are discussed here.

"Stoege" is natural affection, kinship, or acquaintance, such as that felt by parents for offspring.

Annie and Sherry are two really dear friends, who met at a nursing home while their parents were suffering through diseases due to dementia. That was the first thing that they had in common; the affliction of their parents and the torment it was bringing upon them. However, one month after admitting her mother in the nursing home, Annie bore the loss of her mother. Annie truly recognizes that her love has great value and should be reciprocated by family and close friends. She does not take love for granted. Once, while narrating her family life to Sherry, Annie speaks about how her mother raised her up and relentlessly expressed, out of maternal love to her. In her own words, Annie says, "As time went on, Mom's dementia was really bad. She was talking about seeing people, mostly family members, who had been dead for years. Mom had always been very sharp and alert. She was quite smart. I watched my Mom suffer for two long years in the nursing home before she passed away. But during all that time, she never failed to tell me that she loved me. Every night before I left her, she would always say, "I love you, you know I do"."

"Philia" is the feeling of affection in close friendships and with companions. Philia denotes composed virtuous love. It includes loyalty to friends, family, and community, while it entails honesty, equality, and understanding.

Sherry inquired about Annie's husband's demise and said, "Your husband must have been very supportive of you." Upon this, Annie replied, "My Johnny was the ideal husband. He was always supportive, gentle, kind, loving, sensitive, and most considerate of my emotions. There was little that he could do when I had a problem to alleviate my feelings right away or alter my situation. But, he simply kept quiet, respected my privacy, and left me alone to do what I wanted until I felt better. Johnny and I had an incredibly strong marital relationship, and we worked closely together. We were perfectly compatible as a couple."

She continued, "My Johnny was taken away from me too soon. I loved him so, and I still do. No man can ever replace him."

"Eros" means the search for beauty and sexual or romantic desire. It depicts passionate love, with sensual desire and longing. Eros is initially felt for a person. With contemplation, it becomes an appreciation of the beauty within that person, or it even becomes the appreciation of beauty itself.

Upon curiosity of knowing their relationship, Annie insisted that Sherry told her about her husband, so Sherry went on, saying, "Well, I am 63 years of age, and yes, very happily married. My husband and I have a great loving and sexual relationship. I have always felt that love, intimacy, and sex are basic needs that transcend the aging process. Sherry also said, "We both communicate every chance we get, mostly by phone or text, and sometimes even by email. I firmly believe that communication between partners throughout the day and spending time doing non-sexual things together enhance intimacy and bring the couple closer together."

"Agape" is the bestowal of love and affection for the divine powers. It is a self-emptying or divine love. For instance, Christians believe, "Whoever does not love, does not know God, because God is love." [1 John 4:8, New International Version, NIV].

Here's a brief narration concerning *Agape* love:

"I knew that no matter what door you knock on in a Cretan village, it will be opened for you. A meal will be served in your honor, and you will sleep between the best sheets in the house. In Crete, the stranger is still the unknown god. Before him, all doors and all hearts are opened. Night had already begun to descend as I entered the village. Upon thinking a lot, I thought I should go to the priest's home, where all strangers find refuge. Christ lives in their hearts, and sometimes they see Him with their eyes, if not by the pillow of a wartime casualty, then sitting beneath a flowering almond tree in springtime."

A woman came out from a small door, and upon my request, she guided me to the priest's house. *"Thank you, my fine woman,"* I said. *"Sorry to bother you. Good night."*

I knocked on the priest's door, and I heard heavy steps in the yard. The door opened; standing in front of me was an old man, and without interrogating about who I was or what I wanted, he extended his hand. The man said. *"Welcome. Are you a stranger? Come in."*

I heard voices as I entered. Doors opened and closed, and several women slipped down hastily into the adjoining room and vanished. The priest had me sit down on the couch and then said, *"My wife is a little disposed; you'll have to excuse her. But I myself will cook for you, lay the table for your supper, and prepare a bed so that you can sleep."*

His voice was heavy and afflicted. I looked at him. He was extremely pale, and his eyes were swollen and inflamed, as though by weeping. But no thought of a misfortune occurred to me. I ate, slept, and in the morning, the priest came and brought me a tray of bread, cheese, and milk. I held out my hand, thanked him, and said goodbye. *"God bless you, my son,"* he said. *"Christ be with you."* The next moment I left, and at the edge of the village, an old man appeared. He asked me, *"Where did you spend the night, son?"* I replied, *"At the priest's house."*

The old man sighed. *"Ah, the poor fellow. And you didn't catch wind of anything?"* Upon hearing such a question, I surprisingly asked, *"What was there to catch wind of?"*

Soon the man said, *"His son died yesterday morning. His only son. Didn't you hear the women lamenting?"* However, I told him that I absolutely heard nothing at all, for what was true. So, he responded, *"They had him in the inner room. They must have muffled their laments to keep you from hearing and being worried. Pleasant journey!"*

Upon hearing the sad reality, my eyes filled with tears, and so the man asked me in astonishment, *"What are you crying for?"* Without me having to say anything further, he said to me, *"Oh, I see; you're young, and you haven't gotten used to death yet. Pleasant journey!"*

Chinese Conceptualization of Love

- *Benevolent love* is a core concept of *Confucianism*, which developed from the teachings of a Chinese philosopher, Confucius. This concept emphasizes the duty to care about different people in different degrees via actions.

- *Universal love* is a concept of *Mohism*, which was an influential, philosophical, and religious movement that flourished during the Warring States era of ancient China. It stresses that love should be unconditional and offered to everyone without expecting even the slightest bit in return.

- *Passionate caring love* is regarded as a fundamental desire in Buddhism, which adopted the concept of '*Ai*', the traditional Chinese character for love. It is similar to the Western concept of love.

Categories of Love
Interpersonal Love

There is no universal definition of 'LOVE'. Humans express love interpersonally in the form of positive sentiment with romantic overtones. Interpersonal love is closely associated with interpersonal relationships. Love facilitates relationships among people, family members, close friends, acquaintances, creative artists, and couples with a deep, enduring, and strong attachment to each other. Love also acts as a safety measure by which humans protect each other from dangerous situations and propagate the species.

Unrequited Love

Love may be one-sided, called unrequited. Such love is not openly reciprocated, returned, or understood by the beloved. The beloved may either be unaware of the admirer's romantic affection or may consciously disapprove and reject it.

Impersonal Love

In contrast to interpersonal love among humans, impersonal love arises out of unselfishness, a compassionate approach, and intense feelings toward life, material objects, animals, activities, and strong spiritual or political convictions.

Sexual Fetishism and Paraphilia

There are situations where impersonal feelings toward non- humans involve unusual and intense sexual passion and arousal, which is generally referred to as sexual fetishism. However, extreme sexual attraction, passion, and arousal to non-humans are considered abnormal and are labeled as sexual deviation or 'paraphilia'.

Erotomania

When an individual, who is often suffering from a psychotic or bipolar disorder, believes that another secret admirer is in love with him or her, such as a famous person or a stranger, it represents a delusional psychological disorder referred to as Erotomania, also called 'de Clérambault's syndrome.' The deluded individual imagines the perceived affection by various means and returns it by unexpected and often unwanted letters, phone calls, gifts, and visits.

Poetic Deliverance of Love

Pablo Neruda wrote the following in Sonnet XVII in Spanish:

"I love you without knowing how, or when, or from where. I love you straightforwardly, without complexities or pride; so I love you because I know no other way

than this: where I does not exist, nor you,

so close that your hand on my chest is my hand, so close that your eyes close as I fall asleep."

Triangular Interpretation of Love

Under the triangular theory, love can be understood having three components, each of which manifests a different aspect of love.

- *Passion* – that leads to romance, physical attraction, sexual consummation, and desires in a relationship aboding with love.

- *Intimacy* – feelings of closeness, connectivity, warmth, and attachment in loving relationships. It is the most strongly predicted couple satisfaction.

- *Commitment* – a promise or vow, in the long term, to maintain love without wandering anywhere else.

These three aspects of love generate several possible kinds of love when considered in combination, including:

- *Infatuation* which involves passion;

- *Liking someone* which involves intimacy;

- *Empty love* which involves commitment;

- *Fatuous love* which involves passion and commitment;

- *Romantic love* which involves passion and intimacy;

- *Companionate love* which involves intimacy and commitment; and

- *Consummate love* which involves all three components.

The three components of love interact with each other, but no relationship is likely to be a pure case of only one of them. For example, greater intimacy may lead to greater passion or commitment, just as greater commitment may lead to greater intimacy, or with lesser likelihood, greater passion. In general, the components are separable but interact with each other. Although all three components are essential parts of loving relationships, their importance may differ from one relationship to another.

Basis of Love

Love is a natural and biological drive, which is as powerful as hunger or thirst. It results from chemical reactions in the brain, involving norepinephrine and dopamine. Oxytocin is another brain hormone that causes a decrease in stress response and an increase in feelings of attachment. At the beginning of a romantic relationship, Oxytocin surges and then becomes relatively stable throughout the love relationship. The higher the surge of Oxytocin, the greater the likelihood for couples to stay together. Oxytocin also helps increase positive interpersonal behaviors, such as trust, humanity, and empathy.

Overestimation of love leads to discouragement. The desire to possess the partner results in the partner wanting to escape. The quality of a love relationship may be determined by two factors:

- romantic attraction based on genes and culture

- emotional maturity

People who fall in love report higher feelings of self-worth and self-effectiveness than those who do not. Men tend to seek healthy women of childbearing age to become the mother of offspring.

They tend to be susceptible to youth and beauty. In contrast, women may seek men who are willing and can take care of them and their children. They tend to be more susceptible to status and security. Compatibility is something that one creates. It is the critical stew of traits and personal characteristics that matter dearly to humans, such as listening to doubts, celebrating triumphs, sharing laughter, and jumping in the car for impromptu getaways. Compatibility is a lifelong process of negotiation, pillared by the willingness to work, a positive attitude, and a pleasant disposition. As traits and personal characteristics are being developed, the term 'Chemistry' is often used as an element of a good relationship. Couples connect and interact chemically and embrace each other in a positive light. They build acquaintance, discover, and respect each other.

Love Values

Values run very deep and are vital, including finances. Apparent values, such as sports, travel, and epicure food and drink do not matter as much. The biggest reason people get separated or divorced is distancing. The most contented couples are those with excessively healthy views of and respect for each other without inquiring about the love between them. They know things about each other that no one else does. They share common interests, disagree on an emotional consideration, and are willing to compromise on mutual understanding.

Chapter 2
Unconditional Love

The Origin of Unconditional Love

The most powerful words that any person can say to his beloved are:

"I shall always love you, unconditionally."

A quote by Talidari is widely known and appreciated by many authors, which expresses that,

"Unconditional Love is not the case of being blinded by love but rather the resolution that nothing is more important than love."

In 1997, Elisabeth Kübler-Ross wrote a quote in The Wheel of Life, and its modified form says,

"The ultimate lesson all of us have to learn is unconditional love, which includes not only others but ourselves as well."

Furthermore, Denise Hill made it prominent that,

"Unconditional love is a gruesome, painful and sacrificial way to care for another human being. It isn't

butterfly kisses, a steamy night of passion or the joy a son brings to his mother's heart. It is so much deeper than that. It is endless. It is profound. It's powerful."

Barrie Davenport stated in the renowned, *Unconditional Love: The Key to Lasting Relationships*:

"Within the relationship itself, unconditional love is the ability to love the other person as they are in their essence. If you have fallen in love with this person and want to build a lasting relationship with them, then you must view them as a unique individual — not as an extension of yourself."

The majority of the time, we do not love people unconditionally. But an essential ingredient of a lasting relationship is unconditional love. If you do love someone unconditionally, take a moment to tell that person that you do. That beloved person maybe your child, parent, sibling, spouse, relative, friend, or significant other. Tell that person freely, honestly, and truthfully without any hesitation, for it would only require a few expressions of love such that; '*My love to you is infinite and measureless.'* More often, when the other person feels burdened and pressurized under your complaints and demands, maybe you could make the situation better by providing reassurance, saying, *'What I say to you is an act of my feelings for you without the need for a reward.'*

Significantly noteworthy is the need to make it known to your beloved that you do not desire any alteration in their personality and character, but instead, you love and respect their originality for which you fell in love with them saying, *'My love to you stands apart from all other types of love, I love you unconditionally in your essence, as you are, no matter what you do or fail to do.'*

The Prominence of Unconditional Love

It is inherent in our genes to love deeply, limitlessly, and passionately. But unconditional love is partly learned. An exceptional illustration of unconditional love is the mother's bond with her offspring. I always remember my mother fondly on Mother's Day. I vividly remember her affection and dedication to her five children. Her devotion, love, and affection were without limitations, conditions, illusions, or expectations. It was complete, boundless, and invariable love. It was true love between her and every one of her children. Like most children these days, I did not appreciate or comprehend what unconditional love was. I had to grow up and learn about it as an adult.

Unconditional love is not established on specific outcomes. It is most closely equated to 'Agape' love, which is defined as the selfless love of one person for another without sexual implications. But it requires action. It is more than a feeling of love. The lover strives for the well-being and happiness of the beloved person by acting with love. Love is given freely under all conditions and circumstances, without regard to the beloved's choices and actions. It is more about what the lover gives and not what he/she expects to receive from the beloved. Learning to love unconditionally is an excellent way to achieve inner peace.

It implicates loving with a comprehension of the other person, what causes them to pulsate; not attempting to change who they are, but having total acceptance of the person that they are. It is certainly not an attribute that will perfectly come to you on its own, but it is instead learned and practiced over time. Even though it takes a whole lot of time to adapt and acquire, it is also true to understand that love is actually perfect in its own imperfections. To be able to offer unconditional love, one should be able to initially recognize, accept, and absolve his own faults, flaws, imperfections, and shortcomings. Then one can truly love unconditionally by helping the beloved grow by knowing they are loved. When the beloved says something hurtful, the lover may inform them but must always forgive and accept that person without control. An excellent daily routine is to do something small but special for a loved one, a friend, or acquaintance without expecting anything in return. Do it privately and quietly, and watch your love expand and grow. You may call, email, text, or send a letter to someone. Keep a smile on your face. Say nice things to people and try to find something to give them a compliment sincerely on a piece of good news about them or their family members.

During tough periods of growth when pain, discomfort, and suffering are pronounced, make your beloved happy and comfortable; soothe them with love, kindness, and empathy. Be genuinely supportive and truthful when protecting their feelings in the face of adversity or financial difficulty. Confront dire situations, such as illnesses and financial crises, with zest and eagerness to work harmoniously and come up with reasonable and acceptable solutions to the problems at hand.

This concept needs understanding "too", that there need to be boundaries for two people to exist healthily in a reciprocal and loving partnership. Without conditions, one will likely find themselves in an emotional free-fall, as in zero gravity.

Unconditional Love V/s Unconditional Relationships

Jeremy Nicholson distinguished unconditional love from unconditional relationships as follows: "Unconditional Love is very important. When you find someone who loves you for 'who you are' through dating, it is an incredible experience.

Similarly, it is rewarding to love someone else 'as they are.' I certainly believe that such a bond is priceless and should be nurtured with great affection. On the contrary, relationships are an entirely different thing. They are operational partnerships. They involve contemplations, motives, and resolutions. They require two or more individuals in communication, commitment, and mutual exchange."

Relationships Require Attention

To love unconditionally is a long-term personal and conscious choice that is learned and practiced, such as loving children. It is a true kind of love that requires action, attention, a great deal of thought, and trust.

I am a grandmother who adores my grandchildren. I am incredibly proud of all of them. It is true that grandparenting is much more fun than parenting. Indeed, I do miss having my own children at home. I miss hugging them daily, loving, and parenting, as well as disciplining them. But now, I am grateful to be a grandmother who deeply loves and enjoys her grandchildren. It is such a wonderful feeling to occasionally pick them from school, have them over to visit, watch them practice and play their games of sports, attend their graduation, and so on and so forth.

My teenage grandchildren are developing their own interests and friends. Fortunately, my children inherited great values and further provided the grandchildren with loving support and a solid foundation of exemplary parental guiding principles. My job is to sit back and enjoy them. Occasionally, I offer some words of wisdom as an experienced grandparent but mixed with a degree of mentoring or advice. My grandchildren love to talk, while I am always 'all ears' and very eager to listen. I have all the time in the world to dedicate and contribute toward them. I love to hear them talk about themselves, their school, their friends, their social media pictures and stories, and what car they like to drive when they are 16. If I cannot see them in person, I encourage them to talk to me on Skype or FaceTime. I love to engage with them in something that they love doing, too, like when they talk on their phones.

My grandchildren slightly deviate from the ordinary modern U.S. teenagers who are obsessively fond of smartphones. They do not just like communicating through social media conversations, but they also love and adore the idea of receiving cards, notes, and letters. So, I try to write to them as often as I can, especially on their birthdays, holidays, in sickness, or whenever I feel the urge to write to them. They love to hear stories about their parents, upcoming trips, holidays, jokes, hobbies, and school events, projects, and friends; that is precisely what my duty as a grandmother is.

Affection and unconditional love can make children emotionally happier and free of stress, according to a study from the University of California, Los Angeles. The study found that a lack of parental cordiality can make children more stressed, since parents already pressurize them a little too much to succeed, without balancing the necessary burden with affection. It eventually leads to health risks for children, like high cholesterol, cardiovascular issues, and high blood pressure. However, if provided with unconditional parental love and affection, children are less likely to face those health risks.

Unconditional love makes children physically healthier. Parental affection and attention contribute to the child's physical well-being. A study from the McGill University of Montreal explains that children under authoritative parents who are success-demanding and less affectionate are more likely to be obese than children whose parents often show affection.

This is because such demanding parents tend to tell their children that they are eating the wrong kind of food but not explain why. This tends to lead the children into becoming destructive and acting against their parents' will, just to prove to them that a certain unexplained statement from the parent does not mean anything. Hence, it does not affect their life. Such studies authenticate an aspect that seems to be impulsive, which shows just how important nurturing parents are in shaping adaptive human beings. Children exhibit positive emotions from early childhood when their mothers show affection rather than dictating ways to play with the child. Regardless of culture, status, or circumstances, the fact that children need to feel loved has not changed over the centuries, and neither will it ever change.

Ways to Harvest Unconditional Love

In 2016, Aha! Parenting noted that healing a parents' ability to

love their children takes daily attention and commitment, by following certain steps to unconditional love:

- **Forgive Yourself for not being Perfect** – For unconditional love means dropping that list of ways you need to be different before you are good enough in your own eyes. Your goal is to love yourself and others at the same time.

- **Unconditional Love is like a Muscle, which**

Desires Daily Workout – Compassion is the substantial elation of life. If you could choose compassion while interacting with everyone, including yourself. You would see for yourself that you were progressive by the end of the month

- **If You Want to Wake up Jazzed about the Day Ahead; Commit to Radical Self-Care** – We all know that when we can stay connected to our internal fountain of well-being, it overflows onto our children. And we become more patient, loving, and joyful parents.

- **Heal Your Childhood** - If you desire to liberate your heart, you have to heal your old wounds.

- **Love Unconditionally when You're Angry** - Anger and punishment never exist in love. Maybe you can now move your game up a notch and commit to parenting from love and not from anger.

- **Take the High Road** – Seek positivity, excellence, and motivation; establish goals and always aim for better in life.

- **It wasn't a Crime to Make Mistakes as a Parent** – All you have to do is stay contemporary and choose love instead of fear.

- **Secrets to Love Your Child Unconditionally** – Unconditional love is not just what we feel. It is what the object of our love feels: love without strings attached.

- **Practice Makes Perfect** – Research shows that repeated experience actually rewires our brains. Healing our ability to love unconditionally requires daily practice, as we catch the curved balls of life.

Reconstruction of Confidence in a Dilemma of Love

There often arise situations when you need to help your loved ones feel confident about themselves or re-establish poise and intellectual stability in dealing with troubles, distress, or any unexpected situations. If you can understand a few concepts of handling such dilemmas, you can very well deliver the same understanding in a better manner to your beloved too. Initially, the idea that there is no greater foundation for confidence than unconditional love is significantly essential to absorb and lay as a concrete base. Under any such sudden traumatic condition, try to take yourself away from the toxic situation, and acknowledge the factor that destroyed your confidence. No matter what the situation may be, you always need to remember the person who you were before your confidence was destroyed; because self-confidence and self-reassurance lie within. You are truly the same wonderful person; to attain a guarantee in such a situation, you should always mingle and engage with the people who admire you, seek inspiration in you, and think that you are awesome.

Seeking recourse to your mentors and friends whom you trust implicitly, for help, is always a safe and great idea. You must ensure that you have all your goals, aims, and ambitions written down; understand that even though it will take time and that it is a long journey, it is still worth walking this way and fulfilling every little bit that you plotted throughout. This is the kind of reassurance that you could seek refuge in and also make your beloved feel comforted with.

Love Needs Reassurance

In 2016, Carol Mary, a blogger, contributed a poetic elucidation that one may want to dedicate to their beloved in times of deep trouble, and here is an extract:

"Don't quit.

When things go wrong as they sometimes will, When the road you're trudging seems all up hill, When the funds are low and the debts are high, And you want to smile, but you have to sigh, When care is pressing you down a bit, Rest if you must, but don't you quit.

Life is queer with its twists and turns, As every one of us sometimes learns, And many a failure turns about

When he might have won had he stuck it out; Don't give up though the pace seems slow-- You may succeed with another blow, Success is failure turned inside out--

The silver tint of the clouds of doubt,

And you never can tell how close you are, It may be near when it seems so far;

So stick to the fight when you're hardest hit--

It's when things seem worst that you must not quit."

Love Does Not Entail Reciprocation

David K. William stated that;

"Love that has no expectations cannot be betrayed. Betrayal is only possible when an exchange is expected."

Expectation will undeniably lead your love into betrayal. There are certain ways to follow to avoid betrayal in your relationship. If you can do these things and have no expectation for any particular outcome, it is a glorious sign of emotional maturity, and you turn out to be a better person and take the reins in a certain relationship.

There are some ways that can aid humanity to learn to love without expecting. As humans, we have a selfish attribute of expecting the same, or either too much for ourselves, whenever we invest our efforts into another being. However, this should not be the case; you ought to forget your personal investment in the person you love or in that relationship. Learn to love yourself first, totally and unequivocally. Believe and have faith in the good intentions of the person you love. Respect and treat that person like a gentleman or lady, with dignity; make sure to voice your love and affection openly to them.

Find more and more reasons to smile, laugh, and spend time with that person. While doing so, exhibit greater emotions of compassion and understanding. Be a listening ear to them when they need it the most, a shoulder to cry on or someone to uplift their spirits, and also encourage and support them whenever you can. Perhaps, you could surprise them with deeds of kindness when they least expect it.

Moreover, you must clearly abstain from criticizing, whining, nagging, or complaining all the time; clearly ensure not to blackmail or manipulate them to do your bidding, for it is absolutely unhealthy and sickening. When you initially promised to accept that person just the way he/she is, you need to stop underlining that person's flaws or things that upset you about them too much. In fact, cultivate a thick skin in the relationship, knowing that challenges are an inevitable part of life; stay calm, collected, and keep working on making your relationship better.

Nevertheless, if there is certainly a necessary problem or issue that needs to be addressed, talk transparently and face to face with that person about what's bothering you; ensure to be truthful and honest in your interaction with them. And while you give them the chance to speak, carefully listen to what they have to say with an open mind. Do not lie or cheat on them, do not keep unnecessary secrets from them, and do not shift blame to heap it on them. Instead, take responsibility for your own actions. If you are the one to be accountable for any mistakes in the relationship, apologize, and learn from them and make amends when appropriate. Simultaneously, learn to forgive offenses committed by the other person, too, and move on. Life is too short to hold on to grudges and be unhappy.

If you truly love them, hold them in great respect and esteem in front of others, too, especially your family. Hence, it is your responsibility to protect and defend him/her always. You can undoubtedly express your affection physically as well, for it is healthy to maintain intimacy and physical affection between two souls as well as bodies. Lastly, just be positive to celebrate that person when they are in your life, and let them go when they leave.

Love Grants Inner Peace

Inner Peace is an attribute of humanity and aspect of life that every person yearns for. Without inner peace, unconditional love is challenging to achieve. Also, remember that the possession of material riches is like dying of thirst while bathing in a lake, so it is safer and wiser to develop a sense of inner peace.

Inner Peace is a State of Mind

In any situation, first relax, then think carefully and act. Inner peace develops over time. Be smart, stay calm, and be careful with your inner peace. Soothe and replenish your spirit! Sit quietly to free and empty your mind of thoughts. Rest frequently in a comfortable spot to unwind, relax, or take a nap. Inner peace is achieved by doing a job that one enjoys or loves. Be curious to try things out and see what your loved one thinks of them. This produces a natural peace that arises within and leads to greater success than if one has a lot of inner turmoil.

Simplicity in Life

Use limited to-do lists and boundaries. This brings inner peace, well-being, and places harmony in life. Know that you have to say "No" at times to diminish stress and produce better results. Let go of biases and expectations, let go of the need to control! Be open to experience and consider only what is at hand. Be happy and make time to do the things that help you secure that happiness; satisfy your desires, indeed. Take pride in your individuality and accept yourself unconditionally for who you are. You deserve to love your strengths, weaknesses, and all that is good about yourself.

Acceptance of Others

While accepting yourself, also make sure to accept others with their looks, behaviors, and beliefs. This brings inner peace and tranquility. Acceptance places oneself in a better position to take action, if and when it becomes necessary.

Acceptance produces a feeling of stillness inside, seeing more clearly, and focusing on appropriate actions to alter unpleasant situations.

Practicing forgiveness of others and yourself, and letting go of the past, which includes the correction of our misperceptions, are essential to healing the suffering caused by inner turmoil.

Forgiveness frees the individual seeking inner peace from such agony. Every individual makes mistakes, for we are not as perfect as God. All you need to do is admit when you are wrong.

Focus on the positive in life to remain peaceful and in control. Warm your heart by being pleasant, kind, and courteous, and caring for others. See the beauty in everyone and everything, instead of what is wrong and negative.

Insecurity – It creates a false image of oneself. Think about or listen to a song that will keep you busy and at peace. Look at the bright side, regardless of how silly it may seem. Be sure to stick to a positive mind, for it is your choice, belief, and thought that make or break "you." When you really feel the urge to speak about such insecure feelings, while knowing it is wrong and may cause your loved one to be disappointed upon learning, then maybe you can talk to your *"Best Friend,"* whom you trust with anything that is bothering you and about your inner feelings.

Chapter 3
Close Friends Love

Friendship

Friendship is infamously hard to define. For Aristotle the Greek philosopher, friendship or *philia* is a virtue 'most necessary with a view to living, for, without friends, no one would choose to live though he had all other goods.' For a person to be friends with another, he says, 'It is necessary that they bear goodwill to each other and wish good things for each other, without this escaping their notice.'

A person may bear goodwill to another for one of three reasons; that they are good, that is, sensible and righteous, that they are pleasant, or that they are beneficial. While Aristotle leaves room for the idea that relationships based on benefit alone or desire alone can give rise to friendships, he believes that such relationships, to a lesser extent, can be termed as friendships than those based partly or wholly on virtue. 'Those who wish good things to their friends for the sake of the latter are friends most of all, because they do so because of their friends themselves, not coincidentally.' Friendships that are based partly or wholly on virtue are desirable not only because they are related to a higher degree of mutual benefit, but also because they are associated with companionship, reliability, and confidence. In such a friendship, it is more important to exercise reason and virtue, which are the distinguishing functions of human beings, and which, in Aristotle's system, amount to happiness.

Love

If friendship is hard to define, love is even more so, not least because there are several types of love. The one commonly present in modern minds is **eros**, which is sexual or obsessive love. In Greek myth, it is a madness brought about by one of Cupid's Arrows. The arrow fissures us, and we 'fall' in love. In modern times, *eros* has been incorporated with the broader life force, something similar to Schopenhauer's will, a fundamentally blind process of striving for existence and replication.

Until perhaps the 19th Century, people thought of love more in terms of *'agape'* than *eros*.

Agape is universal love, such as the love for foreigners, nature, or God. Also called charity by Christian thinkers, it can be said to include the modern concept of 'altruism,' which means unselfish concern for the well-being of others. *Agape* helps to build and maintain the psychological, communal, and relatively environmental materials that protect, endure, and nurture us. Concerning the inclining fury and disunion in our society, we could all make do with the more old-fashioned *agape*.

There are also other types of love, most remarkably **storge** and **pragma**. *Storge* or familial love is the love between parents and their offspring. More widely, it is the fondness born out of familiarity or dependency, and unlike *philia* or *eros*, it does not depend on our personal potentials. People in the early stages of a romantic relationship often expect unconditional *storge*, but find only the objectifying *eros*, and, if they are fortunate, a certain degree of *philia*. Over time, *eros* often mutates into *storge*, and if we are lucky, there is some *philia* as well.

Pragma is concrete love, based on reason or duty and one's longer-term interests. Sexual attraction takes a back seat in favor of personal potential, compatibilities, and common goals. In the days of arranged marriages, *pragma* must have been quite common. Although outdated, it remains prevalent, most visibly in certain high-profile celebrity and political pairings.

Discovery of Love in Your True Friend

This book depicts two adult women, Annie and Sherry; daughters of demented patients. Annie and Sherry are in their sixties and develop a meaningful friendship. They met at the Lakewood nursing home in Wichita, Kansas, where their parents resided. They developed a close friendship. Both ladies enjoyed great marriages that were joyful, happy, deliciously sexy, intimate, and loving.

Nevertheless, love was always an essential aspect of their life, and they never took it for granted. Annie's first true love was Johnny. He was her soul mate. He adored and loved her unconditionally. They met in high school when Annie was 14, and Johnny was 17. They instantly knew that they were meant for each other. They dated for two years, then they got married at Annie's home. They were madly in love.

Like most newlywed young couples, Annie and Johnny initially struggled to make ends meet. Instead of going to college, they had to work after finishing high school. They were both highly capable of entering college and becoming professionals. Johnny got a job with the government, which helped not only with income but also with health insurance. After three years of marriage, Annie and Johnny were most fortunate to have their only child, a lovely son, James. When James finished high school, they made sure he had an opportunity to go to college. They made absolutely certain that their only child attained higher education. Despite his reluctance early on, James did attend college and graduated with a Master's degree.

Annie and Johnny were inseparable. They were devoted to each other and was the love of her life. They constantly traveled on business and vacation trips. He always followed through the commitments he made to Annie. He would say "I'm sorry" and "forgive me" when he made a mistake, which was rare. He always discussed household responsibilities with Annie. He sought consultation from her on home and work decisions.

Johnny told Annie frequently how well she dressed and how gorgeous she looked. He initiated fun family outings for the relatives and friends on the spur of the moment. Johnny honored Annie in public and encouraged her to be herself as an individual and pursue her own interests, talents, and hobbies.

Annie had the shock of her life when Johnny suddenly developed cancer and died within a few months at 67. Her life began to deteriorate rapidly. A year and a half later, Annie's father passed away, and about three years later, her mother died. Fortunately, she had a nice son, a lovely daughter-in-law, an adorable grandson, and Johnny's siblings and their families to support her. But life was never the same after Johnny died. Annie confronted numerous challenging hurdles and disappointments.

Certainty of Your Feelings Concerning Your Friend
You Daydream about Them

If you are sitting around thinking about your friend in class or at work, you have feelings for them. "Romantic fantasies when you are apart" are a massive giveaway. Your heart beats faster when you see them, know you are going to see them, or hear from them. Basically, if you cannot stop thinking about them, it means you have got it bad for them.

You are Madly Jealous

When you have "envious feelings" about a friend, you are crushing. A relationship coach and psychic medium Cindi Sansone-Braff, the author of *Why Good People Can't Leave Bad Relationships*, tells us: It can often strike hard when you find out that your friend is in a relationship, or if they get into something new as your friendship unfolds. Here is how the scenario goes: "You thought he or she was just your friend, and you loved talking with this person and hanging out with him or her, but then you find out he or she is in a relationship, and all of a sudden, you start feeling jealous," she says.

You might even go as far as destructively affecting their relationship. "You start sabotaging their relationship in subtle and non-subtle ways," she says. "For instance, if he tells you that she seems to be too busy to see him, you start filling his head with a million motives why she just might not be that into him. At this point, you need to come forward and admit your true feelings for this person, even if it means losing the friendship, or you need to back off from this person altogether," Sansone-Braff says.

They Look at You in a Funny Manner

Danielle Sepulveres, sex educator and author of *Losing It: The Semi-Scandalous Story of an Ex-Virgin*, tells us, "Strong eye contact that results in a vibe that feels almost palpable, even if you're not reciprocating" can mean that your best friend wants to become a boyfriend or girlfriend. "They go out of their way for you more than necessary, and there's a thoughtfulness that almost feels surprising," she says. "They listen and remember things that you have said that even you yourself have forgotten." After all, this is someone who is already loyal, supports, and loves you through good times and bad. If there is a certain glint in their eye, this may mean they are into you, paying close attention.

You Can't Wait to See Them

If you are dying to see your friend at all hours of the day, and secretly perhaps, they feel the same, you want something more. Rob Alex, who created *Sexy Challenges and Mission Date Night* with his wife, says, "I have had lots of great friends, but there is a magic in the air when that friendship moves to something stronger." Although you might not be sure at first, when you get to know, you know it. "You will start making up excuses to go see that special friend, you start remembering tiny details of when you are together, and when you look at each other, there is more of a deep soul connection that just a passing glance," Alex says. And the rest is history if his marriage is any indication.

You Want to Make Out

New York-based relationship expert and author April Masini tells us, "When you want to make out with and sleep with a friend, that's no longer a friend." That line is crossed, not when you act on your feelings, but when you simply feel them.

Watch out, though: *"Those feelings of lust create dishonesty — you start criticizing your friend's boyfriend or girlfriend, sometimes without even realizing, because you want to be that person, and you're jealous of that relationship,"* Masini says. *"The minute you've got sexual feelings toward a friend is the minute they're more than just that."* Fess up or give the friendship some time to chill. Otherwise, you will probably just wind up acting like a freak.

Wish to Sleep with Them

Sansone-Braff also tells us that when it reaches this point, it is already too late to put out the flames. *"Here's where you have to figure out if this person could turn out to be a friend with benefits, or if this could turn into a real relationship,"* she says. Or, of course, there is a third option; your friend might want to just be a friend, in which case a little dose of acceptance needs to come into play. *"Being honest about your feelings is necessary in all relationships, but in this instance, truth telling is paramount, or you can find yourself giving each other a lot of mixed messages that could ruin your friendship and your chances for a real relationship in the future,"* she says. Again, coming clean is vital – unless you know there is no chance of romance, in which case, backing off is wise.

You Feel Butterflies

That feeling you get when you are around them is a confirmed giveaway, Kia Grant, Lovapp's relationship correspondent, tells Bustle. Not only do you feel all tingly every time you see them, Grant says, but there are also other factors at play. "You want to spend as much time with them, of course," she says. When you find yourself getting territorial, give some serious thought to your feelings for this person.

You Think and Feel about Them Differently

Somewhere along the line, the way you think and feel about this person changed. *"You enjoy being around them in a way that is unlike from how you are with your other friends,"* psychologist Nikki Martinez tells us. *"You see abilities in them, others don't, and when something happens, good or bad, you automatically want to tell that person about it."* They are the first one you want to talk to in the morning, and the last you want to speak with at night. *"They are the first one that comes to mind that you want to share with,"* Martinez says.

The Way You Touch Changes

Although you have not made an actual move, and neither have they, if you are analyzing the way you physically interact with your pal, something is afoot. *"Your physical habits, even if not sexual, are changing,"* Armstrong says. *"You have moved from quick hugs to kisses on the cheek, hugging for longer periods of time to flirtatious touching,"* he says. Not only that but if it feels natural, get ready. When this type of more intimate touching happens on both sides and is "prevalent, natural and reciprocated," your friend likely feels the same, he says.

Can't Ever Get Enough

Take a look at yourself if this is the case, Sansone-Braff says, *"You used to be happy talking to this person once or twice a week, but now you find that he or she is your go-to person and you want to talk every day."* Whatever the case may be, speak up. If they feel the same way, awesome. If not, think about the next steps. *"You can still choose to be friends, if you can handle it, or you might choose to separate before you get your heart ripped out when this person falls in love with someone else, and you have to bear witness to this,"* she says.

"Accidental" Touching Becomes Constant

Maybe you do not mean to do so, but do you find your hand brushing your friend's arm a little too much. "The strongest relationships usually start as friendships, so the lines can get a bit blurred at times," dating expert Noah Van

Hochman tells us. *"However, proximity is the great indicator."* So if you are touching a lot, beware! *"If your movements always seem to bring you into just rarely obvious contact with one another, it is a sign enough of being more than friends."*

You're Texting Recurrently

"You are texting more frequently, and at all hours of the night," Armstrong says. Maybe you used to check in with your pal every few days, but now you are sending *"good morning"* and *"night-night"* texts. "Who we think about is who we connect with when we are alone," Armstrong says. If they are reciprocating, there is a good chance that something is building up.

Your Friendship Fluctuates in Elusive Ways

"The two of you wind up talking a lot and ignoring anyone else around," Tina B. Tessina, aka Dr. Romance, psychotherapist and author of *Love Styles: How to Celebrate Your Differences*, tells Bustle. *"You start touching each other in a new way: He puts his hand on your shoulder, you touch his arm."* Or perhaps, you are interacting in other ways, they check in with you to see if you are going

somewhere, Tessina says. Regardless of whether this guy or gal has expressly divulged feelings for you, there is a strong possibility that they exist.

You Talk about Them almost All the Time

In addition to the fact that you daydream about them, you do not flinch at the thought of being close, and you prefer to be with them than to be isolated when you are in a bad mood. As other experts have said, the biggest sign you are worrying about your pal is that you are a total motor-mouth about them when they are not around. If you are continually finding ways to work them into discussions with other friends, life coach Kali Rogers tells Bustle, the romance bug has already attacked.

They Call You Something Sweet

This one applies more to a situation where you have initiated dating a friend, but you are unsure where things stand between the two of you. "A great sign to watch for is how the person addresses you," Samantha Daniels, a professional matchmaker and founder of The Dating Lounge dating app, tells us. "If he or she claims you to be their girlfriend straight out, then it is evident. However, if they use a pet name that has a romantic implication, like 'my baby', 'baby', 'my sweetheart', 'my babe'; that is a good signal," she says. That said, if you are being introduced to your maybe-new-partner's friends as something vague, it might be time for a heart-to-heart. "If the pet name is 'my buddy', 'my bestie', 'my number one'; that is more of a sign that you are still in the friend-zoned," Daniels says.

Friendship-Oriented Love is Eminent

Andrew Sullivan, at Brain Pickings, writes:

"For me, friendship has always been the most accessible of relationships, certainly far more so than romantic love.

Friendship, I learned, provided a buffer in the interplay of emotions, a distance that made the risk of intimacy bearable, a space that allowed the other person to remain safely another person."

He argues that our world has failed to give friendship its due as *"a critical social institution, as an ennobling moral experience, as an immensely delicate but essential interplay of the virtues required to sustain a fully realized human being."* And yet, he concedes, the cultural silence around friendship also reflects an inherent truth about the nature of the bond itself:

You can tell how strong the friendship is by the silence that envelops it. Lovers and spouses may talk frequently about their "relationship," but friends tend to let their regard for one another speak for itself or let others point it out.

Reflecting on the tragedy of loss that prompted his meditation, Sullivan adds:

"A part of this reticence is reflected in the moments when friendship is appreciated. If friendship rarely articulates itself when it is in full flood, it is often only given its due when it is over, especially if its end is sudden or caused by death.

Suddenly, it seems, we have lost something so valuable and profound that we have to make up for our previous neglect and acknowledge it in ways that would have seemed inappropriate before... It is as if death and friendship enjoy a particularly close relationship, as if it is only when pressed to the extreme of experience that this least extreme of relationships finds its voice, or when we are forced to consider what really matters, that we begin to consider what friendship is. "

Friendship, for Aristotle, seems to be the cornerstone of human society and flourishing, an integral part of happiness and bound up inextricably with the notion of virtue. For Aristotle, the defining feature of friendship was the trifecta of reciprocity, equality, and the physical sharing of life. Sullivan tackles the first element:

"Unlike a variety of other relationships, friendship requires an acknowledgement by both parties that they are involved or it fails to exist. One can admire someone who is completely unaware of our admiration, and the integrity of that admiration is not lost; one may even employ someone without knowing who it is specifically one employs; one may be related to a great-aunt whom one has never met (and may fail ever to meet). And one may, of course, fall in love with someone without the beloved being aware of it or reciprocating the love at all. And in all these cases, the relationships are still what they are, whatever the attitude of the other person in them: they are relationships of admiration, business, family, or love. "

However, friendship is different. It uniquely requires mutual self-knowledge and will. It takes two competent, willing people to be friends. You cannot impose a friendship on someone, although you can impose a crush, a lawsuit, or an obsession. If friendship is not reciprocated, it simply ceases to exist, or more accurately, it never existed in the first place.

Perhaps, more challenging to grasp is the condition of sharing in one another's physical life. Sullivan has an argument based on why do two friends need to have consistent physical and vocal contact. Sullivan writes:

"It has been said that a person's religion is best defined not by what he says he believes, but simply by what he actually does. Equally, it could be said that one's friends are simply those people with whom one spends one's life. Period. Anything else is a form of rationalization."

Friendship is almost a central symbol of human autonomy, and also the most accessible example of that autonomy in practice. This notion of autonomy is what takes us to Sullivan's most central point; the supremacy of friendship over romantic love, or Aristotle's notion of *eros*, despite our culture's compulsive fetishism of the latter:

"The great modern enemy of friendship has turned out to be love. By love, I don't mean the principle of giving and mutual regard that lies at the heart of friendship [but] love in the banal, ubiquitous, compelling, and resilient modern meaning of love: the romantic love that obliterates all other goods, the love to which every life must apparently lead, the love that is consummated in sex and celebrated in every particle of our popular culture, the love that is institutionalized in marriage and instilled as a primary and ultimate good in every Western child. I mean eros, which is more than sex but is bound up with sex. I mean the longing for union with another being, the sense that such a union resolves the essential quandary of human existence, the belief that only such a union can abate the loneliness that seems to come with being human, and deter the march of time that threatens to trivialize our very existence."

Eros, Sullivan points out, blinds us to even such universal concerns as time and death – why else would lovers promise one another eternal love and swear that they could not live without each other? More than that, they even "insist upon it, because to trap it in time would be to impair the inherently unbounded nature of the experience" and "because anything else implies that love is just one competing good among others." However, this quality of *eros* comes with a dark side:

"Love is a supremely jealous thing. It brooks no rival and obliterates every distraction. It seems to transport the human being — who is almost defined by time and morality — beyond the realm of both age and death. Which is why it is both so irresistible and so delusory."

Chapter 4
Romantic Passionate Love

Romantic Love

"Romantic love," which is illuminated by "depth, engagement, and sexual interest," can last a lifetime.

Neuroscientists believe through careful research that the brains of couples who experience this kind of love can keep the fire within their hearts and bodies alive for each other, the same way they had when they first met 20 or so years earlier. Romantic love is linked with marital satisfaction, happiness, immense self-respect, and relationship durability. Although it seems like such love has all the ideal qualities we associate with the thrill of falling in love, there is another category known as "passionate love" or "obsessive love" that most of us encounter and enjoy in the early stages of a sparkly connection. However, somehow, it is less favorable to become a lasting romance. Romantic love seems to combine many key elements of passionate love it but has the added benefit of keeping both partners happy and in love for the long-term.

A romantic relationship is the peak of love, security, engagement, communication, and sexual chemistry. It is all things compassionate, sexually substantial, lively, and perhaps even a bit exploratory. Despite having been together for quite some time, couples still enjoy the simple pleasures of kissing, holding hands, and leaving love quotes on the bathroom mirror for one another. There is a healthy comfort level, which gives each individual in the partnership the sense that they will always be there for each other.

First Love Nurtures Romance

The movie, Innocence from 2000, certainly makes it evident as to how your 'First Love' can always spark a desire and emotions of affection and love; a sense of attraction, no matter at what point in life you might encounter them; be it once or repeatedly. The film offered its audience some reflections on lo emotional and insightful love. The plot revolves around Andreas (Charles Tingwell), who was a recently widowed musician, and Claire (Julia Blake), who was still married to her first husband, John. Andreas decided to get back in touch with his one great love, Claire, after more than 40 years apart. The couple discovered that the intense passion they shared when they were young was still there. They became involved in a rekindled love affair that was as strong, passionate, and reckless as when they were young lovers. Andreas observed, "Each stage of life has its own kind of love. Now it's deeper, pared down to the essentials. We spend years destroying that part of love that gives us pain. I love you a lot less selfishly now."

However, as they continued aging, Andreas and Claire confronted additional novel complications, including the impact their relationship might have had on John, and the possibility of ill health and death. They realized that the joys and pleasures of re-mating in the later years came with 'leftovers' from other lives, including adult children, grandchildren, health concerns, previous living situations, sexual expectations, financial situations, divorce, caregiving experience, grief, and loss. They had to, with eyes wide open, deal with the 'leftovers' with maturity and wisdom. They had to make adjustments and compromises and then arrive at their own individual decisions and arrangements.

Romance is Evergreen and Youthful

There were two residents living at a nursing home, and this is how their story goes. The woman was single, and the man was a high profile married person, John Jay O'Conner III. They were elderly and suffered from Alzheimer's and dementia. John was born on January 10, 1930. He grew up in San Francisco, California. He developed Alzheimer's at a relatively young age. His beloved wife, the Honorable Justice Sandra Day O'Conner, took care of him at home for 17 years before she had no choice but to move him to an assisted living center in 2006.

The O'Conners truly loved each other very much. Sadly, however, Alzheimer's affected John's behavior in such a way that it became so hard on his wife to handle and care for him at home. He wanted his caregiver wife to stay by him all the time. She did most of the time. She even gave up her extraordinarily powerful and prestigious job as the Justice of the U.S. Supreme Court to be his full-time caregiver. She dearly loved her husband of 55 years. No woman has ever done more to advance the cause of Alzheimer's than Justice O'Conner.

In 1988, Justice Sandra was diagnosed with breast cancer, which, to her good fortune, was successfully treated. Not so lucky was her husband, John, who was diagnosed with Alzheimer's. Sandra took care of him for 17 years until he was admitted to an assisted living center in the summer of 2006. In 2005, Justice O'Connor announced her retirement from the Supreme Court. She cited her age as reasons and the need to spend more time with her ailing husband and with her family. When John was admitted to the nursing care facility, he was initially unhappy and grumbling. So, he was moved to another cottage area in the nursing home. 48 hours after moving to the new area, he was a happy teenager in love.

He struck up a romance with a woman, Kay, who had Alzheimer's. When Justice Sandra visited John at his new place, he seemed happy. She saw his 'girlfriend' sitting with him on the porch swing holding hands. Amazingly, that was a relief for Justice O'Conner to see her husband so improved after a prolonged and painful period. She was not jealous of the relationship. Instead, she was pleased that her husband was relaxed, happy, and comfortable at the center. She understood that people with Alzheimer's need intimacy and sometimes develop romantic attachments with fellow residents. After his placement in the assisted home, John O'Conner embarked on a love affair with another woman, who also suffered from Alzheimer's after being placed at the care center. His wife, Sandra, was far from being jealous. She was thrilled with their romance. She was relieved that her husband, who had become depressed and introverted and barely recognizing his own family, had found happiness in a new relationship with a fellow patient in his care home. Sandra and John were husband and wife, lovers, partners, and best friends for over five decades, and that was gone. To Sandra, the scenario was tragic, but with a sense of humor and a bittersweet irony.

She said that sometimes things that seem tragic can be turned around. Accept life. It is the Buddhist way. John's mental condition deteriorated rapidly until love blossomed with another resident identified as Kay. He was like a teenager in love. Yet these days, her life is dominated by her husband's condition and the unique love triangle in which she has found herself. Her husband cannot remember her. He did not choose to leave her. He had no memory of her. However, his desire for love and intimacy continued. At the same time, Sandra's willingness to sacrifice and care for him remained."

Passionate Love

"Passionate love" has most of the constructive features as romantic love. However, it also includes feelings of indecisiveness and nervousness. According to scientists Elaine Hatfield and Richard Rapson, Passionate love describes *"a state of intense longing for union with another."* Yet, it also brings into play "an obsessive element, characterized by indiscreet thinking, ambiguity, and mood swings. So, to be brief, passionate love is the kind that can work well initially in a relationship, but it does not guarantee lasting love and can be painful in the long run. After long surveys and researches, scientists and researchers have devolved a certain understanding that passionate love would usually either flare up and vanish out like a firecracker or quietly fuse into a less blistering and a safer, friendly acquaintance. This helped explain why couples move on from the honeymoon phase to more of a solidarity one.

Passionate Love Fades

When real passion exists in harmony, just as romantic love does, then the vulnerability of it fading should have been evidently less. But that is not true. Passionate love apparently fades; it fades in the worst manner. People tend to push love away by allowing it to drive them deeper into their own obsessions, insecurities, protectiveness, or by becoming more fearful and detached, less thrilled, and more scheduled in their relationships.

During the starting months of marriage, feelings of love, and being loved are everywhere. This is because both the male and female concepts of "love" are fulfilled. Youthful potency and the absence of children make it easy to maintain a high level of physical intimacy and closeness. Since we base our idea of "love" on such pining feelings, it's no wonder that more mature couples feel that they are 'out-of-love'. The longer you are with someone, the more challenging it becomes to maintain that initial level of passion. Children, careers, and responsibilities make it more challenging to stoke the fires of passion.

Considering the high tendency of passionate love fading away, we can ponder upon the contributing factors elaborated here. They can limit our capacity for experiencing love in our relationships: our attachment forms, psychological barricades, and the concept of the unreal bond.

Attachment Patterns

Our attachment patterns are established in our early childhood relationships, and they continue to function as working models for relationships throughout our lives. Our early attachments shape how we expect other people to behave as well as how we go about relating and getting our wants and needs met by others.

"Our style of attachment affects everything from our partner selection to how well our relationships progress to, sadly, how they end. That is why recognizing our attachment pattern can help us understand our strengths and vulnerabilities in a relationship. When there is a secure attachment pattern, a person is confident and self-possessed and is able to easily interact with others. However, when there is an anxious or avoidant attachment pattern, and a person picks a partner who fits with that maladaptive pattern, they will most likely be choosing someone who isn't the ideal choice to make them happy." said Dr. Lisa

Firestone. People sometimes feel a "spark" with someone who fits their early attachment pattern. However, in the long term, they may struggle to feel close to that person. They may feel flames of passion but lack a sense of security that will allow the relationship to be consistent and satisfying.

Psychological Defenses

Our early experiences in relationships, starting with the ones we had with our parents or primary caretakers, heavily influence the psychological defenses we form and often face throughout our lives. These defenses may have been strategies we adopted to survive in less than ideal conditions in our childhood. We may have become isolated or reclusive to avoid a needy or intrusive parent, or we may have learned to be emotive or clingy toward a parent who was absent or rejecting. We may have found ways to take care of or soothe ourselves because we did not always feel nurtured, or we may have discovered that the way to get what we needed was to get upset and make a big fuss. These adaptations may have helped us as kids, but they can go on to hurt us in our adult relationships.

Oftentimes, when we first fall in love, we are in an undefended state, where we are more open to another person. However, as we get closer, we may experience certain fears around intimacy and fall back to our old defenses. We may become more critical and guarded or become more anxious and controlling, depending on our defense system. Additionally, we may even be attracted to people who are likely to hurt us in the same ways we were hurt as children. For instance, we may be especially drawn to someone more aloof or unavailable, or someone who is highly aggressive or pursuing.

Unfortunately, we often feel fireworks with people whose defenses fit with ours and who reaffirm old, familiar, often unpleasant ways of feeling about ourselves and others. While we may feel passion and excitement in the initial stages of these relationships, our defenses will eventually get in the way, as we find ourselves either becoming more and more distant or increasingly pursuing our partner in ways that trigger their own defense system.

The Fantasy Bond

There are two ways that fantasy can undermine real love. For instance, if our attraction to someone is based on form or something superficial, we may be drawn to the fantasy of being with that person without having the feelings of a more profound love for that person. Falling in love can feel like a dream come true, but it is not a fairy tale in the sense that it has to be based on reality: real affection, respect, and attraction toward another person. Sometimes, people fall in love with the form of being in love, so all the passion they initially feel eventually fades because it is not based on substance.

In another sense, fantasy can intrude on relationships, even after we have truly fallen in love with someone. In fact, Dr. Robert Firestone developed the concept of the fantasy bond to describe an illusion of connection between a couple substituted for feelings of real love and intimacy. A fantasy bond forms when a couple replaces the personal relating involved in being in love with the form of being a "couple". Couples in a fantasy bond tend to fall into a routine and forgo their independence, often functioning as a "we" instead of a "you and me." This bond tends to diminish feelings of attraction and reduce passion.

Sustain Passion by Engaging in Romantic Love

Couples need to feel a physical attraction between one another.

However, this attraction is just one piece of the puzzle. If a relationship is primarily based on passion, then, when the fire begins to wane, the relationship will be doomed. Physical beauty fades, and our concepts of "attractiveness" alter over time. If your relationship is based entirely on your passion for your partner, you are in for a rude awakening as your relationship matures.

Commitment is the resolution to avoid mere attractiveness that weakens your bond with your partner. It is a selfless love that barely has anything to do with sensual pleasure. It is a love so powerful that no matter what happens, there will always be perseverance and loyalty. This kind of emotion is an expression of love that surpasses all passion.

Love is not a passive state that happens to us, but an active force we have to nurture to thrive. If we want to stay in love for long, we have to engage in loving actions. In a recent blog, Dr. Lisa Firestone listed, *"Some essential characteristics that fit the description of a loving relationship"*. These include expressions of affection, both physical as well as emotional. They are followed by tenderness, compassion, and sensitivity to the needs of the other. Your wish to offer pleasure and satisfaction to another must be active and effective. A desire for shared activities and pursuits between two individuals living together helps with believing and reuniting them as one soul and one body. More than anything, the concept of an ongoing, honest exchange of personal feelings, the process of offering concern, comfort, and outward assistance for the loved one's aspirations is highly demanding and needed of you to ensure a loving and lasting relationship. If we commit to these characteristics as principles that we uphold within ourselves, we are much more likely to stay in touch with our loving feelings. We can then keep passion, attraction, respect, and admiration as living forces in our relationship.

Behavioral Impact of Passionate Love

An article at www.kinseyconfidential.org recently highlighted the effects of passionate love on the brain. It stated that "a person who is love-smitten will often make choices that will seem illogical to others, such as prioritizing the object of their affection above work, friends, and family, no matter what they need to trade for it." Studies have also revealed that parts of the brain are activated when people fall in passionate love. The author says, "In many ways, the brain scan studies demonstrate that the maddening feelings of love are fundamentally a major mental-health crisis. The chemical explosion of brain changes it produces is strikingly parallel to drug addiction and obsessive-compulsive disorder. Love really does make us crazy."

Other studies have linked passionate love to addiction. A recent study published in *Frontiers of Psychology* concluded that "individuals in the early stage of intense romantic love show many symptoms of substance and non-substance or behavioral addictions, including euphoria, longing, patience, emotional and physical dependency, withdrawal and degeneration." It is essential to know when the intense feelings we are experiencing are not healthy. If we are struggling or experiencing a lot of pain around our feelings of love, it is important to speak your mind out and seek assistance. For many of us, love can open up old injuries and activate us in ways that are important to make sense of.

Relationships present many challenges, and therapy can help us in understanding what is going on inside us and feel more secure within ourselves.

Ways to Spark Passion in Your Love

Passion makes life good. It is the essence of desire, feeling excited, and experiencing a fire within you. Unfortunately, passion often fades in long-term relationships since our everyday life gets boring and predictable. While this experience is somewhat normal, by no means should we quit ourselves due to passionless love. Because let's be honest, passion is part of the deal. It is what keeps us intrigued, interested, motivated, and coming back for more. If passion has faded in your relationship, you do not need to panic out of fear: there are things you can do to feel it once again. Some ways of enhancing and reigniting that fire in your relationship again are expounded here.

Take Space

Space is a necessary component for fueling passion in a relationship. *Fire needs air to burn.* When we put space from the people we love, we inevitably long to be close to them again. This is a good thing! Notice that you have to separate *first* to want to come back together. Hot relationships include waves of being close and waves of spending time apart. It's a dance. Sometimes, the dance is a little uncomfortable but believe it or not, that discomfort is not the worst thing. It can add fuel to the fire. Consciously incorporate space into your relationship to heat things up again.

Leave Room for Mystery

Contrary to popular belief, your partner does not need to know everything about you. In fact, it is probably better if he or she does not. Sometimes, we confuse intimacy with sharing every little detail. Intimacy is sharing the *vulnerable* parts of yourself with another person. And yes, this will produce a feeling of deep connection in your relationship. But divulging every little detail is not vulnerability; it's just too much information. Keep in mind that mystery helps you feel alive in a relationship. This does not mean you should withhold from your partner. It just means that you get to consciously decide what to share, and what to keep to yourself.

Prioritize Passion in Your Relationship

A common issue in relationships is that we want one person to be everything to us. That means that your partner is your best friend, business partner, co-parent, lover, housecleaner, and handyman. Unfortunately, the more roles we put a person in, the more diluted the relationship becomes. If one of the main priorities of your relationship is to grow passionate love, you have to prioritize that experience above the others.

One person cannot be everything to you, and they do not have to be. This is why we also have best friends, parents, children, and many other relationships. A charge can be reintroduced in your relationship when you start treating your partner like your lover, rather than your roommate.

Experience Yourself as a Passionate Person

We often rely on other people to make us feel a certain way, rather than cultivating that experience in ourselves. If you want to feel more passion in your life and your relationship, you have to become passionate. Whatever turns you on, keeps you alive, and passionate, you must do those things. The fire that comes forth when you are experiencing passion makes you undeniably irresistible to others. Through your passion, you get to express your imagination, love, heart, and drive. This rekindles your life too. By pledging to be a passionate person, you invite passion for entering all capacities of your life, including your long-term love.

Grow

Passion inevitably dies down when the mundane takes over, and new experiences fade into the distance. Some people believe that this is how long-term love goes, but I disagree. Passion comes from having new experiences, and lucky for you, you are human, which means you are growing and changing all the time. If you can show up the growth happening in your partner and you, it will inspire a passionate connection that renews itself over time. A commitment to your own evolution is the fuel for a passionate life. Your personal expansion will expand your relationship, too. Again, passion is something that we all crave. Life would not be nearly good without it. Commit yourself to a path of passion, and you will light up your relationship and the world while you are at it.

Chapter 5
Companionate Love and Sexless Love

Defining Companionate Love

Companionate love refers to the love that is equitably slow to develop. It is characterized by interdependence and feelings of affection, intimacy, and commitment.

Companionate love is also known as affectionate love, friendship-based love, or attachment. Since the development of such love takes a reasonable amount of time to develop, this kind of love is often seen between intimate friends or romantic partners who have been together for a long time. Such love is deeper than friendship because it is defined by a long-term, mutually agreed commitment between two people. In this kind of relationship, there might not be that same passion that you had when you first meet a new person, but there is a deep sense of commitment and allegiance to another person.

Theories of Love

It might be helpful to briefly discuss some theories of love to situate the definition of companionate love in social research. A critical theory of relationships is called the **'Triangular Theory of Love,'** developed by psychologist **Robert Sternberg**. Sternberg set out to understand the different kinds of feelings that might characterize people's relationships. In the context of personal relationships, the three components of love, according to Sternberg, are "an intimacy component, a passion component, and a commitment component."

Passion – Passion can be associated with either physical arousal or emotional stimulation. It is further elaborated in three ways:

- A strong feeling of enthusiasm or excitement for something or about doing something

- A strong feeling that causes people to act in a dangerous way

- Strong sexual or romantic feeling for someone

Intimacy - Intimacy is described as the feelings of closeness and attachment to one another. This tends to strengthen a tight bond that is shared between two individuals.

Additionally, having a sense of intimacy helps create the feeling of being at ease with one another in the sense that the two parties are mutual in their feelings. Intimacy is predominantly defined as something of a personal or private nature.

Commitment – Unlike the other two elements, commitment involves a conscious decision to stick with one another. The decision to remain committed is mainly determined by the level of satisfaction that a partner derives from the relationship. There are three ways to define commitment:

- A promise to do or give something

- A promise to be loyal to someone or something

- The attitude of someone who works very hard to do or support something.

The love that one experiences depends on the absolute strength of these three components. Different stages and types of love can be explained as different combinations of these elements. However, the relative emphasis of each component changes over time as an adult romantic relationship develops. A relationship based on a single element is less likely to survive than the one based on two or three elements.

That's where **companionate love** comes in. According to this theory, companionate love is a form of love primarily based on the commitment component of love. So, there might not be a lot of passion left, but the two people are committed to one another and care about one another.

Other forms of love include **empty love**, which is the presence of commitment but a lack of passion or intimacy. However, it is essential to note that this is different from companionate love because, in companionate love, there might not be a passion, but there is undoubtedly deep affection.

Alternatively, **romantic love** is characterized by passion and intimacy but a lack of long-term commitment.

Consummate love is an ideal kind of love, representing a relationship that has a strong emphasis on all three components of love. People often strive to attain this kind of relationship, but it may be hard to achieve. Moreover, if passion is lost, consummate love could quickly turn into companionate love.

Defining Sexless Love

A sexless marriage concerning sexless love is one where there is little or no sexual activity at all, where sexual intimacy occurs fewer than ten times per year "approximately".

Although rare, if both husband and wife feel that a sexless marriage is fine, they can be happy with it. When the sexual desire is permanently lost between the married couple, the relationship becomes like that of a brother-sister. It is called enmeshment, where the couple dearly loves each other without seeing each other as sexual beings.

Adversity of Sexless Love

Sex is far too important in the grand scheme of a relationship to be ignored. It brings you closer to a person in a way that nothing else can. If you are in a sexless relationship, no amount of talking or cuddling can bring you as close as having sex. In my personal opinion and experience, I believe that a sexless relationship won't last.

We have all heard how vital sex is in a relationship, but we have never heard if you can last without it. However, believe it or not, sex can have a substantial impact on your relationship, and its lack can make things incredibly challenging for you. Overall, each relationship is different, and it depends on what you think of sex in a relationship that determines whether or not it can last.

A 39-year-old lady, married for 19 years, described her sexless marriage. Her husband is a loving, nice, and dependable man. He is loyal to her, and they appear to be close in the societal sense of marriage. They hold hands. He constantly reminds her that he loves her, and he does nice things for her. Both spouses have similar interests, and they engage in conversation all the time. They are like best friends. Both are employed and have a good income and a beautiful suburban home while their two children are adolescents. Despite all of this, the lady has been unhappy and depressed for many years, because her sexual desires are not satisfied. She felt as though a considerable part of her life was missing.

Shortly after their marriage, the couple had sexual relations about once a week. After their first anniversary, that frequency dropped to twice a month. After a few months, sex dropped to once a month, followed by a decline to every three months. After their third anniversary, it dropped to twice a year. This deceivingly happy relationship was not what she desired. The lady finally decided to seek sexual gratification by resorting to an affair.

She wanted a discreet lover to revive something that might be wonderful. She still has sex with her spouse occasionally. Even though she feels guilty cheating on her husband, she is always in a confused state of mind, as to whether she should remain married to him or not.

Sexless Love is Not Enough – Sex is Essential

This is an Australian story of a daughter, who hired a sex worker for her late 93-year-old father. He had dementia and lived in a nursing home when he said to her, "You'll need to find me a woman." The daughter did not react by uncomfortably laughing off his request, or voicing disgust or refusal. She did not tell her dad that he should not be thinking about sex anymore. Instead, she took his request seriously and started looking for a woman.

Her father's reasoning function deteriorated to the point that she began caring for him due to dementia. The daughter was a disability support worker. She had seen how an individual's sexuality needs to be considered. She also knew that her father may eventually need help with his personal, intimate life. Upon the seriousness of his want, she asked him if he wanted her to find him a companion or someone to have sex with. He wanted both. She began searching for a sex worker online, and through disability support groups, she was given the name of a person they thought was the most suitable: 'Emma'.

The daughter called Emma, but one could tell in her voice that she was quite nervous. However, she knew what she wanted for her dad; he missed the intimacy of sex. The desire for physical intimacy did not disappear when dementia set in her father. The daughter was delighted with Emma and what the sex worker gave to her father. At first, 'Emma's' services appeared costly, but the daughter soon found out it was on par with what other sex workers charged. However, 'Emma' gave much more. She spent an entire afternoon and evening with her father for the same price. Her time with her father included having drinks and a chat, a gentle massage, a cuddle, and whatever else he wanted. If he fell asleep, she would wait until he was ready to wake up. After time with Emma, her father's well-being and behavior consequently improved. His nocturnal wanderings ceased where he often experienced falls, resulting in horrid skin tears. He was not agitated. He did not obsess over things like he used to before. He looked serene, happy, and relaxed.

There is much difference between a human with a sexless life and one with sex. It seems quite evident that sexless love may appear to be affectionate, composed, and adorable. However, practically speaking, a man longs for the desire of love with sex.

Contrary Panel of Sexless Love

Sex Brings You Closer – There is a bond, unlike anything else when you have sex. You can spend as much time as you want, going to the movies and cuddling with someone, but it will never amount to how beneficial sex is. When you are in a relationship, you have to be really close to your partner.

You have to know them better than anyone else because it makes your relationship last a long time. Sex is a huge and significant part of making that happen.

It Makes You Empathetic toward the Other – When you get intimate involving sex, it is tough not to feel what the other person is feeling when it comes to emotions. Therefore, having sex can make you more empathetic toward your partner. Not only does this make you feel connected to them, but it can also prevent arguments and hurting each other. When you are sexually active with someone, it makes it challenging to hurt them in any way, which will eventually make your relationship much stronger.

It Reduces Stress – We all know how much stress and tension can add to the downfall of a relationship. Stress leads to outbursts that may cause harm to the other person's feelings, and that can get bottled up until they no longer want to be with you. When you have sex with them, you are reducing that stress and tension and allowing yourself to relax with them. This is hugely beneficial to making a relationship last.

It can Heighten Your Self-Esteem – Having confidence and high self-esteem in a relationship is an incredibly vital part of making a relationship last because it stops the jealousy and accusations. When you have sex with your partner, it makes you feel loved and positive about yourself, and you feel as if they sincerely care about you. Feeling all of those things from your partner is what makes a relationship last for a long time.

Without it, you may start to wonder how they feel.

It Creates Affection – When your partner does not walk up to you, give you a hug or a kiss on the forehead, or tell you how much you mean to them, the relationship is likely to fizzle out quite quickly. Sex can make that affection happen naturally. When you sleep with someone, you automatically feel affectionate toward them. Many couples struggling with affection are told to have more sex because it plays such a big part in being affectionate toward each other.

Sex isn't Love – Having sex with someone does not decipher that you love them. You can be completely in love with someone and never even touch them in a sexual way. Therefore, you can definitely have a relationship based entirely on love if you both have the mindset where physical intimacy is not something you want to do to show your love.

Not Having Sex Can Make You Question Their Feelings – When you do not have sex with your partner, it can be hard to recall how they feel about you. There is really nothing strengthening the fact that they find you attractive, sexy, or even likable. When you do not have sex, it can be quite easy to forget how someone feels about you – especially if they are introverted and have a hard time expressing their feelings, even generally. Many sexless relationships do not last because people no longer think their partner has feelings for them.

Sex Makes You Feel United as One – One of the most important things for making a relationship last is acting as though you are one. You have to be connected with someone in a way that feels like you are just one complete package.

When you have sex, you attain that feeling. It is like you are just one soul together, and no one can split you apart. When you have a sexless relationship, you can become too separate, which can drive a rift between the two of you.

Causes of Sexless Love

In 2015, *Tracy Clark-Flory* in **'How People Plot Their Escapes from Sexless Marriages'**, discussed some contributing factors to sexless marriages, along with examples.

Loss of Passion

"I feel like I die more every day. I have so much love and real

passion to give and it's not wanted, appreciated, or returned. The man who once loved me is dead. He is like a zombie. I know my husband is a porn addict and is on sex hook up sites yet doesn't want me. I have men flirt with me everywhere. He makes me feel like an ugly old woman just sitting out in the country waiting to die."

Rejection

"But even when I think the mood is right and I try to initiate,

she just brushes me off like I'm a dog trying to hump her leg."

Low Self-Esteem as a Result of Rejection

"I guess since I have gained a few stretch marks and dimples along with my pudginess, I am no longer attractive to him."

Infidelity

"I have sought the physical and emotional intimacy I require outside of my marriage. Please do not condemn me for this."

Stress or Family Commitments

"We used to be able to find ways to have sex when our daughter was younger. While she slept in the swing, we would sneak around the corner, far, yet close enough to hear her cry. Unfortunately, since she refuses to sleep in her own bed, she's still with us for the time being. So now we've been in a fully sexless marriage for the last three years. All the little secret spots we had when she was younger don't work anymore."

Legal Considerations

A marriage solely relying on sexless love could be

relevant to finding fault. When it comes to an absolute divorce, most states have a no-fault system. However, the traditional fault grounds for divorce are still relevant in some instances, such as adultery, abandonment, malicious turning out of doors, indignities, cruel and barbarous treatment, and excessive drug or alcohol use.

Fault becomes significant when it comes to divorce from bed and board, post-separation support, and alimony.

In some cases, a sexless marriage could conceivably rise to the level of or contribute to a finding of constructive abandonment, but that may be challenging to prove on the lack of sex alone.

Withholding affection, including sex, could potentially rise to the level of constructive abandonment. Constructive abandonment is generally defined as **a willful failure of one spouse to fulfill the obligations of marriage.** This means that though he or she might be physically present at the marital home, the spouse is mentally and emotionally absent from the marriage. If the spouse leaves the marital home without consent or justification, and with no intention of renewing the marital relationship, that constitutes spousal abandonment.

Even in a marriage, no one is entitled to sex. Constructive abandonment requires that the spouse willfully refuses intimacy. Also, the behavior is beyond the bounds of what could be considered normal in a marriage. To establish willfulness of withholding of affection by the spouse, evidence should show that the spouse knew that the lack of sex was a problem and discussed. That the spouse refused to work on the problem and continually and repeatedly rejected the other partner's advances. If the spouse withholds sex out of spite, it would be considered willful. If the spouse has a medical condition suppressing libido and knows that the lack of sex is a problem but refuses to seek treatment, that might show willfulness. However, refusing sex because of a medical condition does not show willfulness.

The court looks at a willful indifference or hostility toward a spouse's needs over a long period, but it does not make a finding of constructive abandonment based on sexual frequency. "Is your spouse mentally and emotionally withdrawn from the marriage and perhaps not caring for the children? Is the spouse committing adultery, which is a ground for finding fault? Is the spouse on drugs or alcohol? Is the spouse abusive, indignant, or cruel and barbarous?"

Such factors can cause a judge to find the spouse at fault in the breakdown of the marriage.

Rekindling Romance in a Marriage Clinging to Sexless Love

If a marriage lacks sex, it is surely a big deal; something is off. The longer one ignores the sex problem, the harder the punch will be when one is forced to deal with it.

The man feels hurt, rejected, inadequate. He fears that he is disappointing his wife sexually and questions whether or not his wife loves him at all. He may stay away from home, work longer hours, use porn, or have an affair out of frustration or feeling forced to seek sex elsewhere. Then he shuts down, becomes depressed, and begins to despise his wife but remains civil. Next, the wife starts to pull away from non-sexual physical affection, such as hugs and kisses. Now, the man begins to detach, and many partners leave the marriage.

Brittany Wong stated in, *"How to Take Your Marriage from Sexless to Steamy in 7 Steps"* that sexless marriages have become almost endemic in modern society. However, sex life can be improved by some remedial ways, such as working out your marital issues, practice radical honesty and forgiveness outside the bedroom, or making a joint commitment to move forward. You should also acknowledge that there is a problem in the bedroom by having an honest conversation about the sexual relation. Furthermore, spend a few hours every week getting touchy-feely, then slowly build up to intimacy when both spouses are ready, comfortable, and confident. It is highly effective to use your memories to your advantage.

Reminisce about a sensual experience from your past and how it felt, incorporating all five senses. Always try to find out what your partner is craving sexually, and learn how to give it to them. It does not end here. You can develop new "sex menus" together. There is a limitless number of sex positions, themes, fantasy-based menus, and kinks to explore to keep your sex life vibrant and healthy.

Chapter 6
Monogamous Relationships – Marriage

Definition of Monogamy

Monogamy is when you are **married** to or in a **sexual relationship** with one person at a time. Humans are one of the few species that practice monogamy. A sexually monogamous relationship is one where – during the relationship – neither partner has sex with anyone else. **Monogamy** is a form of relationship in which an individual has only one partner during their lifetime or at any one time. The term is also applied to some animals' social behavior, referring to the state of having only one mate.

Types of Monogamous Relationships

It is vital to have a clear concept of the classification of monogamy since scientists use the term for different relationships. Modern biological researchers, using the theory of evolution, approach human monogamy as the same in human and non-human animal species. They hypothesize the following aspects of monogamy discussed below.

- Marital monogamy refers to marriages of only two people.

Marital monogamy may be further distinguished into marriage once in a lifetime, and on the other hand, marriage with just one person at a time (**serial monogamy**), in contrast to bigamy or polygamy.

- Social monogamy refers to two partners living together, having sex with each other, and cooperating in acquiring basic resources such as shelter, food, and money.

Two people share living space, arrange for each other's basic needs, have sex with one another, and no one else is said to participate in social monogamy. This category of monogamy does not precisely denote sexual practice, but it represents the behavior demonstrative of a cohesive pair of partners. Social monogamy is mostly identical to monogamous marriage.

"Even if we're not actually monogamous in other ways, I want people to think we are." Social monogamy is possibly the most powerful monogamy that exists. Many individuals

and couples have come to me over the years, wanting to explore some aspect of non-monogamy but are quite worried about the consequences of being "found out". Indeed, those consequences can seem frightening. We all want to feel like we belong, and being excluded is not a good feeling at all. Feeling "normal" matters to most of us, and if the social norm is monogamy, stepping outside of that can feel terrifying.

Indeed, for some, the power of social monogamy can seem so strong that it is hard for even monogamous people to talk about wanting it. The expectation of monogamy is almost always invisible, and when folks talk about it, it is in the context

of *not* being monogamous. So, if you are a monogamous person wanting to talk about conscious monogamy or having desires outside your relationship, it may seem like no one wants to hear it. Yet, there is value in pushing back against the forces that shame people for giving the appearance of anything but monogamy.

- Sexual monogamy refers to two partners remaining sexually limited to each other, without having any outside sex partners.

When you have only one sexual partner, that is sexual monogamy. Divorce happens in at least half of marriages and usually at a time when there is a lot of life left to live. Remarriage is a strong possibility, or your spouse may die, leaving you to re-establish another path in life.

So, monogamy means one partner, but theoretically, today's reality needs to include a time factor. That's where the concept of serial monogamy comes in. Serial monogamy is a concept where you may have more than one sexual partner over your lifetime, but you **never** have more than one partner at a time. It would appear that society, at least here in North America, has accepted the existence and decency of serial monogamy as the reality of our modern world.

As considered apt, sexual monogamy is an exploitive religious system since it makes you feel guilty within and tends to raise a question to almost every act out of your normal behavior. For instance, 'Do you kiss your friends hello and goodbye? Can you be affectionate friends with your ex? Is it okay to cuddle or flirt with folks other than your partner? Can you see a practitioner for sexual healing? What about getting a massage?'

- Genetic monogamy refers to sexually monogamous

relationships with genetic evidence of paternity. Genetic monogamy is when genes, **not** social or behavioral norms, decree the practice of monogamy. Dr. Emlan, an expert from Cornell University on evolution, believes that only two species are genetically monogamous: the *marmoset* and the *tamarin*. Since humans can and do mate outside relationships, they are not genetically monogamous.

Monogamy between Sherry and Mortimer

Sherry and Annie visited their parents, then decided to go shopping at a new mall where they could also have a meal. They found a nice Italian restaurant. Sherry ordered lasagna and a glass of wine while Annie ordered an Italian salad with chicken.

"How is your lasagna?" asked Annie.

Sherry said, *"Delicious. But they serve a very large portion. I will take part of the meal home. My husband will enjoy it."*

Upon hearing this, Annie said, *"You speak very fondly of your husband. You must have a wonderful relationship."*

"Yes, we do," said Sherry.

Annie said, *"Go on and tell me more about you and your husband."*

Sherry said, *"Well, I am 63 years of age, and yes, very happily married. My husband and I have a great loving and sexual relationship. I have always felt that love, intimacy, and sex are basic needs that transcend the aging process, even in*

Alzheimer's sufferers like my Dad."

Annie said, *"That's great, Sherry."*

Sherry said, *"I have learned a lot. You know, the majority of elderly individuals and those with Alzheimer's disease and dementia maintain their ability to enjoy love, intimacy, and erotic pleasure."*

Annie said, *"I guess that lovemaking evolves and matures over many years in most people."*

Sherry said, *"Yes, that is true. And sexual activity is an excellent form of exercise that involves the mind and body of partners."*

Annie said, *"So, elderly people and those with dementia may develop physical and mental limitations, but do they gracefully adjust to the change that aging brings?"*

Sherry said, *"Yes, they do. It's fascinating that the erotic flames of elderly people continue to burn hot and bright."*

Annie said, *"I think elderly people spend more quality time embracing and enjoying their partners, and that reduces their level of anxiety."*

Sherry said, *"You know, for partners, like my husband and me, an essential cornerstone of our good sex life is being friends and respecting and trusting each other."*

Annie asked, *"Do you communicate with your husband during the day when he is at work or out of town?"*

Sherry said, *"Oh, yes. We both communicate every chance we get, mostly by phone or text, and sometimes even by email. I firmly believe that communication between partners throughout the day and spending time doing non-sexual things together enhance intimacy and bring the couple closer together."*

Annie asked, *"Do you think that elderly couples enjoy sex as much as younger people?"*

Sherry said, *"I was surprised to learn from my reading that elderly couples may enjoy sex better than in the middle age because they know each other's bodies, feel confident, less timid, less inhibited, more relaxed, and more sensual."*

Annie asked, *"May I ask you if you and your husband plan when to have sex?"*

Sherry answered, *"I do not mind you asking. Mortimer and I have both planned and unexpected sex, which is very gratifying."*

Annie asked, *"What do you and Mortimer do for romance?"*

Sherry said, *"We try to do a lot of fun stuff. I hope that the romance between Mortimer and me will last forever. We hold hands, flirt, and kiss each other wherever we are. Sometimes we enjoy showering together, massaging each other, and making out on the couch without going all the way. We may also enjoy sending each other sexy and naughty text messages on our smartphones."*

Annie asked, *"Do you really do all that with your husband?"*

Sherry said, *"Not as often as we should or could."*

Sherry's phone rang at that moment. It was a call from her husband. She answered, *"Hi, honey."* He said, *"I called to tell you that I love you very much."* Sherry said, *"I love you too, honey."*

Annie said, *"You know, it's fascinating to me that as couples grow older together, they are more in sync with each other and have sexual harmony."*

Sherry said, *"Yes, I'm noticing that. My husband is by no means old, but he is beginning to have a slower arousal, which normally occurs in elderly people. As you know, younger men become aroused more quickly than women, causing sexual discord and complaints that he is finished before she even feels aroused. But in elderly men, erection may be slower and less firm, and wilting may occur with minor distractions. However, I've learned that men can reach orgasm without erections by embracing leisurely, being playful, whole-body touching, and massaging, followed by manual or sex toy stimulation or oral sex."*

Annie said, *"You are on a roll. You must have read a great deal about sex in seniors."*

Sherry said, *"You know, age brings inevitable physical changes, and some are unappealing. And, the compulsion to have sex may diminish with age. But married couples, even if old, get another chance to rekindle their lovemaking by focusing not only on the sexual activity but more importantly on intimacy, closeness, and affection expressed by snuggling, cuddling, kissing, laying together naked, and stroking. Sex in seniors becomes more interesting and intriguing, and it becomes more a matter of choice for them."*

American Conceptualization of Monogamy

As a young child, there was an acquainted playground song that taught us the supposed trail of adult romantic relationships. It leads our minds to be sure that we will live idyllically. The monogamy guarantees happiness ever after, and it goes like:

"First comes love, then comes marriage, then comes baby in a baby carriage."

The American relationship reputations revolve around the idea of what works best for us. Some require a certain position of recognition in a relationship, while others do not. Some individuals tend to stay firm and committed, while others are vulnerable to cheating and disloyalty. While some retain healthy and exclusive sexual associations, others believe in building and maintain more profound expressive bonds and intimacy with the significant other. Monogamy, even today, is a much popular exercise and belief, it does not matter if it may be serial monogamy. The ideology that monogamy surpasses other kinds of non-monogamous interpersonal engagements continues to invade the formation and assessment of theories concerning love and intimacy.

Monogamy is deeply seated in the U.S., even the psychologists and scientists who study it are unaware of its partiality. When speaking about non-monogamy, terms such as "unfaithfulness" and "cheating" arise, which in themselves portray unfairness toward a monogamous model. Statistically, non-monogamous interactions are just as efficient, based on several signs as monogamous ones.

The sexual revolution of the 1960s helped in the eradication of repressive approaches toward sex and relationship. It also facilitated in shifting monogamy from its comfort zone, as the moral custom in the U.S. After 50 years, social and sexual monogamy is still favored by a majority of Americans. Hence, relationships outside the bounds of monogamy remain taboo in the country.

Prevalence of Monogamy

Monogamy has been prevalent and inherent because men chose to stick around one woman to maintain the security of their young, which, in turn, would definitely assure that their children remained alive to replicate and carry their genes in a new offspring. Monogamy favors location and its providences. It is arguably popular in areas where the female population is comparatively low, and where men do not engage in fights over multiple women because they are too diverse and alienated. The distance actually plays a positive role since it makes it harder for men to analyze if the child born of a woman is actually their own. On the contrary, women are too much of an introvert and highly intolerant of other women. Since their dietary needs are greater, they avoid competitors where food is concerned, which aids them stay monogamous.

Antagonistic Relationships to Monogamy
Cheating

Although cheating is considered wrong and objectionable, people all across the world still tend to give into it. Scholars estimate that approximately 20-25 percent of ever-married men and 10-15 percent of ever-married women admit to having an affair at some point in their relationship. However, incidents of cheating have steadily increased over the last decade, primarily because of the negative influence of social media, including Facebook and Instagram, which aids us in finding out long-lost crushes and high school or university mates. Cheating is not just limited to physical sex, but it can also originate from other means like gifting flowers, Skype chat sessions, or a pure lunch date with no physical contact but a meaningful and pleasant conversation.

Polygamy

Polygamy is a form of marriage involving more than two persons, and it has been practiced alongside monogamy for a decently long time throughout the world. Polygamy can be further differentiated into *Polygyny*, which is the most common type of multiple-partner marriages, where one husband has multiple wives, and each wife has her own sexual limitations and privacy with the husband. On the other hand, *Polyandry* is the kind of marriage where one wife is married to multiple husbands. This is definitely a rare scenario since it has not been well-appreciated in terms of social, political, and cultural aspects.

Swinging

Among the recognized forms of non-monogamy, swinging is the best and most popular kind. Explicitly speaking, *swinging* encompasses committed couples exchanging partners merely for sexual purposes, with the consent of each other. It is remarkably diverse, ranging from brief interactions among strangers at sex parties to groups of friends who possess acquaintance for quite some years and often socialize. This practice began as "wife swapping" among U.S. Air Force pilots after World War II, and then it became a norm. Hence, swinging has spread its influence across the globe, mostly via the internet.

Monogamish

Monogamish relationships have come into the limelight just a few years ago and started to gain popularity. Such relationships are those where a couple is chiefly monogamous, i.e., committed to one definite partner in life. However, he or she allows diverse extents of sexual contact with others. Some allow only one-night stands, maintaining the idea of no sex with the same person again; while others have time and location limitations where they may either only engage in sexual contact not more than once a week, or it would be restricted to times when they are traveling or are somewhere distant from home.

Open Relationship

Open relationship is a diverse term for consent-based, non-monogamous relationships founded because a **principal couple** is "open" to sexual contact with individuals. The most common type of an open relationship is that of a married or committed couple that hooks onto a third or sometimes fourth or fifth partner. In contrast, their involvement and role in the relationship are always inferior. A couple involved in such a relationship might participate in sexual activity with the **inferior partner**, together or distinctly. Irrespective of the other connections, the primary couple always remains a precedent.

Chapter 7
Consensual Non-Monogamous Relationships: Polyamory

Polyamory

Consensual non-monogamous (CNM) relationships or polyamory are love relationships in which all partners explicitly agree that each partner may have romantic or sexual relationships with others. Polyamory implies having more than one sexual loving relationship at the same time, with the full knowledge and consent of all involved partners. The CNM partners, called polyamorists, aspire to high standards of loving ethically, honestly, openly, and respectfully.

Polyamory often has a fluid and flexible approach to love relationships. Most polyamorists believe that sexual and relational exclusivity is *not* necessary for sincere, committed, and long-term loving relationships. Usually, they have no preconceptions as to the duration of the relationship, although polyamorous relationships can and do last many years. In 2013, Tammy Nelson stated in her book, *"The New Monogamy: Redefining Your Relationship after Infidelity"* that monogamy is no longer defining marriage. There are more couples experimenting with consensual polyamory by having actual romantic relationships outside a primary commitment and with other consensual open relationships. The couples or partners decide what sexual activities outside their relationship are acceptable. Since these relationships occur with the consent and support of the spouse or partner, it represents ethical non-monogamy and averts the need to cheat or look the other way.

Polyamory Relationships

Gender Equality – Polyamorists generally treat their partners equally without acting and behaving like a patriarchist, regardless of gender. However, the partners may agree to adhere to gender-specific boundaries. For example, individual differences, emotions, and needs of a married couple who are contemplating polyamory for the first time may lead them to negotiate and agree that the wife limits her romantic and sexual relationships to women. The agreement could be for a temporary period, after which it could be renegotiated.

Although polyamorists generally accord all partners with equal standing and consideration, different types of relationships vary to some degree. To begin with, *'Hierarchal Polyamorous Relationships'* may be differentiated as primary or secondary to indicate each relationship's place in a partner's life. For instance, in open marriages, a live-in partner may be the primary partner, and a lover may be the secondary partner with whom intimate relations occur once or more times per week. Contradicting this aspect of relation under polyamory, we also consider what is called *'Mon/Poly Relationships.'* These relationships involve one monogamous partner who approves of his or her partner having intimate relationships with others.

Furthermore, we have *'Open Polyamorous Relationships'*, where both partners allow romantic or sexual relationships with other people outside the relationship. In the case of open marriages or open relationships, intimacy may be limited emotionally and open only sexually, for example, in swingers.

On the contrary, we also have *'Closed Polyamorous Relationships'* (sometimes called polyfidelity), restricted to a defined group of committed partners.

Polyfidelity gives rise to concerns since it involves multiple interpersonal relationships, where sexual contact is restricted to only specific partners in the group. Hence, it is challenging or nearly impossible to keep check and balance or to expect complete fidelity.

In addition to the associations mentioned above, we also consider *'solo polyamory'* situations. These are the conditions under which an individual possesses no particular desire to adjoin or create a household with their intimate partners.

Who Seeks Polyamory and Why

Extensive changes are occurring in the sexual and relational landscapes, including dissatisfaction with limitations of serial monogamy, i.e., exchanging one partner for another in the hope of a better outcome. Clinicians must recognize an array of possibilities that 'polyamory' encompasses and examine our culturally-based assumption that 'only monogamy is acceptable.' They must also analyze how such biasness affects the practice of this therapy, the need for self-education about polyamory, basic understanding about the "rewards of the poly lifestyle," and the common social and relationship challenges faced by those involved, and the "shadow side" of polyamory, the potential existing for coercion, strong emotions in opposition, and jealousy.

In 2003, Helena Echlin stated in *"The Guardian,"* the six reasons why people choose polyamory. These causes include a drive toward female independence and equality driven by feminism. Also, disappointment with monogamy, in part because of widespread cheating and divorce, followed by an extremely supportive aspect of individual non-matching of the traditional monogamous stereotype. Further, there is a yearning, a dire need for the richness of complex and deep relationships through extended networks, an expectation of honesty and realism for human nature.

Considering the U.S. point of perspective, there was a couple in the U.S., namely, John and Rebecca, who had been married for 16 years and had three children. They both had good jobs. To everyone around them, they appeared to be living the life of a happy and normal married couple. Their home was beautiful. Their parents visited them frequently and took care of the children when the couple went on vacation alone. Still, Rebecca was far from satisfied and had a feeling of emptiness inside.

One evening after the children had gone to sleep, the couple was sitting and watching TV in their bedroom when Rebecca looked at her husband, sighed deeply, and said, *"We need to discuss something long overdue."*

John said, *"About what?"*

She answered, *"What do you think about us becoming polyamorous? A year ago, our neighbors told us all about their consensual non-monogamous marriage."*

John was surprised and shocked with a blank look on his face. He looked at her with amazement and shook his head. Then he asked, *"What's the matter with you, honey? What are you talking about?"*

Rebecca decided right there and then. She told her husband all that she felt and what she was going through. She told him first that she loved him very much, and that she wanted to make their relationship stronger, happier, and more complete. She was not interested in ever leaving him. She told him that throughout their marriage, she had cheated on him. She had to make up stories about where she was going, and she felt guilty. She lived in constant fear of being discovered, although she suspected that he knew something was going on. She said that monogamy had been a struggle for her. She always had two boyfriends. John told her that they would discuss things the next day.

In fact, they had three lengthy discussions about the pros and cons of polyamory. They read about consensual non-monogamous marriage, then decided that they will try a polyamorous lifestyle with separate partners. That was easier said than done! Initially, Rebecca became quite jealous and envious of her husband's lady partner. But soon, she had two lovers of her own, and gradually, her relationship with her husband became increasingly comfortable with their polyamorous lives. Over the ensuing years, Rebecca continued to date men with her husband's consent, and he had his own women partners. The couple remained married, loved each other very much, confided, and openly communicated. They were also open with their children and informed them about polyamory. The couple was satisfied with their stable love relationship, which worked for them.

Polyamory Values

Extensive changes are occurring in the sexual and relational landscape, including dissatisfaction with limitations of serial monogamy, i.e., exchanging one partner for another in the hope of a better outcome. Clinicians need to recognize an array of possibilities that 'polyamory' encompasses and examine our culturally-based assumption that 'only monogamy is acceptable' and how such biasness impacts the practice of this therapy, the need for self-education about polyamory, basic understanding about the "rewards of the poly lifestyle" and the common social and relationship challenges faced by those involved, and the "shadow side" of polyamory, the potential existing for coercion, strong emotions in opposition, and jealousy.

Polyamory advocates certain values, which are elaborated and highlighted below:

Fidelity and Loyalty – Fidelity and loyalty in polyamory mean being faithful to the promises and agreements made about the relationship. An example of a breach of fidelity would be a secret sexual relationship that violates those promises. Polyamorists are committed to practicing responsible non-monogamy. They have consensual relationships and multiple partners with varying grades of intensity, closeness, and commitment, but *not* sexual exclusivity.

Communication and Negotiation – Polyamorists usually recommend honesty and respectful communication and explicit negotiation among all involved, aimed at transparently establishing the consensual terms of their relationships. Polyamorous relationships do not have a standard model that fits all. If and when mistakes or failure to live up to the terms arise, communication takes a very crucial role in repairing any breaches.

Trust, Honesty, Dignity, and Respect – Most polyamorists emphasize respect, dignity, trust, and honesty for all partners. They accept one another as part of their life. They avoid relationships that require deception and secrecy.

Boundaries and Agreements – Polyamorous relationships are generally based on verbal or written agreements, which establish specific rules and boundaries. These agreements are comprehensive but may be altered by the partners over time.

They include how to handle new relationships, duties, and

responsibilities of the partners, frequency of intimacy, work schedules, physical displays of affection, financial considerations, and budgeting.

Gender Equality – Polyamorists typically treat their partners equally without acting and behaving like a patriarchist, regardless of gender. However, the partners may agree to adhere to gender-specific boundaries. For instance, individual differences, emotions, and needs of a married couple who is contemplating polyamory for the first time may lead them to negotiate and agree that the wife limits her romantic and sexual relationships to women and vice versa. The agreement may have a temporary nature and open to renegotiation.

Shortcomings of Polyamory

In 2015, Elisabeth Sheff noted in *'Five Disadvantages of Polyamory'* a few reasons to make it more evident and plausible as to why polyamory does not work for everyone. These reasons were of varying degrees to each other.

Beginning from the foremost cause; *'Complexity.'* Romantic relationships can be highly emotional, and that intensity can be multiplied by the number of people involved. It can be challenging to find time for all of the relationships, or one can lose the valuable alone time.

Following the trauma of complexity comes *'Faulty Negotiation.'* A polyamorous relationship can be destroyed if consent is negotiated under compulsion, which is truly non- consensual. Forcefulness can be of many forms, ranging from financial, emotional, physical, explicit, implied, or even unconscious.

Considered significantly important after the above-mentioned causes is *'Partner Turnover.'* This is an aspect where larger poly groups, after constant experiences, encounter a change in membership, which can be problematic to some partners. Moreover, an undeniably more considerable situation is that some children experience painful loss and disappointment when their parents' partners leave.

This can further result in *'Legal Problems'* since sexual minorities have conventionally fared poorly in court when family members or institutional representatives from the 'Child Protective Services' challenge the custody of their children.

The lawyer has more or less limited liberty in family court and is ultimately driven by what the judge determines to be in the best interest of the child.

Also, *'Too Much Supervision'* is the most daunting disadvantage identified in kids from poly families. It was the difficulty they experienced in getting away with anything they were not supposed to be doing because there were too many adults paying attention to them. Even worse for the kids is that the adults communicate with each other, so any lie that the kids tried to get away with, had to remain consistent over multiple conversations with different adults, who could spot inconsistencies in the kids' stories.

Benefits of Polyamory

In 1987, Robert Heinlein stated "The more you love, the more you can love, and the more intensely you love. Nor is there any limit on how many you can love. If a person had enough time, they could love all of that majority who are decent and just." For instance, the parent who has two children does not love either of them any less because of the existence of the other. But some disagree when one's love is divided among multiple partners, the love is lessened.

In 1996, Kit Peters noted in *'Polyamory 101: Consensual Non-Monogamy for the 21st Century'* that polyamorous relationships have benefits, some of them are elaborated below.

Firstly, individuals can discuss issues with multiple partners, reduce polarization of viewpoints, and potentially mediate and stabilize relationships. If you have problems with one of the people in the relationship, you can often talk to another participant about it, with the added advantage of having a relationship based on confidence and wider perspectives. When one person faces problems, the others in the relationship would be there to help them through it.

Moreover, committed adults within the familial unit provide emotional support to others that need help. Because several partners are in the relationship, there is a wider range of adult experience, skills, resources, and perspectives.

In addition to this, companionate marriages, which can be satisfying though no longer sexually active, maybe supported because romantic needs are met elsewhere. This polyamory benefit acts to preserve existing relationships. There are more emotional, intellectual, and sexual needs met as part of the understanding that one person cannot be expected to provide all. Polyamory offers release from the monogamist expectation that one person must meet all of an individual's needs, including sex, emotional support, primary friendship, intellectual stimulation, companionship, and social presentation.

Religion and Polyamory

Typical Christianity does not approve of polyamory. However, some people consider themselves Christian *as well as* polyamorous. The liberated Christians' views explore their natural tendency toward multiple relationships and provide biblical study material supporting their interests.

Typical Judaism does not accept polyamory either. However, some Jews are polyamorous, and it may be a choice that does not preclude a Jewishly observant and socially conscious life.

Islam neither lodges nor approves of polyamory. However, ***polygamy*** is permitted. A male can marry four women at a time, if needed, for as long as he cares for them equally.

Legal Aspects of Polyamory

In 2014, Elisabeth Sheff noted in '*The Polyamorists Next Door*' the following five most common legal issues facing polyamorists in her words:

1. **Custody** – Sexual or gender minority parents are particularly vulnerable in court proceedings, and the U.S. has a long history of removing children from parents deemed "morally unsound."

2. **Morality Clause** – Some corporations and organizations have morality clauses in their employment contracts and can fire those employees who violate it. Sexual minorities are at a unique risk of firing for violating moral clauses.

3. **Adultery/Bigamy** – Polyamorists and other non-monogamists who are legally married can be accused of adultery and even bigamy. Virtually, no one is prosecuted for adultery unless their spouse brings the case.

4. **Housing** – In some jurisdictions, landlords can legally limit the number of unrelated adults living in a household.

5. **Importance of Location** – Married heterosexuals are generally considered married, regardless of their state of residence. In contrast, people in same-sex relationships can change the relational status by merely crossing state lines. People who are family members in one state can be abruptly barred from family rights in another. Sex and gender minorities are subject to regulations that change their relationship as they travel, making the law capricious for them differently from heterosexuals.

In most countries, it is legal for three or more people to form and share a sexual relationship. Individuals involved in polyamorous relationships are generally considered by the law to be no different from people who live together, or "date", under other circumstances.

There are no laws in the U.S. that specifically address polyamorous marriages. Marriage rights for polyamorous families may be fully supported, according to some legal scholars, by the U.S. constitutional rights of Due Process and Equal Protection. There is a "dyadic networks" model that calls for the revision of existing U.S. laws against bigamy. That model would permit married individuals to enter into additional marriages, but they must first give legal notice to their existing marital partner.

Statistical Overview of Polyamory

In the U.S., polyamory is a growing movement and enlarging community, in part, resulting from the high rate of divorce, the increasing number of unmarried singles, higher women population, and the dissatisfaction with the stringent requirements of monogamy.

It is estimated that, in 1950, only 22 percent of the adults were unmarried (single). While, in 2014, for the first time, unmarried people made up the majority of the American adult population. About 50.2 percent or 124.6 million adults were unmarried. Following this, in 2015, unmarried U.S. women aged 18 and older numbered 53%, as compared to 47% men. However, in 2016, about 4–5 percent of Americans participated in some form of *ethical* non-monogamy. Monogamy is the expected rule for 'couples,' especially those who are married. But, in general, humans have a hard time with it. Close to half of marriages end up in separation or divorce. Of those who are married, nonconsensual extramarital affairs, subject to cheating and adultery are common.

Chapter 8

Termination of Love Relationship: Separation and Divorce

Termination of Love

Steve Duck demonstrates a five-phase model for ending a relationship. Here, we briefly put them in the limelight:

Relationship phase – The relationship is fairly strong, but dissatisfaction gives rise to feelings of 'there's something wrong.' Eventually, the 'I can't stand it anymore' feelings bottle up to a point which hurls you into stages of collapse.

Intrapsychic phase – Nothing much is said. However, the focus is set on picking out blame on the other partner. Probably only seeking chances to seek evidence that could be legit enough, and when sufficient evidence is gathered, the person feels vindicated in withdrawing.

Dyadic phase – The breakdown now comes out into the open, either with one person saying 'I'm leaving' or 'I'm thinking of leaving'. The truth must now be faced by both partners, and exhaustive negotiations may arise. Eventually, the pressure of 'I really mean it' breaks out, and it becomes an open issue.

Social phase – Now, the attention turns away to the perceptions of other people. Friends may be involved to lodge, or whole social groups may end up into open clashes of who is to blame and what should be done. Eventually, it becomes unavoidable that the split will happen, and things escalate into the next phase.

Grave-dressing phase – The relationship now gets its official burying, with clarifications all in place.

Ways of Ending a Relationship

There are certain commonly observed strategies based on a few researches that two people employ when trying to break up a relationship:

- *Positive attitude*: 'I still like you, but…'

- *Vocal cutback*: 'I don't love you anymore.'

- *Behavioral cutback*: Avoiding contact. Seeing them less often.

- *Negative personality management*: 'We each should see other people...'

- *Rationalization*: 'This relationship is not giving me what I want.'

Second Marriages

"Two-thirds of second marriages end in divorce, and those with stepchildren fare even worse."

The most imperative reason people get divorced is finance. It becomes highly significant to resolve a new set of issues that remarriage presents. There are certain helpful suggestions a couple could and should consider alongside the thought of remarriage, such as before setting a wedding date. The couple should and indeed must discuss their finances openly, not only with each other but under the guidance and help of a financial manager. It is quite tempting to avoid discussing certain assets or debts. Often, the financial discussions are discussed only between the couple without any external advice, and this could result in misunderstandings, tension, and hostile feelings.

Furthermore, review state law regarding the rights of the surviving spouse to the estate of the first to die. Before remarriage, consider entering into a prenuptial agreement. If no pre-nuptial agreement was done, consider a post-nuptial agreement to make sure one's rights are solidified and avoid arguments among your offspring, after either spouse dies.

Homeownership is an incredibly significant issue to consider. The remarried seniors should consider not to own the home jointly if they have adult children. Joint ownership results in a windfall for one side or the other. Furthermore, if the owner of the home adds the new spouse as a joint owner. The new spouse inherits the house upon the death of the first owner. Upon the death of the new spouse, his or her children will get the home to the exclusion of the first owner's children. This can be resolved by giving the new spouse occupancy rights with specific conditions.

On the contrary, some seniors choose not to remarry but have a committed relationship and live separately in their own homes wherever they are. This may eliminate some of the problems discussed above.

Second Marriage Patient at the Nursing Home

This is a true love story as narrated by Sherry to Annie while discussing a couple at the nursing home, who were subject to a second marriage. Donna Lou Young and Henry V. Rayhons lost their respective spouses. And they were in their 70s when they met and fell in love. They got married in 2007. More than 350 people attended their wedding reception. Henry was a well-known, longtime Iowa legislator in Duncan, Iowa.

For the next six-and-a-half years after being married, Henry and Donna Rayhons were inseparable. She sat near him in the State House Chamber while he worked as a Republican legislator. He helped with her beekeeping. She rode alongside him in a combine, as he harvested corn and soybeans on his 700 acres in northern Iowa. They sang in the choir at Sunday Mass.

A few years after the couple got married, Donna was diagnosed with Alzheimer's disease, which progressed to the point that she had to be admitted to a nursing home in March 2014.

Henry was devoted to her. Throughout her illness, he neither left nor divorced her. He also wanted to maintain intimacy with her. On May 15, 2014, Henry accepted that his wife did not have the reasoning ability to consent to sexual activity.

On May 23, 2014, Donna's roommate complained to the authorities that during his visit to his wife in the nursing home, Henry went into his wife's room and pulled the curtain closed. Then the roommate heard 'sexual' noises, which indicated to her that Henry was having sex with his wife. The surveillance video showed Henry leaving his wife's room and discarding undergarments into a laundry bag. That same day, one of Donna's daughters learned about the incident. She became quite upset. The daughter wanted that incident followed up, and her mother examined. Many calls between nursing home staff and Donna's daughters followed, and the police were called.

Sometime after midnight, Garner's police chief took Donna to a hospital for a sexual assault test. Her panties and bedding were sent to the state crime lab in Ankeny. The state crime lab completed Donna's rape test on November 20, 2014. It took six months to process because of a backlog at the lab. Examination of the swabs taken from Donna's mouth and vagina showed no evidence of seminal fluid, and no DNA other than hers.

However, there was a stain in her underwear, which indicated the presence of seminal fluid, but no spermatozoa were microscopically identified.

On August 8, 2014, Donna Rayhons died at the age of 78 years. The memorial noted that Donna enjoyed spending time with Henry and being part of his family. She supported Henry as a state representative and enjoyed her years at the Capitol and attending political functions with him. A Hancock County judge ordered that Donna's daughter, Suzan Brunes, be made her temporary guardian. About a week after Donna died, the Iowa Division of Criminal Investigation (DCI) agents arrested Henry Rayhons. He was charged with third-degree sexual abuse, which is a felony in Iowa, after supposedly having sex with his late wife Donna Lou Rayhons while she was living in a Garner care facility. It happened after he was told that she could not consent due to her mental condition, she was suffering from dementia. He was released from jail after posting $10,000 cash as bail.

Henry's trial started on April 15, 2015, in Hancock County District Court. Jurors listened to about two hours of the audio recording of Henry Rayhons' interview of June 12, 2014, with the Division of Criminal Investigation. During that interview, the prosecutors said that he confessed to sexually abusing his wife. The prosecutors said that Donna could not consent to sex because of the effects of Alzheimer's disease. In the interview with a DCI agent, Henry described vaginally penetrating his wife in her room at the Concord Care Center in Garner. At trial, defense lawyers raised fundamental doubts about his guilt, including whether Henry even had sex with his wife in the facility.

Henry denied that he did on the night in question. At trial, Donna's 86-year-old roommate at the time of the incident testified that she heard noises from behind a curtain, but she could not confirm whether they were sexual noises. At trial, it was not clear who initiated the complaint, but the authorities called it rape because the nursing home staffers had stated that his wife could no longer consent to sex. On April 22, 2015, after three days of deliberation, the Jury found Henry Rayhons not guilty of sexually assaulting his wife.

Separation for the Sake of Children

'A Separation' was an Iranian drama film, released in 2011. It focused on a middle-class couple, Nader and Simin, who had been married for 14 years and lived with their 11-year-old daughter Termeh in Tehran. Simin wanted to leave the country with her family and allow Termeh not to grow up under the prevailing conditions. The husband and daughter disagreed.

Nader was concerned for his elderly father, who lived with the family and suffered from Alzheimer's. Simin filed for divorce. The family court found the couple's problems insufficient to warrant divorce and denied the petition. Simin left her husband and daughter and moved back in with her parents. On Simi's recommendation, Nader hired Razieh, a young, deeply religious woman from a poor suburb, to take care of his father while he worked at a bank.

Several problems arose, resulting in accusations on both sides and miscarriage of pregnancy by Razieh. It led to court proceedings and settlement discussions. The court was assigned to determine the cause of the miscarriage and Nader's potential responsibility for it. If it were proved that Nader knew of Razieh's pregnancy and caused the miscarriage, he could be sentenced to one to three years of imprisonment for murder. Nader accused Razieh of neglecting his father. The case settled. Later, at the family court, Nader and Simin re-filed for a divorce. The father had died. The judge made their separation permanent. The judge also asked Termeh about her choice of which parent to live with. She tearfully said that she had made a decision, but asked that the judge tell her parents to wait outside in the hallway before she told him. The parents waited in the hallway, separated by a glass partition.

Alzheimer's Causes Grief in Second Marriage

'A Song for Martin' was a Swedish film with English subtitles that came out in 2001. It was a moving story, considered as one of the most realistic depictions of caregivers on film. Sven Wollter and Viveka Seldahl, who were married in real life, played a married couple, Martin and Barbara. They were prominent. Martin, in his late 50s, met the beautiful Barbara, who was 10 years younger, and the couple fell in love at first sight. They both divorced their spouses and got married. Martin was a talented and famous conductor and composer. Barbara was a violinist. Things

went well until five years later when Martin suddenly started to experience small memory slips, which violently progressed. Barbara found herself helplessly observing her once wonderful and loving spouse turn into a different person, who did not even know her. That caused pain and struggle for both of them. The film presented a compelling but tragic story of how painful and extensive Alzheimer's disease can be. It dove deep into the denial, sadness, and struggle experienced by the person with Alzheimer's disease, and the grief, depression, and desperation experienced by their caregiver.

Reasons Leading up to Divorce

Money Problems – The love for money is the root of all kinds of evil, and it's definitely the cause of arguments, fights, and court actions. Problems may arise when it comes to money if partners possess different value bases. For instance, if one person likes spending money freely and the other is more frugal and prefers saving. So, when there is any issue related to money and finance, it is crucial that you discuss the same with your partner and resolve it soon.

Affairs – If one person is having an affair, it is likely to break down trust and lead to difficulties in establishing honesty in a relationship.

Interfering Ex-Partners – When establishing a new relationship, an ex-partner getting your partner's attention can create tension. It can feel like they are still married to the ex, or that the ex is more significant.

Sexual Incompatibility – In any marriage, physical intimacy is essential, and a problem in this area often causes stress, ultimately leading to divorce. Sexual incompatibility, whether it is due to reproductive incapability or any other issue, varies significantly from couple to couple. This is why any couple who feels that such an issue is affecting their relationship should take professional help and try to resolve the problem.

Remember, improper attitudes about sex can also bring couples to the breaking point.

Differences in Sexual Libido – It is a stereotype but not far off the mark. Many men want more sex than women, and if couples have different levels of sexual libido, this will lead to problems in the relationship.

Children from Previous Relationships – There is a big difference between how people react to their own children and the spouses' children.

Parents make different allowances for children who are their own. However, if they are somebody else's children, it may be more challenging to establish the same relationship.

Intrusive Parents – If parents are interfering, or if a partner perceives them to be, this can be a problem. For example, if one partner spends too much time talking to their mother, this can create a breakdown of intimacy in the relationship.

Difference Approach to Resolve a Conflict – If someone has grown up in a family where arguing is quite common, and they are in a relationship with someone who does not like arguing or is not used to it, this can cause difficulty. Since you have different ways of solving problems, it is likely that your problems will never get resolved.

Differences in Communication – If one partner is the type of person who shares all their intimate thoughts, but their partner is not, this can cause problems, too. If one partner is not sharing with the other, the other will often interpret is as meaning 'they don't love me, they're not interested in me'.

Privacy Problems – Another problem can be when one person has a different view of what should be kept within the relationship. If one person shares all the intimate details of the relationship with their friends or over Facebook, this can be an increasingly difficult thing to manage.

Lack of Communication – For the survival and success of any relationship, proper communication is mandatory. When there is less or no communication, problems arise in any relationship, and marriage is no exception. In fact, the lack of communication is one of the leading causes behind the termination of a marriage. When communication lines fail, both you and your partner will stop discussing your mutual and personal issues. Good and open communication is essential in the relationship of a husband and wife to ensure that both partners understand each other.

Infidelity or Cheating – Marriage is a relationship based on trust, faith, and feelings for each other. When one starts cheating their partner, and the fact gets revealed by the other partner, the trust and faith do not remain the same. Most of the time, the most suitable solution comes in the form of divorce. This is why infidelity often becomes one of the leading factors behind the dissolution of marriage.

Different Expectations – Wrong or too much expectation from your partner can, at times, lead to arguments. It is vital for both the husband and wife not to allow their expectations to reach great heights for a successful marriage. They should be reasonable in what they expect from their partner. If this is not fulfilled, it can lead to divorce.

Commitment – Marriage is an institution that needs commitment from both parties. It is impossible for just one individual to make the marriage successful. Commitment must be provided equally from both the partners, and when one does not care about the relationship, it will certainly die.

Commitment and sacrifice go hand in hand to make a marriage successful. Without a commitment from both partners, there will be a high possibility of breaking a relationship.

Child-rearing Issues – Just like when you are not able to have a child, the issue of child nurturing can also cause cracks in marriage and lead to divorce. Many times, the sexual drought and the increase in the list of responsibilities that often follows childbirth become challenging for couples to handle. One of the ways to manage child-rearing is to write down responsibilities and share them reasonably. This way, you can easily share your responsibilities as parents, and your child will not have to go for emotional torture that actually takes place after divorce.

Job and Career – In a highly advanced society like the U.S., men and women work together. At times, the professional life of partners becomes the reason for divorce. For instance, when career-oriented husbands expect that their wives to sacrifice their careers for the sake of the family, it can lead to differences in thoughts. This is why it is essential for both husband and wife to understand each other's job requirements. Career is important for both the partners, and thus one should have respect for the other partner. Any abrupt decision made in the case of career and job often leads to problems in married life.

Boredom – When there is boredom in marriage, couples eventually grow distant and disinterested in each other. Some of the common factors behind boredom are not the lack of sex, illness, inability to age elegantly, lack of mutual interests, intellectual incompatibility, social isolation, dependent adult children, insufficient financial resources, and lack of humor.

Couples facing any of these situations should remember the good things and accomplishments of their lives and shift the focus from the negatives to the positives. Take care of the first sign of boredom by trying new and interesting things, or otherwise, your marriage might end in divorce.

Reconciliation made Possible for Separated Couples

Very few people who have experienced a broken relationship even try to reconcile. The U.S. statistics on separation and divorce show that almost 87% of separated couples proceed to obtain a divorce. The remaining 13% reunite after separation.

Reconciliation can happen only when there is a hope of making up and winning back lost love. There are a few ways and possibilities that separated couples could consider adapting to or either consult further counseling regarding these possibilities.

Get Inspiration – If you have any doubt regarding reconciliation after living separately from your spouse, look around to how other separated couples have done it. You can get inspiration from other couples that have gone through a bad relationship breakup and thought of living together again. When you talk to such people, you get to see things in a better manner and realize that marriage and love are vital for you. Other people can make you realize that love is sweeter the second time around. This way, you will become positive and proceed to do things to reunite again.

Learn from Others – The secret to save your marriage after separation is to learn from other successful married people. You can learn from them the secret behind their successful marriage. Seek the advice of reunited couples who have experienced the hardships of divorce and ask them how they made it as a couple again. You can even get tips from them on how to make your spouse see the love in your relationship.

Also, learn from them how to build a strong relationship and keep it going if you get the chance again.

Accept Your Mistakes – For any relationship to work, it needs the effort of two persons, and marriage is not an exception. To make the relationship successful, you and your spouse must accept the mistakes made by each other that have contributed toward the breakup. Admit your faults and the role you played in the troubles in your marriage. This will help you build a new foundation in which you both can take responsibility for making the relationship work. Also, never make the mistake of blaming each other. Just lower down your pride and admit your mistakes. It is a fact that there cannot be any positive sign of reconciliation if the effort is one-sided.

Commitment – The most important step in the reconciliation of a relationship is the commitment made by both partners to get back together. Both of you must promise that you are going to work toward reconciliation and make your marriage successful. It is a fact that couples who are not living together cannot reunite successfully if there is a lack of commitment by the partners for getting back together.

Give Time – It is good to rebuild your relationship slowly so that you find yourself ready again for the demands of your relationship. Both of you need some time and space to work things out. When you spend time alone, you can think rationally and figure out what needs to be changed when you get back together. You can see your own faults and realize the importance of your spouse in your life.

Be Ready for Changes – If everything would have been perfect, separation may not have happened at all. There was some problem in the relationship, and the reason can be you or your spouse; no matter what things that were not okay, need to be changed for the better. Be honest with your wants and desired changes. This exchange will help you determine if you both can realistically build a life together that is acceptable to both of you.

Don't Blame – Never blame each other for the failure of the relationship or point fingers to faults. Instead, you both need to say sorry to each other and suggest things that can help in your future relationship. If you notice that your spouse is feeling uncomfortable about talking of the past, stop it at once. Good communication is possible when both of you are ready.

Say Sorry – Couples who want to go down the path of reconciliation must be prepared to let go of anger and pain. You must understand that forgiveness, rebuilding trust, and openness to change are the primary ingredients of reconciliation. It is quite common for a person to say things to their spouse in anger or in the spur of the moment that actually becomes the reason for divorce. Once you realize the fact, just a true sorry from your end can save you from the emotional trauma during the divorce process.

Acknowledge – You need to acknowledge your spouse whenever you notice an effort from their end to reconcile after separation. Make your spouse realize that you are eager to make your marriage successful and tell your spouse about your feelings. Show your real emotions, but do not try to act dramatically. Your spouse knows you in a better way, and when there is a sincere effort from your end, your spouse will surely get a clear message.

Counseling – If required, you can even take the help of a counselor to discuss reconciliation and the issues that led to the divorce in the first place. You and your spouse might also find it easier to talk honestly with a third party. Counseling sessions can help in realizing what went wrong in your relationship and how you can work on it.

Chapter 9
Love Relationships among Seniors

Senior Love Relationships

The question of Seniors Dating – should or should not?

Seniors, like any other person, seek love and companionship. Naturally, if they are without a partner, they will consider various routes to meet new people. Sometimes, this may involve dating in a bid to find a romantic interest. If a single adult wishes to be dating, it is their right. Age should not be a limiting factor. It is often a reason put forth by children, who are at times resistant to their single parent's idea of starting a new chapter in their life.

The idea that seniors have a shorter lifespan at that time and are not physically capable of sexual contact is extraneous. The need for intimacy and companionship is not age-dependent, and where there is a willing partner, a new relationship should be encouraged and accepted if desired. Relationships, or the lack of it, have been shown as factors of depression in the elderly. It even affects lifespan.

Inappropriateness is never a suitable excuse if two willing adults enter into a consensual relationship that does not pose a threat to either party or their close contacts. Social norms may differ among cultures and countries, but these are individual considerations that cannot be applied to a person not willing to follow suit. Therefore, no specific reasons should be needed for considering a new relationship or seeking new partners through dating.

Engaging with New People in the Senior Years

It may not always be about love and intimacy, but seniors may wish to meet new people and initiate friendships rather than intimate relationships. At a time in life where the number of one's social contacts often decreases, it is not merely a matter of being introduced by a mutual friend or hoping to meet another single hopeful in a bar or club. Seniors may take a soberer approach. Often, this is not easy and even downright awkward for a senior who may have last been in the dating scene decades before. Fortunately, there is a host of professional services that cater to seniors. Some of these providers have physical premises where one discusses their intentions and scour through other like-minded hopefuls. However, in this age of technology, the Internet has become a more popular route. Dating websites have sprung up all across the Internet and have become the preferred choice for seniors worldwide.

Sizzle of Love among Seniors

It was early November. Sherry and Annie visited their parents, then decided to go shopping at a new mall where they could also have a meal. They walked around the mall from one shop to another, admiring the new merchandise. They did not find anything they could not live without. They were getting tired and hungry. They found a nice Italian restaurant and ordered food. While they were talking about Sherry's husband Mortimer, and their love life, Sherry explained how some senior people tend to make love and keep the passion alive in their relationship.

Annie asked, "How about elderly women? Do they desire and enjoy sex as much as older men?"

Sherry said, "Sure. Older women can also enjoy, at times, very erotic, orgasmic sex without penile intercourse. They often enjoy kisses, caresses, massages, oral sex, and sex toys with adequate genital lubrication."

Annie said, "So, what you are saying is that elderly couples need not hold back their desire for more sex. They should be more affectionate by touching outside the bedroom, ask for oral sex, or even have fun sharing some wild fantasies."

Sherry said, "That's right. Some couples tell each other to use their erotic imagination and create the best ambiance for romance and sex. Some elderly couples use soft lights or candles in the bathroom or bedroom, place flowers on the dresser, and dark chocolates on the pillow. Others use silky sheets and plush pillows."

Annie said, "Yes, and some elderly women do make themselves feel sexy by wearing sexy lingerie, soft robes, and perfume."

Sherry continued, "I think that elderly people could at times shift the location of lovemaking outside the bedroom to the living room, the den, the kitchen, the backyard, the swimming pool, or even the back seat of the car. That may make the couple feel younger, and a little bit naughty, which adds sizzle to their sexual activity."

Late-Life Love: Romance and New Relationships in Later Years

Sherry continued, "Last week, I spent quite a bit of time researching online the subject of elderly sex. Connie Goldman, who was an award-winning radio producer and reporter, published an excellent book in 2006, entitled, 'Late-Life Love: Romance and New Relationships in Later Years.' She asked some people between the ages of 20 and 45 what they thought about 70-year-old people hugging, touching, having sexual relations, and living together. Some laughed, some just smiled, and one person responded, "Aren't people over 65 beyond all

that?" Love, intimacy, sex, and building meaningful relationships exist in older couples. They feel spiritual independence that comes with aging. Partners make their own plans on how they live together and often disregard what people think. Connie interviewed 22 couples for her book. They had diverse relationships – cohabiting and married couples, long-distance relationships, and same-sex partnerships. She found that "Human needs for closeness, touch, and intimacy remain with us until our last breath. Older people embrace, kiss, and make love. Sexuality is alive and thriving in folks with big bellies and gray hair. Touching, caressing, enjoying each other's bodies, offer intimacy and pleasure. For some, the physical relationship isn't what it was in their younger days. Yet, many have told me that both their lovemaking and emotional lives get richer and deeper in late-life relationships."

Love Making Urge among Seniors

Louise Wellborn of Atlanta, Georgia, was a businesswoman who died in 2012. She believed that good sex is beneficial at any age. It is healthy and keeps one active and alive. Louise and her husband were deeply in love. After the children left home and her husband retired, the couple had more freedom to express their sexuality. They had sex three to four times a week when the children lived at home. Once they were alone, they made love almost every day. Louise believed that sex kept her husband alive for so long when he was sick with Alzheimer's.

The couple had a variety of excellent sex acts, and at any time of day they wanted until he died in 1997 from complications of Alzheimer's. Louise grieved for several years over her husband's death. At age 73, she began a new relationship with a man in his 80s. They mostly enjoyed each other's company and had sex occasionally. Although the man was quite virile, it was hard for him to have an erection, probably due to his heart medication. However, they had sex differently, which she did not mind. The couple were very affectionate and enjoyed waking up in the morning next to each other.

A few years later, Louise developed breast cancer and underwent a mastectomy. But that did not alter her self-image as a sexual being, which she attributed primarily to having had a lifelong positive attitude toward sexuality. This attitude is in keeping with experts' contention that patterns of sexuality are set earlier in life when the biological changes associated with aging are less pronounced, and that sexuality is less affected if sexual activity is constant throughout life. Louise expected to make love as long as she could. She had a good loving man and a good sex life. Had she stopped, she would have missed sex terribly.

Satisfaction in Elderly Love

Cornelia met Gerry when he took his wife, who was dying of Alzheimer's, to a kosher nutrition program where

Cornelia, a widow, worked as a volunteer. The couple gradually became close friends. After his wife's death, the couple became intimate. When Gerald proposed, Cornelia accepted with pleasure. They were both 72 when they married. They felt like young lovers or newlyweds. They were able to make love better than when they were younger. They had a whole lifetime of experience. Over the two years that they had been married, Cornelia and Gerry disliked the patronizing attitude that many people displayed toward older people who are intimate. Whenever people asked and found out that they had been married for two years, the people said, 'Oh, that's so cute.' The couple did not know anything about being cute.

Their love life was warm and satisfying.

Married Seniors Experimenting Love and Sex

Some elderly individuals are creative when it comes to sexual activity in various places, whether it is outdoors, in a swimming pool, or during travel. Stewardesses have seen sexual activity on airplanes. It is not unusual for a stewardess to see evidence of ejaculates on the small blankets provided by the airline. One night while traveling from New York to Paris, the stewardess dimmed the light, so people can sleep. However, an elderly couple in their 70's was seated next to each other in the two-seat section of the plane. The stewardess observed them have mutual hand stimulation of each other's genitals under the blanket.

The next time the stewardess walked by, the woman was having an orgasm, but her husband was asleep. Then the woman got up and went to the bathroom. Curious as to what was going on, the stewardess struck a conversation with the woman. She told the woman that she looked like she was having an orgasm. The woman responded, "Oh yes, I never travel without my special vibrating egg. It relaxes me and puts me to sleep." This lady knows what to do when she travels.

Barriers to Seniors and Dating

While seniors desire to love, they face many obstacles beyond social norms and taboos. Biological, demographic, and psychological factors can all make it challenging for seniors to form romantic relationships. Older men often develop a sense of inferiority because they are less virile compared to their younger selves. In contrast, older women often come to see themselves as unattractive because of society's worship of youth. Older men who are eligible often seek younger wives. It is common for them to start a new family instead of pairing up with someone their own age.

On the other hand, women live eight years longer than men. This means that there are many lonely widowed women whose prospects of finding another partner are slim. For instance, there is an average of seven women for each man in assisted living communities.

Seniors Reclaiming Intimacy

In her groundbreaking book, author Friedman explains many of the difficulties that seniors face when approaching love are based on expectations that intimacy and love ought to be the same as it was during middle-age.

Instead, she explains, older people must define new modes of intimacy and sexuality that are not based on the conceptions applying to younger adults:

"Before it is too late, we can choose to tear down the walls that we have built up against intimacy, choose to take

the risks of it and choose to create the experiences and reunions that will keep it alive, over the distance of time and space. But space itself, and time too, must be created anew; we have to use it differently, or maybe move to a different space, for the bonds of intimacy to continue to grow and nourish us in age."

Senior living communities are one place where dating has blossomed. Men and women who had once resigned themselves to isolation have been able to rebuild intimacy with a new companion, in a new place, and in new ways.

The Family's Perspective on Senior Relationships

Notably, honesty was the most fundamental element ofnrelationship success in the collective intelligence structural model developed by the older adult group. Honesty was not identified as an element of relationship success by the younger adult group. Older adults defined it as being 'able to confide in one another in a truthful way.' Honesty is an interesting concept as it involves self-disclosure and risks putting an individual in a vulnerable position. Yet, the ability to disclose honestly in a mindful, trusting, and sensitive fashion can facilitate a more profound intimacy level in the relationship. Furthermore, research has suggested that self-acceptance increases with age as people have a stronger sense of their true self and less of a discrepancy between 'real' and 'ideal' selves. It is possible that the older adult group in Kate's study was able to draw on their broad experience and have come to recognize honesty as critical to the long-term success of romantic relationships.

In contrast, younger participants valued Trust and Communication as fundamental drivers of relationship success. Younger adults defined trust as being 'able to rely on and be supportive of one another' and 'to be faithful to one another.'

Interestingly, older adults also selected Religion as one of the critical elements of successful romantic relationships. They believed that sharing religious beliefs and attending church together provided a foundation for a successful relationship. This element was not identified as necessary by the younger adult group.

Socializing was also highlighted as a crucial factor by older people. During the group session, they emphasized that socializing encapsulated going out as a couple but also individually. During later life, one's social network may reduce in size, but within this context, older adults often enjoy increased frequency of socializing with friends and neighbors. This pattern of increased socializing may facilitate romantic relationships, as it stimulates intimacy and communication amongst older lovers.

U.S. Census (2014)

Elderly sex should gradually lose some of its taboo statuses, particularly as the baby boomers become seniors. The baby boomers will expect to make love as long as they can. There will be more U.S. senior citizens living in the next decades, as the life expectancy will increase markedly. Seniors are now the fastest-growing segment of the U.S. population. By 2030, more than 20 percent of U.S. residents are projected to be aged 65 and over, compared with 13 percent in 2010 and 9.8 percent in 1970. According to the 2014 U.S. Census Bureau, between 2012 and 2050, the U.S. population is projected to grow from 314 million in 2012 to 400 million in 2050, an increase of 27 percent. The population is also expected to become much older.

Rekindling the Passion with your Spouse During the Golden Years

In a 2010 online article entitled, *"Rekindling the passion with your spouse during the golden years,"* some techniques were suggested and recommended including:

Surprise each other. Bring her a present she likes, e.g., perfume, flowers, or prepare him a particular meal he likes and have a candlelight dinner. Book a night at a hotel or motel, and plan a special "menu" for the evening. Try to communicate with one another joys and concerns, and encourage each other to speak openly to help the partners feel closer. Also, experiment something new in the bedroom, but make sure to discuss it with the partner. Both should agree and be open to novel and creative ideas. Moreover, expand beyond just intercourse; share passionate feelings with each other by cuddling, caressing, kissing, and sensual massages. Figure out what time of the day partners are the most energetic and schedule in "meetings" with each other at these times, and both partners will be more satisfied with the outcome.

AARP Survey on Sexual Attitudes and Practices in 45+ Population

Stein pointed out in *'Sex and Seniors: The 70-Year Itch'* that as children and careers take a backseat, one advantage of growing older is that personal relationships can take on increased importance. "Seniors can devote more time and energy to improve their love lives. And while some seniors may be forced to give up strenuous sports, sex is a physical pleasure many older people readily enjoy."

In 2009, the AARP (the organization formerly known as the American Association of Retired Persons) commissioned a survey on sexual attitudes and practices among the 45+ population, similar to earlier surveys conducted in 1999 and 2004. A clear majority of men and women aged 45 and above said that a satisfying sexual relationship is essential for the quality of life. The results of the survey showed that:

- Opposition to sex among those who were not married was down by half over the previous 10 years.

- The belief that there was too much emphasis on sex in our culture today was down since 2004.

- Both the frequency of sexual intercourse and overall sexual satisfaction were down close to ten points since 2004, while the frequency of self-stimulation, sexual thoughts, and fantasies had not changed.

- Men continued to think about sex more often than women. They saw sex as more important to their quality of life, engaged in sexual activities more often, were less satisfied if without a partner, and were twice as likely as women to admit to sexual activity outside their relationship.

- Among 45-59-year-olds with sexual partners, 56 percent said they had sexual intercourse once a week or more. Among 60-70-year-olds with partners, 46 percent of men and 38 percent of women have sex at least once a week, as did 34 percent of those 70 or older.

- The survey indicated that the push to a social environment that was more favorable to widespread sexual activity had run head-on into an economic environment that was adding to the stress and financial anxiety. The previous research showed these factors to be strongly related to sexual satisfaction.

Chapter 10
Consent to Intimacy among Seniors

Consent to Intimacy

When Sherry and Annie met together in late November, they were interested and fascinated to discuss the topic of consent to sex in elderly individuals with Alzheimer's and dementia.

Sherry looked at Annie and enthusiastically said, "I have spent a good part of this month researching the subject of consent to sex. I have also interviewed Dad's nursing home administrator and read many articles on the capacity to consent to sex by sufferers of Alzheimer's and dementia. I even prepared some scenarios about the capacity of Alzheimer's individuals to consent to sex. Would you like me to tell you what I found out about this topic?"

Annie answered, "Sure, I would love to hear about it. How about meeting at my house on the first Saturday in December?"

Sherry said, "Yes. My husband happens to have a meeting

that day, and I have nothing scheduled. Shall we meet around 10:00 am?"

Annie said, "That's okay with me. I shall prepare a brunch for us."

Sherry arrived shortly after 10:00 am at Annie's home. That was the first time she visited. Annie took her on a tour of the house. Sherry was so impressed with how neat the two-story house was. The decorations, home accents, and paintings were all very nice; Annie did the interior decoration. They sat at the kitchen table to enjoy a delicious brunch that Annie prepared. They chatted a while, then turned to their subject for the day.

Annie asked, "Tell me about the consent of Alzheimer's sufferers to have sex."

Sherry said, "Every elderly person with or without Alzheimer's has a right to determine what shall be done with his or her own body, including sexual activity. Intimacy and sexuality are civil rights no different than the right to vote."

Annie said, "Well, surely sex is a basic human need for all people. It is no different from the need to eat food and drink water."

Sherry said, "That's right. Alzheimer's sufferers may lack the mental capacity to consent to sex, and that is generally determined by family physicians, internists, and psychiatrists."

Annie said, "So, doctors determine whether or not there is mental capacity. Who determines if the Alzheimer's sufferer has become incompetent and cannot make rational decisions?"

Sherry said, "Whether an adult of sound mind has become incompetent and unable to consent to sex is determined in court by a judge."

Annie asked, "If a doctor diagnoses Alzheimer's disease in a patient, does that mean that person lacks the mental capacity to make his or her own decisions and understand the implications of those decisions?"

Sherry said, "When a patient is diagnosed with Alzheimer's, the physician will categorize the patient into one of seven stages of the disease. In general, sex is not affected significantly for many years until the sufferer progresses to stages 5 to 7. Interestingly, sexual desire survives long after the sufferer forgets names and faces.

And, even more interesting, physical intimacy may calm agitation and ease the sufferer's loneliness."

Annie asked, "What happens in the early stages?"

Sherry said, "If the Alzheimer's patient falls in stages 1 to 4, where the disease is supposedly 'mild to moderate' that may last from 2-10 years, the capacity to consent to sex is generally maintained."

Annie said, "How about stage 5?

Sherry said, "If the Alzheimer's patient falls in Stage 5, the disease becomes 'moderately severe'. There is significant confusion, but typically, the patient knows his or her family members and remembers details about one's personal histories." Annie asked, "What about sex?" Sherry said, "Often in stage 5, the capacity of the Alzheimer's sufferer to consent to sexual activity is maintained. However, the interest in sex may either stay the same, increase, or decrease."

Annie asked, "What do you mean?"

Sherry said, "At times, stage 5 patients may lose some of their inhibitions, and that may lead to aggressive sexual behavior."

Annie asked, "How about Alzheimer's stage 6?"

Sherry said, "In stage 6, the brain and body functions of Alzheimer's sufferers are severely compromised. And that's when consent issues commonly arise. But the sufferer may still be able to recognize the faces of closest friends and relatives."

Annie said, "What about sex?"

Sherry said, "Some Alzheimer's sufferers do lose their interest in sex. Others, however, may develop major personality changes and potential behavior problems, including loss of inhibitions and possible aggressive sexual conduct."

Annie said, "In stage 6, is it challenging for the nurses and doctors to determine if the patient can recognize who is visiting or talking to him or her?"

Sherry said, "Sure, that is very important. The Alzheimer's sufferer should be able to recognize who the other person is, and additionally, whether the sufferer can say no or to express their wishes in other ways."

Annie said, "So even if the sufferer no longer has legal control over his or her own care or certain aspects of their day-to-day life, he or she may still be able to decide to have sex at stage 6 of the disease!" Sherry said, "That's right." Annie said, "How about stage 7?

Sherry said, "In Stage 7, Alzheimer's has progressed to 'very severe,' and the sufferer is in the final stage of the disease. The lack of capacity to consent to sex in this final stage is no longer an issue."

Annie and Sherry enjoyed the brunch and were drinking coffee while discussing the consent issue in Alzheimer's. Annie commented, "I guess, in Alzheimer's, sexual activity and the need for intimacy must be quite challenging to assess for medical professionals."

Sherry said, "Very difficult indeed. Physicians measure memory, reasoning, ability to dress, bathe, and balance checkbooks. But they have been unable to devise widely accepted scientific methods to assess the ability of Alzheimer patients to consent to intimate relations and sex."

Annie said, "Why is that?"

Sherry said, "Well, because Alzheimer's symptoms fluctuate unpredictably. They may vary at different parts of the day or week. A person may be relatively lucid in the morning and significantly impaired in the afternoon. That makes it challenging for the doctor or nurse to evaluate the sufferer."

Annie asked, "What precisely is involved in the consent to sex?"

Sherry said, "For a person with Alzheimer's to consent to the sexual activity, he or she should understand the request, advance or overtures to have sex, retain that request long enough to be able to make a decision, weigh up the request, communicate their decision either verbally or by sign language, nodding, squeezing hands, or other means that can be understood by the partner."

Annie said, "What about those people that may seem to passively accept sexual overtures without being very responsive?"

Sherry said, "If the person with Alzheimer's cannot express his or her wishes, the partner should watch for non-verbal signs and also stop at any sign of reluctance on the part of the sufferer."

Annie said, "Can you give me some examples of what you have been talking about?"

Sherry said, "I read an article on consent to sex in Alzheimer's by Paula Spencer Scott, which described various scenarios involving the most common consent 'minefields'. Would you like to hear about them?"

Annie answered, "Sure, we have plenty of time. We are not rushed. Go right ahead."

Sherry said, "The first potential minefield is where 'a consenting couple enjoys the sexual relationship, but one party has Alzheimer's. Scott pointed out that the Alzheimer's symptoms can ebb and flow. They are not predictable. The Alzheimer's partner may appear like his or her old self one night, and the next day might have a hard time with reading nonverbal body language and respond appropriately. As the disease progresses, intimacy suffers, and the caregiver becomes frustrated and feels distant despite the continued sexual relationship. As time goes on, the caregiver becomes increasingly aware of these changes than the person with dementia".

Annie commented, "The situation may be different for married people living at home, as compared to those living in nursing homes."

Sherry said, "Yes, Scott pointed out that consensual sex between partners who live in assisted living situations is a hot- button issue in long-term care. *'Who decides when sexual activity should stop where one or both parties suffer from dementia?'* In nursing home situations, the staff should recognize that sexual communication is important to relationships among residents, and they should be treated with respect."

Annie said, "But semi-communal living situations in nursing homes do not generally provide privacy for sexual activity among residents. And the staffers are mostly young people, who are neither trained nor adequately prepared to deal with this reality; they feel awkward."

Sherry said, "A second potential minefield that Scott noted is where, 'The person with Alzheimer's wants sex, but the spousal caregiver, not so much.' As the disease progresses, the sufferer may become disinhibited. This is a common side effect of Alzheimer's where the sufferer may make aggressive sexual advances or strip. However, that behavior may be a function of the disease rather than increased sexual desire. The stressed caregiver may find it hard to tell the difference."

Annie said, "How about the opposite scenario?"

Sherry said, "Scott noted the potential minefield where 'the spousal caregiver wants sex, but the person with Alzheimer's is past the point of consent, or that isn't the object of desire.' If the spouse has sex with the sufferer who is unable to consent, it brings up the subject of marital rape, which we'll discuss at length some other time. The spousal caregiver may also resort to an extramarital sexual relationship, which raises moral and

legal issues. Because Alzheimer's is a chronic disease that may span a decade or more, the gratification of the caregiver's sexual needs can become a real issue."

Annie said, "That can be a big problem. However, I think the caregiver should be realistic and make decisions that are in the best interest of both partners."

Sherry said, "I agree. How about the scenario where, 'The person with Alzheimer's wants sex, or seems to, with anybody?' Scott noted that lack of judgment is a hallmark symptom of dementia, as is disinhibition leading to stripping or making sexual comments. On the other hand, sexual desire is a natural urge. This combination can lead an

Alzheimer's sufferer to act on a natural sexual urge in ways that may or may not be appropriate."

Annie said, "I feel sorry for the hired or family caregivers around this hypersexual behavior. That must be very uncomfortable for them."

Sherry said, "Yes, extremely uncomfortable. But the worst scenario is where 'A non-spousal caregiver or other person takes advantage of the person with Alzheimer's'. Scott noted that sexual abuse is unconscionable. Nursing home workers have been accused of fondling or having intercourse with Alzheimer residents who could not possibly consent to sex.

Those 'rape' cases are rarely litigated because the Alzheimer sufferer cannot remember what happened."

Annie said, "This consent to sex issue is fascinating. I would like to learn more about the capacity of the individual with dementia to consent to sexual activity from the Director of Nursing at Lakeview Nursing Home. What do you say, shall we call and talk to her?"

Sherry said, "That sounds like a good idea. I am concerned about my Dad. He has been away from my Mom for about eight months. He is getting worse mentally, and there is no shortage of women residents in this nursing home. I worry about him. He is an affectionate, loving man. He needs human interaction, intimacy, and love." The ladies ended their nice discussion.

Desire for Intimacy in Seniors

In 1995, the Hebrew Home in Riverdale, New York, established what's recognized as the nation's first Sexual Expression policy for residents of a retirement community. Updated in 2013 to address the matters of consent (which can be especially tricky with patients coping with Alzheimer's disease and dementia), the policy affirms sexual intimacy as a human right and lays out guidelines for appropriate sexual expression in their community along with staff responsibilities in safeguarding residents' well-being.

This document remains revolutionary nearly 20 years after it first appeared. My goodness, old folks, sometimes really old, get to have sex? The knee-jerk reactions to the notion span the gamut from bemusement to embarrassment, but here's the thing. Aging seniors want to have sex, enjoy it, and increasingly expect it.

In late 2013, ASHA convened a meeting to discuss sexual health issues among an aging population, and the experts in attendance agreed on the following points.

Social and sexual relationships remain important with age, as satisfying relationships are associated with quality of life and longevity. The happiest individuals tend to be those with a regular partner, but this can be challenging for older adults. They often report difficulty maintaining relationships and express concerns about sexual function and performance.

I asked Robin Dessel, an Alzheimer's and Sexual Rights Educator with the Hebrew Home, who worked on the updated policy, about the challenges for determining consent among elderly residents, especially when a number of whom have diminished mental capacities. She said the first lesson is not to assume an absence of the ability to make choices in sexual partnership; *"A diagnosis of dementia does not presume someone's ability or lack thereof to have a sexual partner. Almost as if people default to say 'this couldn't be legitimate because one has dementia,' and I'll tell you that's not correct."*

In terms of how the staff works to assess and monitor consent, she said it's important to look beyond language: *"With dementia, so much of what we have to glean from people is nonverbal, as language skills are among the first to be compromised. Just because they can't verbally express choices doesn't mean they can't indicate them, so it's up to us to determine that. They may have memory loss, but have to work in their world to uphold their rights and choices; have to be upheld."*

We should not overlook the mechanics of sex, which can surely get a bit creaky as we age. This was also a major discussion point that emerged during our meeting, the idea that sexual health issues for seniors exist across the spectrum, including medical matters like erectile dysfunction and vaginal dryness, but also other conditions that, while not directly sexual in nature, can still impact one's ability to frisk in Cupid's garden.

A key to address those challenges is that both providers and patients should be empowered to talk about sexual health. Educating consumers to feel comfortable in starting the conversation is vital. We talked at length during our meeting on the need to actually model these conversations.

For instance, a video provider can depict a doctor or nurse discussing sexual health with a patient. On the flip side, a sexual health tip sheet for patients might be just the thing to take to their next clinic visit. You live long enough, you get old. It's a success indeed that the acceptance and encouragement of sex, as we age, is increasing.

Married Couples – Intimacy Consent

Our approach remains a clinical tool, and has as its goal to assess capacity but does not have as its goal to be the ultimate determiner of whether the intimate relationship is sanctioned. If the older adults in the relationship do have the capacity, we feel strongly that older adults should not only be permitted but also be assisted in participating in an intimate relationship. Our assessment method neither states nor implies that all older adults without capacity should not engage in intimate relationships. Instead, the lack of capacity should be recognized, and a set of careful decisions should then be made.

Case 1

A demented widowed woman in her 70's living in a long-term care facility depressed and still grieving the loss of her husband 10 years earlier, started to perk up when she became the object of a 70-year-old male's attention. The man had been married three times and had the reputation of being a ladies' man. At the beginning of the relationship, both residents seemed happier and could be seen walking up and down the halls arm in arm. They kissed and fondled as well. Both expressed great pleasure in the relationship. She said he filled an "empty place" in her heart, and he repeatedly stated what a "fine" woman she was. They also spent a lot of time talking to each other and clearly enjoyed a social relationship.

On the Mini-Mental State Exam, he had a score of 20, while she had a score of 21. In the interview, both patients appeared to be cognizant of the identity and intent of the other. He wished for intercourse, but she did not. It was clear that she could and had said no to unwanted sexual contact, and he respected her limits. She was capable of saying she did not want to get in too deep and get hurt. He was clear about his wishes and also realized the relationship might not last. The staff agreed that both patients were competent and allowed them the sexual contact with the mutual limits set by the couple.

Case 2

In this case, the sexual relationship was denied by a married couple. Mr. Martin was a 78-year-old retired accountant, and his wife was a 74-year-old retired custodial worker. The couple met after Mr. Martin's 30-year marriage ended when he was widowed. For the first four years of their marriage, their relationship was a good one. She then, however, became demented. He, in turn, became angry and physically abusive toward her. As her dementia increased, he also became mildly demented.

Social services responded to many complaints from their neighbors, but could not be awarded guardianship by the court. Finally, due to neglect, Mrs. Martin was hospitalized and sent to long-term care after discharge. Mr. Martin also entered long- term care a year later when social services were awarded guardianship. While the couple did not occupy the same room, they were placed in the same long-term care unit.

Mr. Martin resumed his abusive manner toward his wife. She complied with all of his demands. Her behavior, however, deteriorated as she became uncooperative with staff and appeared depressed. Mini-Mental State scores were 22 for Mr. M and 8 for Mrs. Martin. During the interview, it was clear that Mrs. Martin could not avoid exploitation and privately stated that she did not want a sexual relationship with her husband.

Mr. Martin, interestingly, confided that, although he had engaged in sexual relations with his wife in long-term care, he was not eager to continue this practice. Due to her incompetence, the staff agreed to monitor the couple and prevent sexual intercourse.

Legal Considerations concerning Consent to Intimacy

In 2009, the *Vancouver Coastal Health Authority* came out with the guidelines about how to proceed with intimate relationship decision-making when one or both older adults display a lack of capacity to participate in an intimate relationship. The explicit values of the *Guidelines* stated that; Care facilities have an ethical and legal obligation to recognize, respect, and support clients' sexual lives. Furthermore, the *Guidelines* are intended to guide the care facilities in knowing how best to support healthy sexuality with their clients while supporting staff and care providers.

If the older adult is believed to lack consent capacity, a team is generated, including a family representative, to determine whether the intimate relationship is permitted. The process may follow as; first, if a person has been appointed by the court or the client to make decisions specifically about sexual activity, that person is the decision-maker.

Secondly, if there is no one with legal authority to make the decisions, the family representative and the care facility jointly determine whether sexual activity is in the best interest of the client. Lastly, the allowance of the inclusion of the client in this decision-making process as much as possible is vital.

Chapter 11
Remarriage

Concept of Remarriage

In the United States and most Western countries, there are more widows than widowers because life expectancy is longer for women. And with age, the likelihood of a wife becoming widowed increases significantly.

Is remarriage the answer to the loss of the first true love, the husband of almost 5 decades, and one's life soul mate? There is a lack of research on remarriages in later life. However, according to some fascinating and unknown observations, companionship is the most common reason for remarriage in later life by all seniors. Moreover, senior widows are less likely than elderly widowers to remarry following the death of a spouse. Successful career women who value their autonomy and freedom prefer not to remarry. However, as compared to women, men tend to remarry because they gain a lot more from the emotional support of marriage. On the contrary, some senior women caregivers of overly dependent elderly husbands with chronic illnesses are subject to remarkable responsibilities and may be tied down at times for years, preceding the loss of the spouse. These widows shy away from remarriage.

Furthermore, senior widowers are several times more likely than elderly widowed women to remarry. They have a larger pool of available women, and they may choose significantly younger spouses. Widows are more likely to remarry for economic security, especially those who are dependent on their husbands' retirement benefits. Also, some senior widows elect not to remarry because they experience feelings of freedom, autonomy, self-sufficiency, control, and independence after the loss of their spouses. They may be reluctant to give those feelings up by remarrying. While other senior widows do not remarry out of their vivid and unforgettable remembrance of the wonderful life, they spent with their spouses. Therefore, they avoid adhering to coping strategies, social support from family, friends, or counseling services.

Reassuring Reasons to Choose Late-Life Marriage

Reason to Get Married Over 50: Love

The most traditional reason to get married over 50 or at any age is still the best: love. Couples who live together outside marriage no longer face the societal pressures and judgments they once did. Vows such as "in sickness and in health" and "until death do us part," whether spoken or implied, are not vague concepts to couples who get married over 50. These couples have few illusions about aging and the end of life. Their joy comes from consciously committing to share the best and the worst of whatever lies ahead for them both.

Reason to Get Married Over 50: Cost of Living

While it may be a stretch to say that two can live as cheaply as one, it is undoubtedly true that two people together can live on far less money than two people apart. Married couples enjoy the economies of scale that single people simply can't equal unless they cohabitate. The bottom line is that most living expenses will decrease dramatically when two people begin sharing the cost of one household.

Reason to Get Married Over 50: Social Security & Pensions

Under social security and most pension plans, spouses have benefits that domestic partners and unmarried lovers do not. If your spouse dies, many pension plans include a survivor benefit that will transfer the pension to the surviving spouse. Most do not extend the same privilege to domestic partners.

Furthermore, if the spouse with the higher benefit dies first, Social Security will increase the surviving spouse's benefit to match the amount of the deceased spouse's monthly check.

And it doesn't stop here. If you never held a job, perhaps because you stayed home to care for children, you are entitled to Social Security retirement benefits based on your spouse's work history. If you are divorced but were married for at least 10 years, you can still collect benefits on your former mate's work history. Moreover, if a parent dies and leaves behind children who are still minors, their kids will receive Social Security benefits until they turn 18, and so will the surviving spouse who is left to care for them.

Depression Remedy as a Case of Senior Wedding

John Deurwaarder was an ordinary senior whose life fell

short of light, became prone to darkness, and almost collapsed after he lost his wife in an accident in 2010. Less than a week later, Deurwaarder, an avid tennis player, had deteriorated so rapidly that he had to move into an assisted living facility at Vancouver's Glenwood Place Senior Living.

"I was too weak on my feet and couldn't stay alone anymore,"

Deurwaarder said.

He struggled with loneliness, depression, and poor eating habits. A reversal of fortune seemed unlikely until one day at Glenwood Place's choir practice, he met a woman *named Alta Lunsford.*

"After my wife was killed, I had a difficult life until I met Alta," Deurwaarder said. *"She built me up and gave me a purpose in life."*

After a five-month courtship, Lunsford, 78, and Deurwaarder, 97, were married on Saturday by Glenwood Place's bus driver and retired pastor Carroll Myers in the retirement community's banquet hall. Their love story is just one example of how long life, greater social acceptance, and more evidence of the health and emotional benefits of a loving union have created new possibilities for marriages late in life.

Love in Seniors Contributes to Remarriage
Love is Ageless

Deurwaarder and Lunsford's story illustrates that love does not change much over a lifetime. Surely, there are some stereotypes about romantic relationships in later life, but we should work on clarifying those myths because love and dating are the same at any age. We are social and sexual beings over the entire lifespan. Whether a teenager or a senior, the feelings of excitement and nervousness that come with dating are similar. That fact can be a revelation to older people who unexpectedly find themselves in a new romance.

"The most amazing thing about all this is here I am an old lady, and I am head-over-heels in love," said Lunsford of Glenwood. "I didn't know old people fall in love."

Love Heals

Research shows that a healthy marriage offers physical and mental health benefits. Unmarried people are generally at greater risk of dying at any given period than married people, according to several bodies of research. However, experts are also quick to point out that the quality of the relationship is crucial. It's not simply the institution of marriage itself, but the quality of the relationship, which is the best predictor of health and well- being.

Widowers, men and women, who are divorced are at particular risk for cardiovascular disease compared with married people and interestingly, widows. Divorce amps up the risk for both men and women, but the death of a spouse only increases the incidence of cardiovascular disease in men, according to research by Orjan Hemstrom in 1996 in the *"Journal of Marriage and the Family."* Married people also are more likely to have better mental health than the unmarried, according to *"Social Causes of Psychological*

Distress" by John Mirowsky and Catherine Ross.

Unmarried people, not surprisingly, are generally worse off financially and more likely to need a paid caregiver in their last years, compared with married people who may be able to rely on a spouse to care for them. Just like Deurwaarder, who found Lunsford to himself for care and affection, and now, the couple is inseparable. They share an apartment, eat similar foods, and like the same activities, including singing.

"We have a wonderful reason why we're getting married: We are both lonely," Deurwaarder explained and further said, *"She's changed my life."*

Researcher Analysis of Senior Weddings

"In the past, it would have been seen as silly or ridiculous to be in a passionate romantic situation at 65. If your marriage ended, you were done. There would have been fewer people getting together at all," said Pepper Schwartz, a *University of Washington sociologist* and *AARP's Love and Relationships expert.* Since today's longer life expectancy has changed that perception, "We are looking at very long periods of time," Schwartz said. "If you get married at 65, you could be together for 30 years. That may seem like a long enough time to get married."

About 1.2 percent of nearly 700 people who applied for marriage licenses in Clark County, in July 2012, were 65 and older, according to a review of applications by *'The Columbian.'* Karen Updike, *Clark County deputy auditor*, said that marriages among older people are more common during the holiday season because many want to marry when their families are already together. A review of December marriage licenses showed that to be the case. About 2.3 percent of nearly 400 people who married in December in the country were 65 and older. Whereas, nationwide, an estimated 500,000 Americans at 65 and older remarry each year, according to research by Marilyn Coleman and Lawrence Ganong of the University of Missouri.

"I think people are still a little surprised by remarriage after the age of 65," Schwartz said. "It's a mixture of congratulations and 'Why are you getting married? Why don't you just live together?' Many who marry do so because they have moral objections to living together; others simply enjoy the privileges and status marriage brings," Schwartz said.

More people now assume that older people will just live together if they want companionship. The rates of remarriage after divorce and death of a spouse among all ages have actually declined because more people are opting to live together, according to research by R. Schoen and N. Standish in the *'Journal Population and Development Review.'* Still, older people are likelier to choose marriage over living together if they decide to pair up, said Cory Bolkan, the *assistant professor of human development at Washington State University Vancouver.*

Complications and Challenges Faced by Seniors Who Remarry

Remarriage is not ideal for everyone. It could mean a loss of Social Security benefits or complications with children's inheritance for many people. For instance, if a widow remarries, she will no longer be able to collect her deceased husband's social security benefits and may not be able to afford that loss of monthly income, depending on her would-be spouse's financial situation. Undeniably, adult children may object to the marriage because they are concerned about their inheritance or because they fear their deceased parent may be forgotten. Most seniors who remarry confront various unique challenges compared to most first marriages. To begin with, the negative attitudes, social pressures, and the dissuasion of family and friends, mainly from adult children toward blended families and from peers, represent the most challenging hurdle that seniors confront in remarriage. The approval of friends and family often predicts the success of the marriage. It is essential for the seniors who are considering remarriage to develop a good friendship of several years before marriage and develop common interests and activities with relatives and friends on both sides.

The soon to be newlywed seniors have to decide where they will live, how to suppress, hide, or put away prior cherished memories; and what their relationship will be to their children and other family members. The second marital relationship has to accommodate a variety of friends, relatives, and acquaintances of different cultures, mores, habits, and histories from both sides. It also has to accept and entertain people who have developed and established their way of life. They have their own families, homes, careers, religions, and social networks. The newlywed seniors will have to deal with highly delicate and personal issues, including inheritance and other financial dealings, debts, and expenses incurred by one or both partners. They must be ready to deal with homeownership of both parties before marriage, their other assets, and estate planning. The spouses should be reassured that they will be taken care of in case of the death of one spouse. And the children need assurances that they will not lose all their inheritance.

Wedding of Seniors

Annie called Sherry by phone and said, "I received a phone call from my brother-in-law, George. We had not spoken to each other in several months. I assumed he was calling to tell me how his wife, Sarah, was doing. Sarah had suffered a stroke a few years ago. The stroke had left her unable to walk, and she had suffered some mental debilitation as well. George had retired from his business to take care of his wife. He has devoted his entire life to her care."

Sherry asked, "Well, what did he call you about?"

"To my surprise, George said that one of my husband's sisters, Kathryn, was going to get married at his house on Sunday and inquired if I like to attend. He also informed me that the 'Wedding' was going to be held at his home because he was going to officiate over the ceremony, and his wife (one of my husband's other sisters) would be able to attend along with every in-law that was still living. I thought it might be fun, so I said yes. I had not had the opportunity to see any of my in-laws since my husband passed away seven years ago, so this would be like a family reunion. One of the problems you have, when you lose your spouse, is that you have to go everywhere by yourself. I arrived a little late. Everyone was already there. In the past, when my husband was alive, there always seemed to be a lot of friction in the family.

My husband was one of ten children, six girls, and four boys. As in most families, there was a lot of sibling rivalry and jealousy. I noticed most of the jealousy was between the married spouses of the family. I always called them and me 'Out-laws.' Now, there are only four sisters-in-law left, and one of them is getting married for the second time. Kathryn, the bride, had been married for 42 years to Joe and had two daughters, Rosanne and Jamie. Kathryn's husband Joe passed away 17 years ago. They had lived their entire life in a small town of fewer than 3000 people. Kathryn was approximately 60 when she was left a widow. Her girls were grown and married and had moved to the big city. Mom Kathryn was left alone in the small town.

However, now she was getting married again to the new love of her life, Sid. For 17 long years, she had been in a small town with limited opportunities for meeting someone 'special.' Kathryn was very excited. She had known Sid for years but hadn't seen him for a long time. When they graduated high school, Sid married Kathryn's best friend, Betty. They had even double-dated in high school. Sid and Betty married and moved to California. They lived together for 41 years before Betty passed away. Sid moved back to a town not far from where Kathryn lived.

As fate would have it, Kathryn had attended the funeral of a distant cousin in the small town to which Sid moved to. That is where she saw Sid again. At the time, Kathryn was dating a man named Carl, but she never had that 'special feeling' for Carl. He was a nice man. Kathryn had met several years before when she was at a very low point. She was lonely and depressed and wanted companionship. Carl was a quiet man, sort of a loner. Kathryn loved being around people and going places, but she allowed the affair with Carl to start out of loneliness. Carl had always told Kathryn he would never marry because of his children, even though they were grown and married with children of their own. Kathryn was the marrying kind. She was very happily married and wanted to be married again.

Carl had been fighting prostate cancer for the past three years. He had treatments, and his prognosis was looking very good, but it was challenging t for Kathryn, so she made a decision.

She realized she did not love Carl and did not want to spend the few good years she had remaining with him. So, when Kathryn saw Sid again, she knew that she had to split with Carl. Sid asked Kathryn for her phone number and if he could take her to dinner. One year later, here we are, and they are getting married. Sid said he was so excited to see Kathryn again that he felt like a teenager.

Well, I guess I had better get back to the wedding. When I arrived, everyone was so warm and welcoming. It reminded me of the past when my husband was with me. We had so many good times with his large family. It was hectic but fun. Kathryn looked beautiful. She was glowing, and the groom, Sid, was beaming at her. You could tell they were both delighted with their decision to marry that day. They looked like two teenagers.

The minister, George (my brother-in-law), was getting ready to start the ceremony, and he started out by telling everyone how much he and the couple appreciated everyone coming. He continued by saying these two people are between the ages of 75 and 77 and mentally competent. They should be allowed to make their own decision about marriage. It was not until after the ceremony that I found out exactly what and who he was talking about.

George also said he had been counseling the bride and groom. He had first spoken to the groom about how they both had been married previously and had been alone for some years. He counseled the bride and groom that they needed to be patient with each other. He also told the couple to honor each other's privacy and that each one would need some 'alone time.' The bride and groom both nodded their heads in agreement. George then said, 'let's get the ceremony started.' It was a conventional ceremony with the exchanging of vows and rings. Sid was really excited and could hardly wait. He started kissing the bride early. We all laughed. After the 'I dos' and the 'kiss,' the bride and groom went on to cut the cake and open presents. It wasn't until later that I found out from Kathryn about the problems with her daughters, Rosanne and Jamie, and precisely what George was alluding to in his statements before the wedding.

Kathryn told me that this marriage was a very big decision for her. Both of her daughters were totally against her getting married. Kathryn said that her daughters were not going to attend the wedding, but they were there. I noticed when I first came in that the daughters, Rosanne and Jamie, did not have much to say.

They did not appear too happy. Kathryn was really hurt by their attitude, and she was concerned they would cause problems in the future. Kathryn said, 'They have their own lives, and they don't understand what I go through at night when it is quiet and lonely.' We talked for a while, and everyone seemed to agree that Kathryn was the one to decide what she should do with the rest of her life. As our group continued our conversation, we realized there were six widows among us. All of them were talking about the drastic change in their lives when we lost our spouses. You suddenly become a single and not half a couple. The couples that used to be your friends no longer invite you to their gatherings, as they are all couples, and you are 'one.' The lady part of the couple will call you occasionally to ask how you are and make some small talk, but eventually, the calls become less regular. I do not blame anyone. That is just the way it is. It is truly a 'couples' world.

However, today was a good day, for our widows have one less single and one more couple. Humans were meant to pair up and not to be alone. Many people feel that when you reach 70 years, your life is over, especially if you have lost your spouse, and you are alone. All you are supposed to do is remember when you were part of a couple and live off those memories.

Kathryn and Sid may not have many years together before one passes, but at least they will have and enjoy each other for now with sex, intimacy, and love, hopefully for many years without Alzheimer's or dementia.

Chapter 12
Love Relationships among Alzheimer's Patients

Love Relationships Kindled among Alzheimer's Patients

Alzheimer's does not alter the need for love and affection within a person. However, it definitely changes many aspects of a relationship. People who were always close and dear to someone might be driven away from them due to dementia. They might lose the other person's companionship, maybe forever. A person with dementia may be excessively affectionate at the wrong time or out of place.

This, in turn, often leads to the loss of marital love and the marriage itself in the long run. While in extreme cases, spouses may grow excessively possessive, envious, and less understanding toward their partner. This situation, in turn, can cause the love to eliminate automatically, further affecting the patient's mental condition. Furthermore, a person suffering from dementia may also find trouble and difficulties in their interactions with friends and family. Those people they once called family and friends, and the ones whom they thought they could count on, may now hesitate to spend time with them. Because they're not sure what to expect from an Alzheimer's patient at any particular time.

Romance at the Nursing Home

Sherry went to work at the newspaper office. That morning she was looking forward to meeting the editor, Eddie. She wanted Eddie to read the touching and unique story about love, intimacy, and romance between two residents at a nursing home care center. The woman was single, and the man was a high profile married man, John Jay O'Connor. Both of them were elderly and suffered from Alzheimer's and dementia. John was born on January 10, 1930. He grew up in San Francisco, California. He developed Alzheimer's at a relatively young age. His beloved wife, the Honorable Justice Sandra Day O'Connor, took care of him at home for 17 years before she had no choice but to move him to an assisted living center in 2006. They truly loved each other. Sadly, however, Alzheimer's affected John's behavior in such a way that it became so hard for his wife to handle and care for him at home. He needed his caregiver wife to stay with him all the time, and she even did most of the time. She even gave up her extraordinarily powerful and prestigious job as the Justice of the U.S. Supreme Court to be his full-time caregiver. She dearly loved her husband of 55 years. No woman has ever done more to advance the cause of Alzheimer's than Justice O'Connor.

The Wedding Ceremony

Sandra O'Connor was born on March 26, 1930, in El Paso, Texas. She grew up on her grandfather's ranch. While in law school, Sandra and John met at Stanford when they were both law students. She graduated in June 1952 with honors, and he graduated in June 1953. They were deeply in love. Hence, they soon got married on December 20, 1952, six months after she graduated from Stanford. She wore a white dress with a traditional sheer veil and had two bridesmaids. John's father, Dr. Jay O'Connor, served as the best man. The wedding ceremony was fabulous. It was performed by the rector of All Saints Episcopal Church in El

Paso. The wedding reception was held at Sandra's grandfather's ranch in a new barn with 200 guests attending. The barn was decorated with pinion pine boughs and mistletoe from the mountains near Silver City. Hay bales were covered with canvas for extra seating. A Lazy B yearling was butchered and prepared in a pit barbecue. The guests brought salads and casseroles. Some of the music played at the reception included 'Put Your Little Foot' and 'The Virginia Reel.'

Married Life of an Alzheimer's Patient

Sandra spent five years as a full-time mom. She gave birth to three sons, Scott Hampton, Jay, and Brian, born in 1957, 1960, and 1962, respectively. The O'Connors subsequently had several grandchildren. From 1958 to 1981, Sandra and John lived happily in Phoenix, Arizona, in an adobe residence that they built over an acre of land. Sandra's parents' own hands went into the mudding of each brick that was set. The mud bricks were made near Mill Avenue in the Salt River from Arizona earthen materials. That adobe home was slated for preservation. Sandra worked as Deputy

County Attorney, then became Assistant Attorney General of Arizona. She served in the Arizona State Senate. She was the first woman to serve as a state senate majority leader in any state. She then served as Maricopa County Superior Court Judge, Arizona Court of Appeals. On September 25, 1981, she became the 102nd Justice of the Supreme Court. She was the first woman appointed to the U.S. Supreme Court by President Reagan, who himself died years later of Alzheimer's. Husband John O'Connor worked as an Attorney. He left a partnership at a Phoenix law firm to come to Washington with his wife in 1981. He worked for D.C. law firms but was limited in his ability to take on matters that could come before the Justices of the U.S. Supreme Court.

In 1988, Justice Sandra was diagnosed with breast cancer, which, to her good fortune, was successfully treated. Not so lucky was her husband, John, who was diagnosed with Alzheimer's. Sandra took care of him for 17 years until he was admitted to an assisted living center in the summer of 2006. In 2005, Justice O'Connor announced her retirement from the Supreme Court. She cited reasons her age and the need to spend more time with her ailing husband and family.

S. S. SANBAR, MD, PHD,JD

Married Alzheimer Patient's Life at the Nursing Home

When John was admitted to the nursing care facility, he was initially unhappy and grumbling. Hence, John was moved to another cottage area in the nursing home. Forty-eight hours after moving to his new area, he was a happy teenager in love. He struck up a romance with a woman, Kay, who had Alzheimer's. When Justice Sandra visited John at his new place, he seemed thrilled. She saw his 'girlfriend' sitting with him on the porch swing holding hands. Amazingly, that was a relief for Justice O'Connor to see her husband so improved after a prolonged and painful period. She was not jealous of the relationship. Instead, she was pleased that her husband was relaxed, happy, and comfortable at the center. She understood that people with Alzheimer's need intimacy. They can develop romantic attachments with fellow residents.

Press Publication by a Chicago Association

On November 13, 2007, the Associated Press published an article about the romance between patients at the Nursing

Home, and it spoke about John O'Connor's romantic love in contrast to other Alzheimer Patients' romanticism. The articles spoke saying that when John O'Connor first came to the care center, his son Scott said:

"He knew this was sort of the beginning of the end. It was basically suicide talk." He was shifted to another cottage at the center, and "48 hours after moving into that new cottage, he was a teenager in love. He was happy."

The manager at the assisted-living facility said there were three romances among the center's 48 residents. She described the relationships as almost childlike, with the couples holding hands, hugging, or simply having dinner together. As for their families' reactions, she said, "I've seen total extremes where families just fall apart, the wife doesn't understand, and they'll cry. And then you have the other end, the opposite spectrum, that it is alright, and they have somebody to make them happy."

"Relationships among Alzheimer's patients nationwide are certainly not uncommon and they're definitely understandable," said Dr. Peter Reed, senior director of programs at the Chicago-based Alzheimer's Association. "Whether residents still have a spouse or whether their primary families are their children, people living in these situations are engaging each other all the time and are seeking human contact and seeking social relationships," he said.

Alzheimer's sufferers who forget their spouses and fall in love with someone else is a scenario that is somewhat common. In 2007, the senior director of programs at the Alzheimer's Association in Chicago said that the frequency of Alzheimer's patients forming new romantic relations is hard to estimate.

However, the underlying causes of this are fairly common. They lose their cognitive abilities and experience mood changes, but one of the things that do not go away is the need for relationships. He commended Justice O'Connor for raising awareness and helping to reduce stigmas. On November 11, 2008, John died at the age of 79 in Phoenix, Arizona, as a result of complications from Alzheimer's. In 2010, Justice O'Connor called for the country to commit to developing a national strategy against Alzheimer's, with the goal of finding a breakthrough by 2020.

Sandra O'Connor's Interview Publication

In a caring.com interview by Paula Spencer Scott, the author of

Surviving Alzheimer's: Practical Tips and Soul-Saving

Wisdom for Caregivers, Justice O'Connor talked about what the country needs to eradicate Alzheimer's, and how individual caregivers can cope. Below is the unedited interview as it was published online.

- **"What's the one thing you'd like to see the new Congress do to help put the country on a clear path toward a cure?**

Very little national focus has been given to Alzheimer's, other than by private groups. We need to see the same effort on a national basis to take action concerning Alzheimer's that has happened in the past with other diseases, like AIDS and polio.

We need to take stock of all federally financed resources available. Or perhaps designate a coordinator -- when this nation decided to take on AIDS, we got a leader or two to head the effort. The biggest impediment has been getting the votes. They have not been there so far. Why that is, I am not sure given that Alzheimer's is so prevalent.

- **You've said before Congress that many caregivers lack the resources to take time away from loved ones to lobby for a national Alzheimer's strategy or cure. What do you suggest an individual caregiver do to help bring about change?**

There is still a lot they can do. They can send letters to individual members of Congress who are considering legislation about Alzheimer's policy. Stamps are not that expensive! They can also become a member of any group advocating change for Alzheimer's, and be counted that way. Caregivers can still be a voice.

- **How did you and your family respond when you first learned your husband had Alzheimer's, and at what point did you begin to think of yourself as a caregiver?**

I think my three children and I realized the seriousness and the difficulty of the disease immediately. I do not think we had any misconceptions. We knew how dreadful it is. I thought of myself as a caregiver from the outset. My husband and I were very close. If one needed help, the other was always there.

Hence my caring for him happened on autopilot. That was the deal we made when we married, that we would care for each other.

- **Was there some aspect of your caregiving experience that worked especially well, that other caregivers might learn from?**

One great thing was that I asked my three children to select a care place for their father when his condition went beyond my ability to care for him at home. It is something almost everyone has to do eventually because this is such a degenerative disease. They did a wonderful job, and I was glad. If I had selected a place myself, they may have felt I could have done better. By talking together and collaborating, we avoided internal misunderstandings and disappointments. That was great.

- **You've had some significant challenges in your life. Where does caring for a husband with Alzheimer's rank with things like being accepted**

as a woman attorney or serving as the first female member of the Supreme Court?

It's all hard. Probably the hardest part of the Alzheimer's was early on when John could not drive anymore. We Americans are wedded to cars. They're our independence. I recall so poignantly the day I had to have my husband be told he couldn't drive anymore. I had the doctor do it instead of me. John was in his 70s.

- **And did he listen to the doctor, or put up a protest? That can be so hard for families.**

He did "hear it" from the doctor. His own father was a doctor, so I guess he was inclined to respect that opinion.

- **Given that you're now 80, and by age 8,5 people have a one in two chance of developing Alzheimer's, how much discussion have you had with your children about your potential future care?**

Not much about me because we have just been through that, and all know what has to be done. But we did talk a lot about my husband's care. It's hard for families. You don't want to acknowledge that your spouse or your parent or your child is incapable of managing anything anymore [because of Alzheimer's]. But the problem is, you have to. You have to go through the issues of having someone authorized to have legal action, to file tax returns, and apply for Social Security benefits, for example. Someone has to take those things on.

- **What was the most challenging emotion you had to deal with as a caregiver?**

Seeing someone you love and care for falling to a totally disabling and fatal disease; such sadness.

- **So many families dealing with Alzheimer's can relate to that. Is there one hopeful thing you see happening now?**

What's hopeful is that there are many people and many groups focusing on this problem; and that finally, more of them are recognizing that we need to get together as a nation on this.

Loss of Marriage due to Alzheimer's

In January 2008. Philip Sherwell published an article describing how Alzheimer's robbed Sandra Day O'Connor of the husband she had known for 55 years, while she had never imagined she would lose him again to another woman. The following is a summary of that article. Faced with his rapid decline, she began taking him with her to her office at the Supreme Court. Only a few people knew about this. The O'Connors would be chauffeured into the basement garage in the early morning and take a private lift directly to her office. Justice O'Connor would bring lunch from home, and they would eat together at a table in her office.

His memory had almost entirely gone. By 2005, this unusual set-up was becoming increasingly challenging as Mr. O'Connor wanted to wander around the corridors. The compromise of taking him to the office was no longer working, so Justice O'Connor faced a gut-wrenching decision – place her husband in a special care home or resign from the Court to look after him full-time for as long as that was possible. She opted for the latter, but the resignation was an enormous personal sacrifice.

By the summer of 2006, he had become too difficult for her to handle, and she reluctantly placed him in an assisted home. After placement in the assisted home, John O'Connor embarked on a love affair with another woman, who also suffered from Alzheimer's after he was placed at the care center. His wife, Sandra, was far from being jealous. She was thrilled with their romance. She was relieved that her husband, who had become depressed and introverted and barely recognizing his own family, had found happiness in a new relationship with a fellow patient. Sandra and John were husband and wife, lovers, partners, and best friends for over five decades, but that was gone. To Sandra, the scenario was tragic, but with a sense of humor and a bittersweet irony. She said, "Sometimes things that seem tragic can be turned around.

'Accept life,' for it's the Buddhist way."

John's mental condition deteriorated rapidly until love blossomed with another resident identified as Kay. He was like a teenager in love. However, these days her life is dominated by her husband's condition and the unique love triangle in which she has found herself. Her husband cannot remember her. He did not choose to leave her. He had no memory of her. However, his desire for love and intimacy continued. At the same time, Sandra's willingness to sacrifice and care for him remained.

The Good, Bad and Ugly

A psychiatrist, Dr. Gail Saltz, published an article entitled, '*An Alzheimer's affair: The good, bad, and ugly*' that dealt with the challenges faced by couples affected by the disease. Dr. Saltz asked why would a married man, like John O'Connor, who is in an assisted living home, strike up a sudden romance with another Alzheimer's resident. And why his wife, Sandra, may not be upset about the romance.

Dr. Saltz noted a few aspects with respect to the good, bad and ugly, and it follows:

"Alzheimer's disease ravages memory, mood and the ability to care for oneself. It does not necessarily interfere with libido or the need for intimacy. It is not unusual for people living in either assisted living or a nursing home to "find love". Where patients still have an awareness of their declining state, they may long for companionship to make them feel connected, understood and alive. Few things make one feel more alive than romance, and when you know at some level that you have a terminal illness, the desire to battle back your fears of death with feelings of vitality and excitement is great. Romance is a good defense against anxiety about mortality. It is also not unusual for a person in an assisted living situation to feel "abandoned" by their spouse, even when they also understand that their spouse could really no longer manage to care for them at home. Such feelings of abandonment can lead to a strong desire to connect with another to nurture their own feelings of hurt.

Alzheimer's can affect one's judgment and ability to consider the consequences of one's actions. It is likely that John really did not perceive at that point that he was betraying his wife, Sandra, and also likely that she understood that. Caring for someone with Alzheimer's is incredibly stressful and difficult. Watching the man you love slowly but surely lose his mental faculties is excruciating. Having to constantly be vigilant and watchful is exhausting and "caregiver burnout" is more the rule than the exception.

The caregiver often becomes fatigued and depressed. Anything that lifts that burden may be welcomed; even one's husband having an affair. The caregiver wishes to see the impaired partner happy. Not to feel that all the sufferer's happiness is dependent on the caregiver is enough to make the spouse accepting of some situations that would never have been acceptable before.

The truth is that we as a society are still not very good at helping couples deal with Alzheimer's disease. We need better systems of evaluating both the patients and the caregivers for depression. We need to teach better systems of managing symptoms, and we need more support systems so that caregivers can get a break in an otherwise overwhelming task. No doubt, the O'Connor have done the best they could under very difficult circumstances. While the Honorable Sandra was one of the most important judges of the century, this is a situation where it is best to not judge either her or her family.

Alzheimer's is a ravaging disease that attacks the organ we prize most; it plagues the mind."

Chapter 13
Facts about Alzheimer's Patients

Open-End Discussion at Café Royal

Annie and Sherry got together on several occasions at the nursing home, café, and restaurant. On one occasion, they decided to take Chris and her husband Mortimer with them for a late lunch. That turned out to be an excellent opportunity for the two couples to do something enjoyable and become good friends. On a beautiful Saturday in October, the temperature was growing pleasantly cooler in Wichita, Kansas.

The two couples met at the Café Royal, about a mile away from the Lakewood Nursing Home. They arrived at the Café just before 2:00 p.m. and exchanged greetings. They generally talked about their parents, who seemed to be doing reasonably well. Both Chris and Mortimer were chatting and smiling. They seemed happy, too.

Sherry said, *"Well, this is the famous Café Royal."*

Annie said, *"It is so nice to see us four get together at this impressive Café."*

The Café Royal was a cozy, French restaurant. It had a coffee bar and served light meals and refreshments. It had an outdoor section, where the two couples decided to sit. The waiter was a neat looking young man. He welcomed the two couples, provided each person with a menu, and explained what is available on special for the day. Then he asked what drinks they would like. The tabletop had a picture of an old French Café, which was opened in Marseille in 1660. There was a note on the picture that stated,

"The coffee beverage was introduced in Venice around 1615 and in France around 1650 by merchants and travelers who had been to Turkey and Egypt."

"Do you serve old French coffee?" Asked Annie.

The waiter said, *"Yes, we do. The owners are very proud of their French heritage. They used to grow their own coffee, but now they import it from France."*

Sherry said, *"We would like to try your old French coffee and some of the pastries."*

They ordered an assortment of pastries. Within a short time, the waiter brought the coffee and pastries and placed them on the table. He also brought cream, sugar, and sweetener. The two couples truly enjoyed the delicious coffee. The pastries were fresh and tasted great. They had fun visiting and making small talk. Then the discussion turned to Sherry's Dad, his Alzheimer's, and dementia.

Annie asked, *"Are there a lot of people with Alzheimer's disease like your Dad?"*

Sherry answered, *"I was reviewing last week online the Alzheimer's Association Facts."*

"How come?" asked Annie.

Sherry said, *"I was collecting recent information about*

Alzheimer's and dementia before completing my newspaper columns about this terrible disease."

Annie said, *"What did you found out?"* Sherry said, *"I was really disappointed and shocked to find out that Alzheimer's is the only disease among the top 10 causes of death in the U.S. that cannot be prevented, cured, or even slowed."*

Mortimer said, *"That's hard to imagine that nothing can be done to help Alzheimer's sufferers."*

Chris said, *"That makes it very difficult for family members and caregivers to see their loved ones get worse in front of their eyes with no hope of a cure or even improvement."*

Sherry said, *"Yes, it takes a devastating toll on caregivers both at home and nursing centers."*

Annie asked, *"Are Alzheimer's caregivers, mainly women?"*

Sherry answered, *"Yes, as a matter of fact, about two-thirds of the caregivers are women."*

Chris asked, *"What age are those women caregivers?"*
Sherry said, *"All ages. Two-thirds of the women caregivers are below 65."*

Chris said, *"So, one-third of the caregivers are age 65 or older, right?"*

Sherry nodded her head and said, *"Yes."*

Annie said, *"I imagine the caregivers are relatives of Alzheimer's sufferers!"*

Sherry said, *"You are right. Most of the elderly women are spouses, like my mother. They take care of their husbands until they can no longer manage them at home. But over half of primary caregivers are the children of the people with Alzheimer's and dementia due to various reasons. Both of us are such examples who care for their parents."*

Mortimer said, *"Judging by you, Sherry, I bet those caregivers spend untold hours caring for their loved one with Alzheimer's."*

Sherry said, *"Interestingly, in 2014, friends and family of people with Alzheimer's and other dementias provided an estimated 17.9 billion hours of unpaid care, which translates to a contribution to the nation valued at $217.7 billion."*

Annie said, *"Do you happen to know how many people have Alzheimer's disease in the United States?"*

Sherry said, *"Well, some 5.3 million Americans of all ages had Alzheimer's disease."*

Chris asked, *"What ages are they?"*

Sherry told him, *"About 96 percent of Alzheimer's sufferers are 65 and older, like my Dad. Only a small number of sufferers, less than 4 percent, develop the disease quite early, below the age of 65 years."*

Mortimer asked, *"Are men more likely to have Alzheimer's like Dad Jacob?"*

Sherry said, *"Just the opposite. Almost two-thirds of Alzheimer's sufferers are women. And unfortunately, older African-Americans and Hispanics are more likely to develop Alzheimer's than Caucasians."*

Annie said, *"You sure are full of information, but you are scaring me. I am becoming more concerned, being an older female, and my mother also has dementia."*

Sherry said, *"I am just as concerned as you are, and my Dad has Alzheimer's, which is more common than Parkinson's."*

Chris asked, *"So, what are the projections for the next few years about Alzheimer's?*

Sherry said, *"I read that by 2050, the number of people at the age of 65 and older with Alzheimer's is projected to be 13.8 million."*

Annie asked, *"Wow, that's a lot of people to care for. How deadly is Alzheimer's?"*

Sherry said, *"That's another thing. This year, about 700,000 people in the United States at the age of 65 and older are expected to die with Alzheimer's."*

Annie said, *"It has become so expensive to care for dementia sufferers in adult care centers and nursing homes. I have been paying a lot of money monthly for my mother's care. How do people manage financially?"*

Sherry said, *"Yes, it is very costly to care for dementia. According to the Alzheimer's Association, the disease is one of the costliest chronic diseases in society. In 2015, the direct costs to American society of caring for those with Alzheimer's are expected to be about $226 billion, and half of the costs will be borne by Medicare. Sadly, in 2050, Alzheimer's is projected to cost over $1.1 trillion."*

Mortimer said, *"This is incredible!"*

Annie asked, *"It seems like a lot more people are being diagnosed with Alzheimer's and dementia."*

Sherry said, *"You know, Annie, most people living with Alzheimer's are not aware of their diagnosis, even though the diagnosis was made."*

Annie asked, *"How come?"*

Sherry said, *"Well, the sufferers, or their caregivers, are not being told the diagnosis by the health care provider to avoid frightening or upsetting them or their loved ones."*

After finishing their coffee and pastries, the two couples decided to take a stroll in the downtown area. The shops were full of Halloween decorations and paraphernalia. There were all kinds of candy. That was a lot of fun. They looked at the displays of merchandise. They were most interested in antique stores. They walked inside jewelry and antique stores to view and admire the displays.

Annie said, *"Sherry and Mortimer, it has been so enjoyable visiting with you today. Let us all get together again soon. I would also love to learn more about Alzheimer's and dementia."*

Sherry answered, *"That will be wonderful."*

Annie said, *"How about next week? Let's meet then."*

"That is okay. I look forward to seeing you next week," said Sherry.

They all returned to their cars. Annie and Chris said farewell and went to visit Lucy. While Sherry and Mortimer went to visit Jacob at the nursing home.

A Broader Perspective - Fact File

A German doctor named Alois Alzheimer was the first person to observe Alzheimer's disease in 1906. He remembered and described a patient known as Auguste D., who had memory loss and other problems with thinking. After the patient's death, Dr. Alzheimer discovered that some elements of the patient's brain were shrunken. Later, a psychiatrist who worked with Dr. Alzheimer named this condition in 1910.

Alzheimer's disease is an irreversible degeneration of the brain that causes disruptions in memory, cognition, personality, and other functions that eventually lead to death from complete brain failure. A person with Alzheimer's disease may lose their sense of smell, according to the National Institutes of Health (NIH). A study included in the *Journal of Neurological Sciences* suggests that changes in the sense of smell may be an early sign of developing this disease.

Alzheimer's Disease Is a Leading Cause Of Death

The Alzheimer's Association states that this disease is the

sixth leading cause of death in the United States. About one in three seniors die with Alzheimer's or another form of dementia. Moreover, in 2010, the Centers for Disease Control and Prevention (CDC) reported that Alzheimer's disease claimed more than 84,000 lives in the U.S., while the Association also states that Alzheimer's is the only disease, among the top 10 causes of death in the U.S. without any methods for prevention, cure, or decline.

Certain medications can help to relieve a few symptoms. However, research into a vaccine is still in process, but so far, there are no sure ways to prevent Alzheimer's disease from developing.

Role of Heart Disease

Heart disease escalates the chances and risks of developing Alzheimer's disease. Due to this connective factor, there are other conditions that result in heart disease. These conditions also become linked to accelerating the risks of the developmental process of this disease. These heart conditions may include high blood pressure, high cholesterol, diabetes, poor diet, and a non-active lifestyle. Heart disease may also arise from vascular dementia, which results from constricted blood vessels in the brain. This leads to a decrease in oxygen to brain tissues.

Education Can Lower Your Risk

It is a relatively unbelievable fact indeed that has been stated by the National Institute on Aging (NIA) that the possession of higher education can lower risks of getting Alzheimer's disease. By keeping the brain active during old age through activities, such as attending classes, attempting to learn various languages, and playing musical instruments or even light sports, one can definitely reduce the risks of developing Alzheimer's.

A Costly Disease

Total payments in 2017 for all individuals with Alzheimer's or other dementias are estimated at $259 billion.

Health care systems are expected to cover $175 billion, or 67 percent, of the total health care and long-term care payments for people with Alzheimer's or other dementias. Out-of-pocket spending is expected to be $56 billion.

Health care costs increase with the presence of dementia since people with Alzheimer's or other dementias have twice as many hospital stays annually, as compared to healthy seniors. Such people constitute a large chunk of elderly people who receive adult day services and nursing home care.

Moreover, the per-person health care costs and long-term care payments in 2016 for Medicare beneficiaries with Alzheimer's or other dementias were over three times as great as payments for other Medicare beneficiaries. While the average per-person *out-of-pocket* costs for Alzheimer's and other dementias are almost five times higher than average per-person payments for seniors without these conditions.

Total annual payments for health care, long-term care, and hospital care for people with Alzheimer's or various dementias are projected to increase from $259 billion in 2017 to more than $1.1 trillion in 2050. This sharp rise includes more than four-fold increases, with the government spending under both the health care systems, including Medicare and Medicaid, while also in *out-of-pocket* expenditure.

Alzheimer's Is Probable to Cripple the Healthcare System

Total payments for health care, long-term care, and hospice for people with Alzheimer's and other dementias are projected to increase from $259 billion in 2017 to more than $1 trillion in 2050 (in 2017 dollars). This dramatic rise includes a four-fold increase in government spending under Medicare and Medicaid and a nearly four-fold increase in out-of-pocket spending.

Prevalence

An estimated 5.5 million Americans of all ages have Alzheimer's.

Among the estimated 5.5 million Americans living with Alzheimer's dementia in 2017, an estimated 5.3 million are 65 and older. Whereas, approximately 200,000 individuals are under 65 and have a younger onset of Alzheimer's. One in 10 people aged 65 and older are suffering from Alzheimer's dementia. Furthermore, almost two-thirds of Americans with Alzheimer's are women. Alzheimer's is now a growing epidemic. More than 5 million Americans currently have it. By 2050, nearly 14 million Americans over

65 could be living with the disease, unless scientists develop new approaches to prevent or cure it. However, estimates based on high-range projections of population growth provided by the U.S. Census suggest that this number may be as high as 16 million. It is also estimated that nearly 500,000 new cases of Alzheimer's disease will be diagnosed this year.

Due to the increasing number of people aged 65 and older in the United States, the number of new cases of Alzheimer's and other dementias has significantly escalated. Present-day statistical views state that someone in the United States develops Alzheimer's disease every 66 seconds. While it has also been estimated and assumed that, by mid-century, someone in the United States will develop the disease every 33 seconds.

Caregivers

In 2016, 15.9 million family and friends provided 18.2 billion hours of unpaid assistance to those with Alzheimer's and other dementias, a contribution to the nation valued at $230.1 billion. Approximately two-thirds of caregivers are women; among these, 34 percent are 65 or older, while 41 percent of caregivers have a household income of $50,000 or less. Almost one-quarter of dementia caregivers are *"sandwich generation"* caregivers, which means that they don't just cater to the needs and nurturing of an aging parent, but also for children under the age of 18.

A prevalent issue is that many caregivers remain unpaid. Caring for a person with Alzheimer's or another dementia is always incredibly challenging. Many families and other unpaid caregivers experience high levels of emotional stress and depression as a result. It is true that in comparison to caregivers of people without dementia, there are twice as many caregivers of those with dementia who indicate tremendous emotional, financial, as well as physical turmoil. It has also been discovered that caring for someone with Alzheimer's disease eventually has a negative impact on the health, employment, income, and financial security of many caregivers.

Chapter 14
Capacity to consent in
Dementia and Alzheimer's

Basic Insight into 'Capacity to Consent'

When Sherry got home, she was still thinking about the capacity to consent and what to include in her newspaper column. She sat at her computer desk and reviewed the following questions and answers from an article by Elaine K. Sanchez entitled, *"Who Has the Right to Control the Sexuality of a Person with Dementia?"*

Who Has the Right to Decide When a Person with Dementia Can No Longer Have Sex?

It's not unusual for a person with Alzheimer's to forget their loved ones' names and have entirely different concepts of time, place, and reality from their caregivers. However, regardless of how many memories have been stolen and how many skills have been lost, most people do not lose their desire for intimacy, closeness, and human touch. We are born as sexual beings, and we die as sexual beings. And even diseases as devastating as Alzheimer's don't destroy that part of our humanity.

"Do You Need a Sexual Power of Attorney?

Most people understand and accept the need to assign a durable power of attorney to handle their finances if they become mentally incapacitated. They also understand the need to appoint a healthcare representative to make sure their wishes about life support and tube feeding are followed, but the idea of assigning a sexual power of attorney is unfamiliar, possibly even radical for most of us. However, unless we explicitly state our wishes regarding our sexual choices and activity in the event of incapacity, we could end up leaving that decision to our children or possibly the nursing home staff person who has the most Victorian attitude toward sex."

"How Do You Distinguish Between Sexual Pleasure and Sexual Abuse in People Who Have Dementia?

Elder sexual abuse is generally defined as coercing an older person through force, trickery or threats. It includes sexual contact with elders who are unable to give consent for unwanted sexual contact between care providers and their elder clients. Here's one thing I do know for sure: If something happened to my husband and I was in my right mind, I would not be interested in another man. However, if I developed dementia and lost all of my memories of my husband and my marriage and I found comfort and companionship in the arms of another man, I would not want my children or a nursing home staff member to decide that my behavior was inappropriate. So, I have written a draft of my sexual power of attorney. I will take it to my attorney soon and get help refining it and adding it to my advance directive.

In case you may be considering something similar, I've included a first draft of what I plan to take to my attorney to ensure my wishes are carried out in the event I'm unable to express myself at a later time. Please feel free to use this as a template for your own language to use if you decide to draft something similar for your family and legal counsel."

Elaine's 1st Draft of Her Sexual Power of Attorney

"To: Eric, Robert & Annie, as my healthcare representatives, I am directing you to not place me in a nursing home that doesn't respect its residents' right to privacy and intimacy. If I develop dementia and lose all of my memories of my marriage and my love for Alex and I get romantically involved with another man, it is my wish that you do not interfere. As long as I am conscious and aware of the things that bring me pleasure and joy, let me make my own choices about what I eat and drink and with whom I sleep. Unless you have reason to believe that I am being bullied, forced, manipulated emotionally or physically abused, let me enjoy whatever companionship and pleasure I receive from any intimate relationship. If the nursing home does not provide locks for residents' doors, you might want to provide me with a Do Not Disturb sign. If I forget that I need to put the sign on the door, please be sure to knock before you enter."

"What's the Future of Sexuality and Dementia in Nursing Homes?

Sexuality is a part of our humanity, and if nursing homes are committed to person-centered care, they will need to recognize this fact and establish policies and train staff on how to respond properly when older people and residents with dementia display surprising, uninhibited and inappropriate sexual behavior. Professional caregivers need to be able to recognize the difference between intimacy and sexual abuse, and they need to understand how to respond in both situations to protect the rights and the dignity of the people in their care."

Capacity versus Competency

It is crucial to make a distinction between capacity and competency, which has overlapping meanings, but the context of use is different. The capacity to make one's decisions is fundamental to the autonomy of the individual. It is a functional assessment made by a clinician to determine if a patient is capable of making a specific decision. It refers to a person's ability to make a particular decision at a particular time or in a specific situation.

Capacity evaluation for a patient with dementia is used to determine whether they are capable of giving informed consent, participate in research, manage their finances, live independently, make a will, and can drive. While competency is a global assessment and legal determination made by a judge in court. It is a threshold requirement imposed by society for an individual to retain decision-making power in a particular activity or a set of activities.

Alternate Decision Makers

Patients with Alzheimer's may have notably decreased ability to give adequate informed consent to research. This may be the case even in the disease's earliest, mild stage. It is indeed quite common for patients with Alzheimer's to make healthcare decisions for themselves for as long as they can, as long as they live. Psychiatrists should support the expressions of individual preferences of patients with Alzheimer's throughout their participation in medical examinations in every way possible.

Patients should be allowed to participate to the degree to which they will, both when they can still legally consent and after they have lost the capacity to consent, and then they may legally only provide the agreement. In many other areas of research, consent requirements are sharply defined. However, it is not the same when it comes to research participants with dementia. Once patients with Alzheimer's disease lose their consent capacity, surrogate decision-makers can generally decide, depending on the patients' prior values. Thus, even when patients do lose competency during study participation, these surrogate decision-makers may follow through with what these patients would have wanted. Sometimes, surrogate decision-makers want to maximize what they think is best for their patients, as opposed to pursuing what they believe their patients want. This is not an uncommon occurrence in the clinical context. The best "therapy" for this is to have patients with Alzheimer's discuss their future desires as thoroughly as possible with their chosen surrogate decision-makers before they enter a study.

A core concern that a psychiatrist should have when a patient with Alzheimer's disease is considering enrollment in a study is the extent of how great a risk the patient is willing to take. As a common rule, the greater the risk, the stronger a patient's capacity to consent should be. For instance, a patient may experience pain, such as a headache, after a lumbar rupture. It might be optimal that a patient shows a better degree of understanding risks such as this than the patient should show if he or she were only giving blood. Patients with Alzheimer's may be willing to take on higher risks, and they should be allowed to do so, as long as they are legally capable and can give "advance consent."

Capacity and Dementia

A person's capacity to decide and make choices is an essential part of who they are and how they wish to live. The assessment of one's capacity, as discussed, falls on a spectrum and varies according to the situation. It is the duty of health care systems, including nursing homes, to provide ample conditions for the optimal level of functioning of the individual to enable them to make a decision.

This includes spending time to educate the person and their families, alleviating their anxieties, taking into account lucid intervals, and any physical conditions, such as difficulty in speech that may interfere with the capacity. Patients with dementia should not be assumed to be incapable of making decisions. Patients with mild to moderate dementia can evaluate, interpret, and derive meaning in their lives. The law assumes that all adults have the capacity unless there is contrary evidence.

Capacity must be assessed concerning the particular decision that an individual needs to make. For instance, if a person at the decision-making time is incapable because of mental disability to decide on the matter at hand, or if he is unable to communicate a decision on that matter because of subtle unconsciousness either; this is where it becomes evident that person does not possess the capacity to consent. Capacity is required for valid informed consent. Although dependent on cognition, it is not the same as cognition. It is also different from functional activities. A person who is unable to decide if he can do the task on his own may yet be capable of determining who can help them to do that task.

For any decision, in particular, the person either has the capacity or not. Most life decisions are made by people independently. Decisions are often controlled by our personal choice, morals, relationships, and culture. Decisions may not always be based on logic or deliberation. Education and occupation profoundly influence decision-making. There are four decision-making abilities that characterize capacity, which includes understanding, appreciation, reasoning, and expressing a choice.

Decision-making never remains static, and fluctuations that affect this capacity are bound to occur, which may arise due to medications, infections, lethargy, and hallucination. Diminished decision-making was found in 44-69% of residents in nursing homes. The ability to express a choice and provide some reasoning is often preserved in patients with Alzheimer's. They can decide about daily care choices but are not well-trained anymore to make a decision about complex treatment options. Even a patient with advanced dementia may have the capacity to appoint a health-care proxy, but he would still lack the ability to make a living will.

Patients with amnestic mild cognitive impairment were able to express choice but lessened on appreciation, reasoning, and understanding than controls. In a study on research consent capacity, patients with Parkinson's disease with borderline cognitive impairment had decreased decisional capacity.

Assessment of Capacity

Capacity should be assessed in a semi-structured direct interview with the patient. The patient should have adequate and relevant information about the issue under discussion, which could be about the disease, treatment options, sex, relationships, and any other concerns. Capacity evaluation is a two-step process. First, the concerned clinician evaluates a person's decisional abilities. A judgment regarding the person's capacity for a particular decision is reached using results obtained after a session of questions. While determining capacity, one should strike a balance between respecting patient's autonomy and acting in their best interest. A clinician has a clinical and ethical responsibility to accurately assess the decision-making capacity of a patient. It is also possible that these decisions are sometimes reviewed critically in a court of law. Capacity assessments should be done carefully, cautiously, and completely.

If the patient is harmed by the treatment, the doctor could be held responsible for not making a thorough assessment of the patient's capacity. Capacity assessment must be quite rigorous in situations where there are serious consequences of decision-making. All four components of the assessment may not carry equal weight, and it would depend on each situation and context.

A person's capacity is a point along a continuum. Capacity can be rated as adequate, inadequate, and marginal. Sometimes, the patient refuses assessment, or the family disagrees with the assessment. In such situations, the clinician should be not only tactful and cautious but also transparently communicate the need for further assessment or describe the reasons for inadequate capacity and keep adequate records. If the clinician makes a diagnosis of impaired capacity, there may be several implications depending on the severity of cognitive impairment, situation, and decision.

Measures such as the Mini Mental Status Exam (MMSE) have not been accepted as sufficient guides to whether or not patients with Alzheimer's should have adequate capacity to consent. This is because a patient's capacity to not only understand but also to appreciate what he or she is consenting to in an affective or emotional sense may differ greatly, regardless of how the patient performs on the MMSE.

The "gold standard" for measuring capacity to consent to be in clinical research is the MacArthur Competency Assessment Tool for Clinical Research. This standard should not suffice on its own, however. Instead, those assessing the capacity of consent of a patient with Alzheimer's should ask the patient-specific questions about his or her understanding of the particular study in which he or she wishes to be enrolled. This tool, even if used only as a primary screening measure, takes time to administer. Personnel who administer it must have specific training.

Thus, there may be other preferable measures.

Care providers assessing the capacity of consent in patients with Alzheimer's should also seek to discuss the potential study with the patients more than once. Since some patients with the disease may only "understand it and absorb it" after discussing it for a second or third time. The person assessing the capacity of consent and level of understanding in a patient with Alzheimer's disease must also try to determine whether or not the patient is merely repeating what people around them have just said. A patient suffering from the disease may often pass statements without any understanding of what they are actually speaking about.

Assessment Tools

MacArthur Competence Assessment Tools for Treatment (MacCAT-T) is a frequently used tool to assess the competence and has been validated in patients with dementia. The test consists of a hospital chart review followed by a semi-structured interview and scored for four domains of capacity. Tests such as the Assessment of Capacity for Everyday Decision-making are useful to understand if a person who has a functional deficit, understands and appreciates this problem, understands and appreciates the risks and benefits of solutions to that problem, and can reason through choices about how to solve this problem. The formal assessment of capacity is not required in each patient. It may be evident that the patient may have adequate capacity for a particular decision in mild dementia or may lack the capacity as in severe dementia. Formal testing may be required in situations in which capacity is unclear, and there is disagreement among family members or surrogate decision-makers, or a judicial involvement is anticipated.

Continuation of Assessment of Capacity to Consent

A patient's capacity for understanding and consent should be determined not only before participating in a study, but also periodically during the study. Researchers should plan, before the study's beginning, who will make the subsequent capacity determinations and how often these determinations should be made. Ideally, those making the subsequent assessments should be independent of the study personnel to prevent favoritism. Researchers, possibly with the patients' psychiatrists, may determine beforehand the method and the frequency of patient capacity evaluation. If researchers wish to use a scale, such as the MSSE, to track and screen study participants, they should keep in mind that due to the nature of Alzheimer's disease, mild variations in these scores can likely occur.

Working with the psychiatrists of study participants, researchers should also determine in advance what establishes a refusal by a patient to continue participating in the study overall, or perhaps for just one small aspect of the study. For instance, a participant may, at some point during the study, refuse to have blood drawn. However, this may not necessarily indicate that the patient wants to discontinue participation in the trial.

A patient with Alzheimer's disease may refuse this blood drawing procedure just this one time, but later, he may be willing to let blood be drawn and want to continue to participate in the study. Furthermore, researchers may want to determine earlier, as to how many "sticks" they should attempt before they take a patient's refusal as a definitive "no" to having blood drawn.

Chapter 15
Nursing Homes - Intimacy Consent Policy

Tang's Article concerning Consent Criteria

When Sherry arrived home, she called the director at the Lakewood Nursing Home and asked her if she and Annie could visit to talk about consent issues and sexual activity policies about residents. Sherry also explained that she was writing a column for the newspaper on the topic and would appreciate her input. She agreed to meet.

Sherry asked the director if she would email her curriculum vitae to know more about her. The director also agreed and obtained Sherry's email address and phone number. The same day, Sherry received the Director's curriculum vitae in an email attachment by email. She quickly opened it. To her amazement, the director was not only a nurse but also a lawyer. Sherry felt honored and grateful. In her email, the director suggested that Sherry read a pertinent and timely article, written by Attorney Stephanie

L. Tang, entitled, "WHEN ''YES'' MIGHT MEAN ''NO''": STANDARDIZING STATE CRITERIA TO EVALUATE THE CAPACITY TO CONSENT TO SEXUAL ACTIVITY FOR ELDERLY WITH NEUROCOGNITIVE DISORDERS."

Sherry looked up Tang's article online and proceeded to read it. It dealt with the challenging issues of consent to sex in elderly individuals whose cognition is impaired. Sherry spent condensing Tang's article for the rest of that day. She wanted to be well informed before meeting the nursing home director. This extract of information would also be included in her newspaper column on the consent topic.

Consent Policies of the Nursing Home

Three days later, Sherry and Annie went to meet with the nursing home director at her office. The receptionist greeted them warmly and asked them to sit in the waiting room next to her office. The director was notified by phone that the two ladies were waiting to see her. A few minutes later, a tall, blond, and pretty lady walked toward Sherry and Annie, introduced herself as Pamela, and then invited them to her office. The three ladies first exchanged a short conversation.

Then Sherry thanked Pamela for advising her to go through Tang's article.

Pamela asked Sherry if she actually managed to read the article. Sherry's response was an enthusiastic yes, and she handed Pamela the condensed version of the article. Pamela was thoroughly pleased.

Sherry said, *"Annie and I have prepared a few questions regarding consent and sexual activities in nursing homes."*

Pamela said, *"Okay. I hope I can answer your questions to the greatest extent. But some of my answers may be derived from Tang's article too. Please proceed to ask your questions."*

Annie asked, *"Could you explain what consent is generally among nursing home residents?"*

Pamela answered, *"Every resident in this nursing home has to agree voluntarily to either an act or a proposal of another person, whether an employee or a visitor. That may range from eating a certain food, drinking any liquid, taking medication, bathing, or even dressing up for the sexual activity. When it comes to sex, there has to be a meeting of the minds and willingness of both parties that the sexual act shall occur."*

Annie was perplexed as she questioned, *"But how does the resident consent?"*

Pamela said, *"Generally, the resident consents to sex by actually performing the sexual act that is recommended by another resident, spouse, or partner. In this situation, the consent to have sex is exercised freely, unaffected by fraud, duress, or even mistake."*

Sherry proceeded with her question, *"So, should I understand and imply of what you are saying that when residents engage in intimacy and sexual activity, consent is generally implied in those activities?"*

Pamela said, *"That's right."*

Annie asked, *"What about an elderly person who has dementia like my mother?"*

Pamela answered, *"The capacity of the elderly with dementia to consent to sexual activity is extremely important. Whether the elderly have sex at home or in a nursing home; if one of the individuals does not consent to sexual activity by outright refusal or inability to refuse, that raises the question of rape. What I worry about most is* sexual abuse or rape, where one of the residents has not consented or is incapable of consenting to the sexual act."

Sherry asked, *"Are your nursing home residents competent to give consent?"*

Pamela answered, *"The vast majority of our nursing home residents are legally competent. They decide where to live, what food to eat, what to drink, and how to dress. They may exercise their right to vote and can decide on many aspects of their lives, including sexual activity."*

Annie asked, *"Is there anyone in this nursing home who determines if a resident is incompetent?"*

Pamela said, *"No one makes that determination in this nursing home. Many of our residents exhibit some cognitive impairment. But every resident, with or without dementia, remains legally competent unless a Judge adjudicates that person as incompetent, and we receive a court order to that effect."*

Sherry asked, *"How common is cognitive impairment in the elderly?"*

Pamela said, *"Cognitive impairment ranges from mild to severe. According to what Tang noted in her article, about one out of 10 elderly individuals, ages 70 and older have moderate to severe cognitive impairment. Impaired individuals have trouble remembering, learning new things, concentrating, or making decisions that affect their everyday life. At some point, issues such as deciding if the individual has become so impaired that one's mental capacity to reason is abridged, or if the individual can hold appropriate values and goals, appreciate one's circumstances, understand the information that is given, and if the individual can communicate a choice, become questionable. These capacities can change over time."*

Sherry said, *"But people suffering from Alzheimer's may be confused one day and lucid the next."*

Pamela said, *"That is certainly true. That makes things even more difficult for the nurse and the doctor to evaluate the patient. Mental capacity is a continuous quality that may be present to a greater or lesser extent. Nevertheless, those individuals that exhibit moderate to severe cognitive impairment are often thought to lack capacity and are consequently deemed incapable of providing valid consent to any sexual behavior. Both the government and society are generally uncomfortable with the idea that cognitively impaired seniors engage in sexual activity. But I might add that there is a lack of laws, regulations, policies, and general guidelines on the subject."*

Annie asked, *"Do you have policies regarding sexual activity in this nursing home?"*

Pamela said, *"Yes, this is one of the few nursing homes that have implemented standardized policies and procedures regarding sexual relations. And you know that an essential step in determining the legality of sexual relations is defining the capacity to consent. Unfortunately, nursing home residents who have cognitive impairment or are demented, are negatively stigmatized by society. In fact, the word dementia has a Latin root meaning 'madness,' which originates from **de** indicating 'without' and **men** indicating 'mind.' Dementia is a medical disorder. It damages the brain causing mental symptoms. In 2013, the American Psychiatric Association published the Fifth Edition of the "Diagnostic and Statistical Manual of Mental Disorders" ('DSM-5'). It eliminated the term 'dementia,' while placing it within the category of 'Neurocognitive Disorders,' in part to diminish the stigma attached to dementia."*

Annie asked, *"What is your perspective, and what are your thoughts about sexual activity in nursing homes?"*

Pamela said, *"It appears that sexual activity and intimacy in the elderly and in people living with dementia are beneficial for both mental and physical health. But, the vulnerable residents must be protected from psychological and physical abuse and sexually-transmitted diseases. We should be very careful, and we must do everything we can to prevent non-consensual sexual contact or sexual contact with any person who is incapable of giving consent. Unfortunately, the risk of sexual abuse is increased in elderly individuals with diminished capacity."*

Sherry asked, *"Do you have an estimate as to how active are your Alzheimer's residents, sexually?"*

Pamela said, *"No, I do not have an estimate. However, it is my understanding that many elderly individuals, with and without Alzheimer's, remain active sexually. Sexual sensations remain pleasurable and gratifying, even when Alzheimer's is advanced. And patients with Alzheimer's often assert their privacy, individuality, and autonomy. Some of them might need physical contact more than younger people. Interestingly, younger people think that sex should be reserved for individuals who are cognitively intact, and they are repulsed by the idea of sexually active elderly individuals with dementia."*

Annie asked, *"Can you tell me how judges determine the capacity of Alzheimer's patients to consent to sexual activity?"*

Pamela started to explain, *"When determining capacity to consent to sexual activity, all states employ what is called a functional approach. It focuses on the elderly victim's ability to understand information related to the sexual act."*

Sherry requested, *"Can you please elaborate?"*

Pamela said, *"First, let me read to you the three things that Judges consider.*

First*, the Judge considers the elderly individual's knowledge of the relevant facts concerning the decision to have sex and the individual's understanding of the sexual nature of the act.*

Second*, the Judge considers the elderly individual's mental capacity and intelligence to realize and rationally process the risks and benefits of engaging in the sexual activity; and,*

Third, the elderly individual's voluntariness to engage in sexual conduct without coercion. Most states require an understanding by the elderly individual of both the sexual nature of the act and the voluntary nature of participation in sex. But in some states, judges also require an understanding of the associated potential consequences, such as contracting sexually transmitted diseases. Only a few states require an understanding of the moral quality of engaging in sexual activity."

Annie asked, *"Is there a standard way for the court to determine the capacity of Alzheimer's patients to consent to sex?"*

Pamela said, *"Not that I have any knowledge about it! States utilize different tests and varying thresholds to determine the capacity of Alzheimer's patients to consent to sexual activity."*

Sherry asked, *"I would love to hear you explain the thresholds used in court to determine capacity."*

Pamela responded by saying, *"Well, the lowest threshold employed by the court is to determine that the nursing home resident has an understanding of the sexual nature of the act and that he or she voluntarily consents to sex. A resident is unable to consent if the mental state is such that he or she cannot comprehend the distinctively sexual nature of the conduct, or is incapable of understanding or exercising the right to refuse to engage in such conduct with another. And there should be no coercion, unfair persuasion, or inducements. This test has proven vague and seems to encroach upon the sexual autonomy of individuals with mental disabilities.*

The intermediate threshold, which is applied in some states, adds the requirement of understanding the potential health risks and consequences of the sexual activity, in hopes of balancing the states' interests in protecting individuals from sexual exploitation against the individuals' rights to sexual autonomy. This test is similar to the informed medical consent, which requires that a patient understands the nature and consequences of a given medical procedure. The highest threshold, applied in a few states, adds the requirement of understanding the 'moral quality' of the sexual conduct to evaluations of victims' capacity. The nursing home residents are required to be mentally capable of understanding the social mores of sexual behavior. This test is strict and strongly favors the state's 'protection from harm' interest. This standard infringes on people with both mild and major cognitive disorders. And care must be taken not to restrict the freedom of persons in cases where this test is applied. Some courts apply the evidence of mental disability test to determine an individual's capacity to consent to sexual activity but set no guidelines as to what is sufficient and what type of evidence a court is seeking. Interestingly, Georgia and Minnesota apply the Judgment Test, which looks at whether an individual can exercise judgment to consent to sexual activity.

Thus, an individual is incapable of consenting to sexual activity where, due to her high degree of mental impairment, he or she is unable to give intelligent assent and exercise judgment regarding sexual activity. Thus, Judges generally use two methods to determine the capacity of an individual to consent to sex. First, the clinical determination method based on evaluations by a qualified psychiatrist, psychologist, or physician. Second, the judicial determination method directly evaluates a victim's competence by evaluating evidence and expert testimony."

Annie asked, *"Are there possible solutions to the issue of consent to sexual activity by an individual who is cognitively impaired?"*

Pamela said, *"According to Tang, there are several possible solutions.*

Giving a legal guardian the right to consent to sexual behavior on behalf of the individual with a neurocognitive disorder.

- *Adoption of an upper limit for the age of consent, similar to the lower limit imposed in statutory rape cases.*

- *Mediation between the parties as a means of understanding the sexual interests and determining the capacity of a victim.*

- *Education of Doctors and Cognitively Impaired Elderly.*

- *Adoption of Model Assessment Tools for Judicial Determination."*

Annie and Sherry thanked Pamela for being so generous and taking the time to explain them so clearly and analytically, this difficult consent to sex topic. They went to visit their parents before going home.

Sex Policies at the Nursing Home

In the U.S., there are no national standards pertaining to sexual expression in nursing homes by senior residents. Some nursing homes have established sex policies for residents and have also developed guidelines for their staff to communicate willingly and comfortably about sex with the residents and their families.

Firstly, the need for sex doesn't disappear as we age, yet many facilities for the elderly have no policy on sex at all. They only acknowledge that it happens when there's a problem, like a concern that an Alzheimer's or dementia patient is being abused. Whether it's out of ageism or just discomfort with the idea of senior sexuality, nursing homes are not eager to raise the issue, leaving a massive gray area where the line of consent is blurry. Secondly, Alexander Warso published an article in 2015, entitled, "Something Catchy: Nursing Home Liability in The Senior Sexually Transmitted Disease Epidemic."

The author pointed out that the growing incidence of sexually transmitted diseases among the elderly population necessitates a substantial, mature discussion. The author stated that elders are often under-educated about the risks of unprotected sex, and many do not even understand the diseases to which they are inadvertently exposing themselves. Warso noted that various state and federal regulations address the problem of disease and infection in nursing homes and similar communities, but few cases have been decided regarding sexually transmitted illnesses.

Warso also noted, "In order to combat a real and growing problem among our elder population, we must increase sex education for elders and begin to hold nursing homes civilly liable for the spread of infection among their populations. The combination of education and enforced liability would lead to a more comprehensive, proactive approach, ensuring the health and comfort of our elder population." Some U.S. nursing homes, such as Genesis HealthCare Corp. of Kennett Square, Pennsylvania, and Golden Living of Plano, Texas, address the issue of sexual expression by nursing home residents on a person-by-person basis, and their broader programs incorporate training about sexual situations.

In 2003, Doll addressed the scope of sexual activity of nursing home residents, the staff's reactions to sexual behavior, and the policies and guidelines used in nursing homes. The results showed that:

Nursing home resident sexual expression covered a wide variety of activities from flirtation to sexual intercourse and was evident in nearly every nursing home.

- The reactions to these sexual activities by family and staff members, especially nursing staff, could be quite negative and interfered with the residents' quality of life.

- Sexual expression policies and staff/family training and education could improve the likelihood that residents' intimacy needs are met.

In 1995, the Hebrew Home at Riverdale in the Bronx developed a Sexual Expression Policy, which recognizes and supports the older adult's right to engage in sexual activity. Patients with dementia and Alzheimer's can give consent to sex, either verbally or non-verbally. The policy is explicit. It respects the emotional and physical intimacy of all seniors. It regards human interactions among seniors as a normal and natural aspect of life. The Hebrew Home Sexual Rights Policy defined sexual expression as "Words, gestures, movements or activities (including reaching, pursuing, touching or reading) which appear motivated by the desire for sexual gratification."

The policy applied to all older adult residents was based on the assumption of autonomy, civil and privacy rights of all people, including the protected rights of seniors residing in Medicaid/ Medicare settings. It applied to all nursing home residents, including those with physical and cognitive impairment.

Furthermore, it recognized and supported the right of seniors residing at the nursing home to engage in sexual activity, provided there was consent among those involved to ensure their safety and well-being. The nursing home staff of professionals and caregivers were expected to set aside personal biases and judgment about senior sexual activity.

The right of nursing home residents to sexual activity precluded non-consensual acts, acts with minors, acts between persons if there is any possibility of the transmission of an STD, and acts that impact negatively on the resident community as a whole through public display.

Ombudsman Fact Sheet

In Georgia, the members of the "long term care council of community Ombudsmen" prepared a fact sheet which was intended to help and educate the community about issues regarding long term care facilities in Georgia. 'Ombudsman Fact Sheet' dealt with sexuality in the nursing home. The following is a summary. It stated that "Sexuality is part of human nature throughout life. It doesn't automatically stop at the nursing home door. Being elderly and sick does not necessarily mean sexual desires decline. Family members and nursing home staff should expect sexual behaviors to occur and be ready and willing to respond appropriately."

Reasons Why Residents May Show Sexual Interest in Others

They feel a need to maintain intimate relationships, which residents can still maintain and treasure after losing their homes, health, independence, and often life partners. While there is also a need to be touched, which indicates acceptance and positive regard by others. The lack of touch may cause depression, withdrawal, diminished responsiveness, and death. Moreover, physical or mental illnesses have a tendency to decrease or increase sexual desire and activity. Similarly, medications may affect sexual behavior too. The theory of "transference" may cause sexual interest in another person whose mannerisms or looks may remind a resident of someone significant in their life. Also, inappropriate sexual behavior may be a part of a resident's personality, and past behavior, or the inappropriate behavior may be "acting out" an expression of anger or frustration, concerning the president's health and living conditions.

Responses by the Nursing Home Staff

The appropriate responses by the Nursing Home staff toward sexual activities within the nursing home, include:

- Informing the resident who the staff is and what is to be done before providing care.

- Avoiding touching that might be construed as inappropriate by the resident or family members.

- Avoiding being taken by surprise;

- Refraining from expressing negative emotions toward the residents;

- Checking for indicators of tendencies toward

sexually inappropriate behavior;

- Becoming educated through regular in-service training about handling inappropriate behaviors according to enacted nursing home policies and procedures for identifying and dealing with unwanted and inappropriate sexual behavior;

- Avoiding negative labeling or punishing the resident;

- Identifying gently but firmly unwanted behavior and pointing out that such conduct is unacceptable;

- Discussing the incident with appropriate staff and keeping it confidential;

- Remaining as objective as possible and not making moral judgments;

- Determining whether the behavior is healthy for that individual;

- Attempting to redirect the inappropriate behavior by giving the resident something else to be doing with his/her hands.

- Not encouraging unwanted behaviors or inappropriate jokes by responding to them or telling them.

- Avoiding suggestive dressing and the use of suggestive or inappropriate language.

- Respecting the privacy of alert and consenting residents and not interrupting their sexual activity in private locations.

- Encouraging family involvement and providing a place for private visitation during normal visiting hours, in addition to the residents' room.

Chapter 16
Advance Care Planning for Alzheimer's

Advanced Care Lecture

Annie and Sherry attended a lecture on Advance Care Planning for Alzheimer's. About fifty people including the nursing home doctor, physician assistant, nurse practitioner, registered nurses, social worker, and several relatives of residents at the Lakewood nursing home attended the lecture on advance care planning (ACP), which was scheduled for 7:00 P.M, during the first week of October. The weather was just perfect.

The temperature was 72 degrees, and the sky was blue with a few clouds and minimal wind. The lecture attendees were seated comfortably at tables in the large dining room area. The residents were fed early that day, then they were requested to clear the area unless they wanted to attend the ACP lecture with the visitors. After being seated, the attendees were served with cookies, soft drinks, and coffee. There was a table upfront reserved for the speaker, Attorney

George Sweeney, and the nursing home administrator, Lenora Smith. There were a microphone and a laptop computer on the reserved table, and a projector and screen on the side.

A few minutes after 7:00 P.M., Lenora stood up, picked up the microphone, and said, "Good evening, ladies and gentlemen. We are so glad that your schedule has allowed you to be with us this evening to attend a timely and important lecture on advance care planning. Here to tell us about this subject is Attorney George Sweeney. He has been practicing elderly law for 29 years, and he advises me on legal matters that arise in this nursing home. Ladies and gentlemen, please help me welcome Mr. Sweeney."

The attendees welcomed the speaker with applause. He stood up and took the microphone from Lenora and bowed slightly, acknowledging the attendees. The projector was on.

George wasted no time and started his lecture by saying, "Thank you, Lenora, for the introduction. Ladies and gentlemen, thank you for coming today, and I welcome you to comment or ask questions."

Answers to Common Scenarios

George continued saying, "One of the most common scenarios that family members ask me about goes like this: My father has moderately severe Alzheimer's. His condition is getting pretty bad, and he is difficult to handle at home. There are times when he does not seem to recognize his family.

What legal and non-legal issues should I be considering now that my father is incapacitated?

My answer generally goes like this. "The housing of Alzheimer's sufferers is critical in making certain legal and financial decisions. Staying at home is the best option. If feasible physically and financially, the family would think of moving him to a retirement facility or a nursing home, depending on the level of care needed. Some people consider a rental or a "buy-in" arrangement. There are several legal options available to protect the person, preserve his or her estate, and provide distribution upon death. These include Last Will and Testament, Advance Directive for Health Care (Living Will), Durable Powers of Attorney for Health Care, a HIPAA release for medical records (Protected Health Information), Revocable and Irrevocable Trusts, Gifting of

Assets, Joint Tenancy Accounts, Payable on Death Accounts, Transfer with a Retained Life Estate, Durable Powers of Attorney for assets, Designation of a representative payee, and Conservatorship (Guardianship) of the estate and of the person."

Another common question that family members ask me goes like this: I am a caregiver. What kind of an attorney should I consult with to help me with the advance care planning for my wife, who is suffering from Alzheimer's?

There are a couple of essential things that should be emphasized for advance care planning:

- First, the medical condition of Alzheimer's sufferer. Advance care planning involves health care providers advising the patients and their families on a range of issues and options, from minimal medical interventions to demanding that every treatment possible be offered near the end of life.

- The second primary consideration is the legal aspect. There are some attorneys who specialize and maybe are certified in health law. In general, attorneys who advise caregivers on planning for long-term care of chronically ill elderly individuals should know he following areas of law.

- Medicare and Medicaid (Medi-Cal) laws and regulations;

- Social Security rules and regulations;

- Revocable and Irrevocable Trusts and Special Needs Trusts);

- Conservatorship (Guardianship) laws;

- A durable power of attorney for health care and asset management;

- Tax (income, estate, and gift) planning; and

- Housing and health care contracts, among others.

Another question that is frequently asked regards payment or advance care planning advice!

On October 31, 2014, the CMS revised its payment policies by adding two new practice billing codes, 99487 and 99497. In doing so, it officially recognized the efforts of physicians or other qualified, trained, and licensed health care professionals to engage in ACP with patients. That includes the explanation, discussion, and completion of standard advance directive forms. In May 2015, sixty-six organizations representing medical providers and senior citizens, including the American Medical Association (AMA) and the AARP, Inc., formerly the American Association of Retired Persons, wrote to the Health and Human Services Secretary, Sylvia Mathews Burwell, urging the federal government to establish a way to pay for advance care planning.

The letter noted that "Published, peer-reviewed research shows that Advance Care Planning (ACP) leads to better care, higher patient and family satisfaction, fewer unwanted hospitalizations, and lower rates of caregiver distress, depression and lost productivity. And ACP is particularly important for Medicare beneficiaries because many have multiple chronic illnesses, receive care at home from family and other caregivers, and their children and other family members are often involved in making medical decisions."

In 2014, the Institute of Medicine (IOM) report entitled, *"Dying in America: Improving Quality and Honoring Individual Preferences Near the End of Life"* cited the payment for Advance Care Planning (ACP) as one of its five key recommendations. It noted that the hallmark of good

ACP is open, clear, and respectful communication between the person doing the planning and their clinicians, loved ones, and health care agents. And, the reimbursement for ACP should be based on models that focus on this type of communication, such as Respecting Choices. In the early 1990s, La Crosse implemented the Wisconsin based Respecting Choices (RC) ACP initiative. ACP conversations between clinicians and patients were not reimbursed by any traditional payers. The RC model relied on trained ACP facilitators who volunteered their time and assisted people with the advance care planning process.

ACP facilitators worked with patients and their medical providers to improve the patients' understanding about their disorders, help bridge gaps of medical knowledge, engage patients about their values, beliefs, preferences, and goals, and communicate with their health care proxies or agents and other loved ones about those values and goals of care. The facilitators also assisted patients in documenting their health care proxies or agents, and goals of care in living wills, powers of attorney for health care, POLST, and Do-Not-Resuscitate physician orders. They made sure that the documented plans are easily retrievable by those who may need them, including health care proxies or agents, loved ones, and medical providers.

The La Crosse ACP facilitators were trained and certified by RC to conduct ACP in three distinct stages:

- When adults were relatively healthy;

- when patients began to suffer the effects of a chronic or life-limiting illness; and

- When they were near the end-of-life.

The ACP facilitators included physicians, nurses, social workers, and community volunteers without medical training. They were assigned to work with populations that fit their level of training, and they engaged only with people who wanted to create an advance care plan.

In 1995 and 1996, two years after the communitywide implementation of the RC model, the La Crosse Advance Directive Study (LADS I) was conducted as a retrospective study of 540 decedents in La Crosse. The study found that 85 percent of the decedents had an advance directive and that 95 percent of these directives were documented in their medical records. Only eight patients were found to receive medical treatment inconsistent with their documented preferences in LADS I. In 2007 and 2008, a second study was conducted (LADS II). The results showed that the numbers of decedents with advance directives that were also documented in their medical records rose, respectively, to 90 percent and 99 percent. It found no cases of patients that received treatment inconsistent with their documented treatment preferences. The RC model had an economic impact on utilization and health care expenditures in the last two years of life, which was attributable to reducing wasteful spending related to providing unwanted care to patients at the end of life.

Respecting Choices has been implemented in many health systems and organizations throughout the United States and in Canada, Australia, Singapore, and Germany. Successful statewide ACP programs, such as Honoring Choices Wisconsin, Honoring Choices Minnesota, Honoring Choices Virginia, and Honoring Choices Florida are based on the RC model.

On July 8, 2015, the Centers for Medicare and Medicaid Services (CMS) published a new rule, which stated that starting in 2016, doctors will be paid for the time they spend helping people on Medicare do ACP for a serious or life-threatening disease or condition. This CMS rule is quite remarkable. It supports individuals, such as Alzheimer's sufferers and families who wish to discuss ACP with their physician and care team, as part of coordinated, patient, and family-centered care. As far as health care providers are concerned, ACP has become a standard of care. It improves the quality and outcome of medical care and substantially decreases health care costs at the end-of-life. During these sessions, patients would get advice on a range of options, from minimal medical interventions to demanding every treatment possible be offered near the end of life. Patients can choose whether or not to schedule end-of-life counseling.

Well, our time has come to a close. I would like to thank all of you for attending this evening and also Lenora Sweeney for giving me the opportunity to speak to you. I shall remain here for another 10-15 minutes and attempt to answer your questions individually."

Lenora stood up, shook Sweeney's hand, and thanked him for a very informative lecture. Sherry and Annie were thrilled to have listened to George Sweeney, although the information presented was somewhat overwhelming. However, it served to inspire the two ladies to learn more and make sure they are serving their parents' interests, as well as their families. They decided to review their parents' documents and properly complete all advance care planning forms.

Chapter 17
Nursing Home Intimacy Workers

Touching Base and Nursing Home Intimacy Workers, Australia

Touching Base is a non-profit organization that helps people like sex worker Emma connect with disabled clients. They recommend that nursing home facilities should be obliged to support and facilitate the intimate and social relationships of their residents. However, some of the residents may forget that they have been visited by the sex worker, and they feel like the staff is lying to them. In one case, a token system was set up for the client, where a sex worker would leave the resident a token as proof of the encounter.

Nursing Home Intimacy Workers in England

Chaseley Nursing Home in Eastbourne, England has regularly hired prostitutes, who meet residents in a special room and put a "special red sock" on the door for privacy. Caregivers check on the rooms every fifteen minutes. Chaseley caters mostly to ex-soldiers. The procurement of the sex workers was handled by a third-party consultant. However, the concern of potentially placing vulnerable nursing home residents at risk of exploitation and abuse was significant. The non-profit Para Doxies in Milton Keynes, England, opened a brothel planned and designed specifically for disabled clients who can travel outside the home. They offer transportation and are wheelchair accessible. People have the same sexual urges, whether they are disabled or not. Everyone deserves to experience and enjoy sexual contact.

Nursing Home Intimacy Workers, Denmark

The Kildegaarden residence in Denmark had made several calls to sex workers over several years, according to the news website, but the practice was greeted with skepticism by some politicians. When a male resident at Kildegaarden nursing home in Denmark made an indecent sexual proposal to a member of the staff, the home's director told a nurse to telephone for a prostitute. There was a considerable change in his demeanor after the escort girl had paid him a visit. The nursing home does this for its residents, just as they offer them other services that they need as human beings, according to the director. Bringing a sex worker into a nursing home was an effective way to handle a resident with dementia engaging in "inappropriate" sexual behavior. People living with dementia often lose their inhibitions and are not fully responsible for their behavior. They may exhibit sexual behavior that is challenging for caregivers, including disrobing in public, inappropriate touching, using suggestive gestures or language, or going into another resident's bedroom in an aged- care facility and getting into their bed uninvited.

Nursing Home Staff Duty

Nursing home staff need to look at the person's sexual history to address their unmet sexual needs and reconnect the person to their past experiences and pleasures. The need for Alzheimer's sufferer to express one's sexuality continues to flourish regardless of age or disability. Nursing homes should consider employing a sex worker where appropriate. Some nursing homes do allow sex workers to see residents in specific circumstances. They should find out the sexual history of the person, whether they have used sex workers in the past, and whether they have used sexual aids or toys. It is noteworthy that sex is just one component of sexuality and only one expression of intimacy.

Chapter 18
Adult Toys for Disabled Seniors

Toys for Disabled People

When it comes to adult toys, the elderly and Alzheimer's disabled individuals are not adequately catered for, despite demand from older and disabled people for adult toys. Often, it is not clear which toys are most appropriate for disabled people or how they should be used. Some manufacturers provide ergonomically designed products, which are remotely controlled, easy to grip, and easy to use by disabled individuals with limited mobility and dexterity or suffering from fatigue.

Disabled people often use equipment to help with everyday things. They also use adult toys as aids in the bedroom to enjoy sex. The toys assist those with sexual difficulties or physical, mental, or sensory impairments. The toys are used for pleasure, variety, sexual experimentation, among other reasons. A few examples of adult toys include:

- The Humpus

- The Fleshlight (one version with a suction pad)

- Rends A10 Cyclone

- Butterfly vibrators

- Vibrating panties

- Venus 2000

- The Sybian

- Hitachi Magic Wand

- Ferticare

- Liberator

- Silver Sex

- Literotica

- The Hold It

Furthermore, men who are unable to achieve an erection may use a strap-on dildo in its place, or strap it to their thigh, so their partner can sit on it and play with their penis at the same time. On the contrary, women who cannot reach down between their legs to masturbate may use a Magic Wand, which has a long handle, to stimulate the clitoris. Women also have no-hands toys like the butterfly and vibrating panties, which can get them to orgasm. Since they have the tendency to not be able to lubricate naturally, they need lubricants in an accessible container. Moreover, blind and visually impaired people may use audio erotica to excite them. Also, people who cannot move and want to provide pleasure to their partners may be able to hold toys on them; toys such as vibrators or electrostimulation gadgets to provide stimulation.

People with arthritis or who have difficulty getting into the right positions for sexual interactions might use sex swings or supports to make it easier for them. Some disabled people need sex toys because they are unable to masturbate to orgasm, maybe because they have short arms, their hands get tired and weak, or they cannot move their arms. While other disabled people may have partners who will stimulate them manually or go down on them. Surprisingly, some nursing home care staff may be willing to put a vibrator on the female clitoris or masturbator on the male penis, secure it in place, maybe even turn it on, and leave the room, coming back later to clear up and put the toy away. There is also a toy called 'Happy harnesses,' which will fit the wearer and hold the required sex toy, meaning the sex toy is not only in the right place, but it will also stay firmly in place.

Hands-free Toys

The **'Love Bumper'** used with or without a vibrator, like the **'Mystic Wand'** or **'Hitachi Magic Wand'** allows you to prop your body up for various positions. It's gotten rave reviews from some of the customers with limited mobility or arm/leg strength.

'Leo' is a 100% silicone dildo that suctions to any smooth, hard surface, from a chair to a shower wall too, for hands-free use.

'Butt plugs' in general are designed to be hands-free.

The **'Little Flirt'** is a slim plug that's perfect for first-time anal play.

'Aneros toys' are patented prostate massagers that rock in your body, as you squeeze your PC muscles.

Wearable Adult Toys

Wearable toys like the ***'Fukuoku'*** and the ***'Babel and Remote*** **Vibe Panty'** can be creative alternatives to conventional vibrators.

'**Vibrating Cock Rings**' like the Sonic Ring Kit can be attached to a penis, another toy, or a hand.

If your fingers get tired during masturbation, a '**Vibe**' is the perfect way to save yourself from tired, strained hands and fingers.

'**Strap-ons**' are a whole new world in wearable sex toys.

'**Dildo harnesses**' are equal-opportunity sex toys that can be used by anyone who wants to penetrate a partner.

Adults with limited hip or leg mobility can take recourse to the '**Thigh Harness**,' which allows the wearing partner to remain stationary, while the penetrated partner straddles the dildo-ed thigh.

Virtual Intimacy for Adults

Finally, the digital age is creating new definitions for sex, especially virtual intimacy: Computers and technology are expanding the boundaries of sex and how to connect with another person. Adults and young people are exploring sexuality with new forms of communication. For instance, Sex tech is opening up huge possibilities for sex and intimacy.

Mark Pesce has been exploring how the virtual realm is forcing us to rethink our ideas of intimacy and paving the way for artificially intelligent sex partners. Virtual reality is a form of communication. Sexting is a form of virtual, sexual communication.

Chapter 19
Pre-Alzheimer's

For some 15 years before any mental symptoms of Alzheimer's appear, patients go through a so-called 'silent,' 'latent,' 'asymptomatic,' or 'preclinical' stage.[1] For short, it is referred to here as 'Pre-Alzheimer's.' In the late 20th century, Pre-Alzheimer's was described in cognitively *unimpaired* individuals whose postmortem examination, had brain lesions similar to those who were cognitively *impaired* from Alzheimer's.

In the 21st Century, Pre-Alzheimer's is diagnosed before death using a variety of biomarkers by testing blood, urine, fluid around the brain and spinal cord, and brain imaging. Pre-Alzheimer's is presently believed to be the best time to start treatment aimed at delaying or secondarily preventing cognitive impairment due to Alzheimer's. However, the diagnosis and treatment of Pre-Alzheimer's raise some ethical concerns. Here is a case on point.

---

[1] https://www.ncbi.nlm.nih.gov/pmc/articles/PMC6417794/

The Case of Samantha Dalton, M.D.

In 2016, Samantha, age 47, was happily married to Peter, an accountant, and had two teenage children, a girl, 19, and a boy, 17. They were all healthy. Dr. Samantha had been practicing internal medicine fulltime for almost 20 years in Los Angeles, California. She loved going to her medical office to treat her patients. She had a busy practice. She was attempting to slowly cut back her work hours to spend more time with her family.

Dr. Samantha had routinely undergone annual physical examinations by her Ob-Gyn physician. She had no medical problems. In 2016, she made an appointment with Dr. Jennifer Seymour, a neurologist, who was an expert on Alzheimer's. On her appointment with Dr. Jennifer, she arrived 15 minutes early and signed in at the reception desk. Because she was a new patient, she was seated at a computer and asked to complete several medical forms, which had extensive questions. It took her about 20 minutes to answer the questions. After a short wait, she was taken from the waiting room to an exam room where her vital signs and weight were taken by a nurse. Dr. Jennifer walked in, just as the nurse finished checking the vitals. She approached Dr.

Samantha with a smile and shook her hand while saying, *"I am Jennifer. Pleased to make your acquaintance. May I call you Samantha? And you may call me Jennifer."*

Samantha smiled back and answered, *"Of course, you may. And thank you for seeing me today."*

"Well, what brings you to a neurologist?" asked Jennifer as she walked toward a nearby stand, which had a computer on it. She wanted to review the forms that Jennifer completed.

Samantha said, *"You are a well-known peer and an expert in Alzheimer's disease. You have done the research and published several articles on Alzheimer's. I am here because I am petrified about the possibility of developing the disease. I am concerned about myself and my family. I would like to find out whether or not I may have the propensity to develop this horrible disease. Two months ago, I had my annual medical check-up. All my routine blood and urine tests, electrocardiogram, and chest x-ray were within normal limits. Still, I would appreciate a more thorough work-up. My mother passed away a few months ago from Alzheimer's disease."*

Jennifer said, *"Sorry to hear about your mother. Would you please tell me more about her?"*

Samantha answered, *"Six years ago, my mother, Gloria, began having some cognitive mental symptoms. She was 63 years of age then. Prior to that time, she had hypertension, but her blood pressure was well-controlled with a low-salt diet and medications. She had no other problems. She had no cardiovascular or brain problems. In 2010, she started having difficulty with memory, mainly forgetfulness and some behavioral issues, such as irritability and combativeness with my father, Alfred. After a few months, she began exhibiting some paranoia and fear. She was evaluated by her family physician and a neurologist and diagnosed with early Alzheimer's dementia. My Dad took excellent care of Mom at home. She specifically requested that Dad care for her at home. She loved her home, which was on five acres of land in a small town. She enjoyed seeing the beautiful trees, the small pond, the birds, the squirrels, and her dogs, cats, chickens, and a horse roam around. She loved sitting on the porch swing, watching the sunrise early in the morning, and the sunset before retiring to bed.*

Mom dreaded being placed in a nursing home. She was treated with several medications for Alzheimer's, but they were essentially ineffective in stopping or slowing down her disease process. About five years later, she became severely demented. Her physical condition deteriorated until she became bedfast. She died a few months ago at 69 years of age."

Jennifer listened silently while jotting down some notes. When Samantha stopped talking, she raised her head, and for a few seconds, she gazed at Samantha with empathy and concern then said, *"My condolences."*

Samantha's eyes were teary. She returned, *"Thank you."*

Jennifer resumed her questions and asked, *"Do you have any physical or mental symptoms?"*

"None whatsoever," answered Samantha. *"I am an only child. I do worry that I may have inherited something from my Mom that may put my children or me at risk of developing Alzheimer's. During Mom's illness, I read a great deal about Alzheimer's disease and dementia. And, as you can imagine, I have seen a number of patients in my office with the disease. I try to keep up with the most up-to-date approaches*

to diagnosing and treating Alzheimer's. And I have adhered to a healthy lifestyle."

Jennifer proceeded to finish a comprehensive neurologic history, followed by a thorough physical examination. She told Samantha that everything was normal.

Samantha was asked to complete a cognition test, even though there was nothing to suggest that she had any impairment. Jennifer said it was merely a baseline test to document the absence of cognitive impairment.

Samantha was thinking privately. She is nearing 50. She knew that age is the strongest known risk factor for the cognitive disease. She would like to find ways to help her retain her cognitive health and independence. She was afraid to be like her mother.

Pre-Alzheimer's Statistics

There are three categories of Alzheimer's:

1. Pre-Alzheimer's - Preclinical (No symptoms)
2. Mild Cognitive Impairment (MCL)
3. Dementia (cognitively impaired)

Samantha thought that if she had any brain issues, she would be in the first category, and that might be challenging to diagnose.

In 2017, Dr. Ron Brookmeyer, Professor of Biostatistics at UCLA, California, estimated that 46.7 million Americans had Pre-Alzheimer's. That represented 35% of the U.S. adults age 45 years and older. Fortunately, many of those people will not develop symptoms of Alzheimer's during their natural lifespan.

By comparison, in 2018, there were a total of 6.08 million patients that had mental symptoms varying from mild impairment to severe in all dementia patients.

Another thing that worried Samantha was the fact that almost two-thirds of the Alzheimer's patients were women, especially those with the gene called APOE4. This is one of the biomarkers of Alzheimer's disease. The risk in men with the same gene was much less.

Samantha was anxious to know if she had evidence of any of the two other biomarkers of Alzheimer's in her brain. They are the two hallmarks of Alzheimer's, which are abnormal proteins. They are called '*amyloid*' and '*tau*,' which respectively appear in Stages 1 and 2 of Pre-Alzheimer's. They are basically the 'silent killers' of brain cells (neurons), which work to slowly destroy the brain over a decade or so.

1. Stage 1 is when '*amyloid*' deposits in the brain outside the cells (neurons). This stage lasts several years, with no symptoms.
2. Stage 2 is when '*tau*' begins to appear inside the brain cells. Still, there are no mental symptoms.

These two stages of Pre-Alzheimer's may be followed by a 'transition" stage with minimal, subtle cognitive symptoms, which are challenging to diagnose and are usually attributed to age.

Cognition Test

Samantha knew about the various cognition tests, such as:

1. The Clock-Drawing Test for Alzheimer's
2. The 7 Minute Screen
3. The Brief Alzheimer's Screening Test
4. Montreal Cognitive Assessment (MoCA)
5. St Louis Univ. Mental Status Exam (SLUMS)

6. AD8 Informant Interview

7. *The SAGE At-Home Test for Memory*

8. *Mini-Cog*

9. Mini-Mental State Examination (MMSE)

Nowadays, healthcare institutions have started screening physicians of a certain age with cognitive and physical dexterity tests. For instance, at Scripps Health system, San Diego, they have about 3,000 physicians; about 150 are aged 70+ years, who are being screened regularly for cognitive impairment, among other medical problems. Testing for cognitive impairment is a condition for re-credentialing every two years to maintain hospital privileges.

The Medicare Annual Wellness Visit provides for a yearly appointment with the primary care provider (PCP) to create or update a personalized prevention plan. This includes:

- Weight and Blood Pressure
- Assess health risk
- Medical and family history
- List current providers and suppliers
- Screening tests
- *Screen for cognitive issues*

- Provide health advice and referrals

At her office, Samantha uses the **SAGE test** on her patients, which may be completed at home. However, Jennifer gave her the **'Mini-Cog' test**. Samantha passed the test and had no evidence of cognitive impairment.

Lab Tests

Next, Samantha had several laboratory tests.

- Her blood test indicated that she had the biomarker gene, APOE4.
- Her urine test was normal.
- The fluid from around her spinal cord, called cerebrospinal fluid, was also examined and showed no abnormal proteins (amyloid or tau). That was good news for Samantha.

Jennifer asked Samantha to return annually for follow up, which she did. She would complete another cognition test; the results were normal every time.

Brain Imaging Tests

In 2019, Samantha surprised Jennifer by requesting imaging of her brain with MRI, CT, and PET scans.

- MRI stands for Magnetic Resonance Imaging. It checks the size and structure of the whole brain using radio waves and a strong magnetic field.
- CT, Computerized Tomography, examines a specific portion of the brain as slices, which are produced using x-ray.
- PET, Positron Emission Tomography, uses specific radioactive tracers that are given intravenously to reveal a particular feature in the brain, such as areas of the brain with poor metabolism or the presence of *amyloid* and *tau*.

Jennifer was hesitant to do so. She was fearful of over-diagnosis. She wanted to avoid performing highly sophisticated and expensive brain imaging tests on Samantha, who did not have any symptoms and find an imaging abnormality. Even if the brain scan showed an abnormality, it is possible that the abnormality will not go on to cause any noticeable symptoms or health problems during the person's life.

The diagnosis of stage one Pre-Alzheimer's is something that might never become a significant health issue for Samantha. On the other hand, diagnosing Pre-Alzheimer's in Samantha could have downsides, such as fear, stigma, and the potential harms of the experimental treatment.

However, Samantha explained that she is doing this for her children as well. They deserve to know. Jennifer approved brain imaging tests.

- Samantha's MRI and CT scans were normal.
- The PET imaging revealed deposits of '*amyloid*' in her brain.
- There was no evidence of '*tau*' inside her brain cells.

Treatment

Samantha was grateful to know exactly what was happening in her brain. She was searching for answers, not only for her but also for her children. She informed her husband about the results. In due course and at an appropriate time, she will inform her children.

Jennifer advised Samantha to eat healthy foods, follow the MIND diet, be more active physically, avoid even second-hand smoke, and use moderate alcohol intake if any.

She also told Samantha to check her blood pressure monthly to make sure it remains in the normal range, control her workload to reduce stress, and sleep well. Emphasizing key lifestyle facts, Jennifer said, are associated with a significantly lower risk for future dementia, even among individuals who had a high genetic risk.

Still, there are no guarantees. Samantha can do everything "right" and still get dementia in later years.

Jennifer finally told Samantha that there are some ongoing clinical studies that are using FDA-approved medications or experimental drugs to determine their safety and efficacy in Pre-Alzheimer's, such as:

- Cholinesterase inhibitors, which boost the brain's cell-to-cell communication. These include donepezil (Aricept), galantamine (Razadyne), and rivastigmine (Exelon).
- Memantine (Namenda), which slows the progression of Alzheimer's.

Samantha has been followed annually by Jennifer without medications. She elected not to take the experimental drugs.

As of 2020, she has neither cognitive symptoms nor worsening of her brain amyloid deposits.

Chapter 20
The MIND Diet

The **MIND** (Mediterranean-DASH Intervention for Neurodegenerative Delay) diet is actually made up of two diets: (1) **Med-Diet (Mediterranean Diet)**[2], which was initially created to encourage heart health; and (2) **DASH Diet (Dietary Approaches to Stop Hypertension)** diet, which was designed to control high blood pressure and adult-onset diabetes.[3]

The MIND diet is designed to prevent or reduce dementia and the decline in brain health that usually occurs with age. By changing one's lifestyle and adhering to the MIND diet, it reduces the risk of Alzheimer's.

In 1995, Wengreen and co-workers[4] began studying the mental effects of the Mediterranean and DASH diets on 3,831 men and women, aged 65 and above, who were

---

[2] https://www.ncbi.nlm.nih.gov/pmc/articles/PMC4663587/
[3] https://www.chaptershealth.org/mind-diet-for-reducing-memory-loss-risk/?gclid=CjwKCAjwssD0BRBIEiwA-JP5rKgB1cdebppQPvDg8ZrM0V9hB4mBOZjrUj02ChNpWRnITmMw6eFMaRoCspAQAvD_BwE
[4] Am J Clin Nutr. 2013 Nov;98(5):1263-71
https://www.ncbi.nlm.nih.gov/pubmed/24047922?dopt=Abstract

residents of Cache County, UT. The cognitive function of the participants was assessed using the Modified Mini-Mental State Examination. After 11 years of follow up, the authors reported that both the DASH and Mediterranean dietary patterns were associated with consistently higher levels of cognitive function in elderly men and women. They also noted that whole grains, nuts, and legumes were positively associated with higher cognitive functions and maybe core neuroprotective foods common to various healthy plant-centered diets.

The MIND diet differs from the Mediterranean and DASH diets by:

(1) Placing emphasis on berries over other fruits due to their antioxidant properties;

(2) Highlighting the difference between green, leafy vegetables, and other vegetables, both of which are essential; and

(3) Eating fish at least once per week.

Importantly, the MIND diet is effective when it is used in conjunction with *"other healthy habits"* like regular exercise, not smoking, and getting adequate sleep.

There are certain factors that seem to increase Alzheimer's risk, and they are tied to a steeper memory decline. For instance:

- Individuals that have some inflammation in the body during midlife are more likely to have dementia;
- Psychological distress also plays a significant role [Danish study];
- Even a slight rise in blood pressure might shrink young brains; and
- Heart disease is present in many Alzheimer's patients.

On the other hand, there are many factors that seem to lower the risk of Alzheimer's, including:

- Youth, genetics, and family history are not modifiable.
- ***Physical activity and exercise*** (See Chapter 21).
- ***Mental activity*** is essential. Brain training is fundamental to the maintenance of cognitive skills throughout life. It helps with attention, memory, problem-solving, reading, and psychosocial functioning. Some examples include crossword

puzzle games, reading, writing, cooking, and playing an instrument.

- *Continued learning* stimulates the brain making people less susceptible to conditions like dementia. It keeps the mind sharp. So, join a book club, take classes at a local community college, or learn a new language.

- *Higher education* is vital too.

- *Social activity* is quite helpful.

- Having a good *socioeconomic status* is also helpful.

- *Sleep* gives the brain cells (neurons) a break from recent activities and prepares the neurons for the next day. Sleep helps the brain to work faster and more accurately. It also improves memory attention and retention.

- *Rocking motion*, such as resting on a hammock or a rocking chair, not only leads to better sleep but also boosts memory consolidation during sleep.

- *Meditation* is associated with improvement in a variety of psychological areas, including stress, anxiety, depression, eating disorders, and cognitive function. It can also reduce blood pressure, pain response, stress hormone levels, and even cellular health.[5] Meditation trains the brain in the elderly to be more attentive and mindful of tasks, and it can control memory loss and impaired concentration.

- *Hyperbaric oxygen* has been found to be helpful. Brain metabolism can be improved by treating Alzheimer's patients with oxygen in a hyperbaric chamber. It helps to get some oxygen from fresh air and take occasional deep breaths.

Smoking does not seem to be a significant factor in harming patients with Alzheimer's. However, it is not recommended for elderly people who suffer from respiratory, heart and vascular disease, diabetes, and obesity.

Tea and coffee are not harmful either for Alzheimer's patients. In fact, caffeine is associated with a lower incidence of Alzheimer's. It may boost brain function, improve tests of cognitive function, and may also have a positive effect on long-term memory retention. However, taking caffeine at night may affect sleep.

---

[5] https://www.huffpost.com/entry/meditation-health-benefits_n_3178731

Wine or Other Alcoholic Beverage is recommended by the MIND diet; one glass daily appears to be beneficial. Avoid excess alcohol, and care should be exercised when taking concomitantly sedative drugs, marijuana, or opioids with alcohol (See Chapter 24).

Dietary Supplements - Caution

In 2019, the Food and Drug Administration (FDA) took action against 17 companies for illegally selling 58 products claiming to treat Alzheimer's disease. Those products were sold as dietary supplements, unapproved new drugs, and/or misbranded drugs that claim to prevent, treat, or cure Alzheimer's. They may cause serious complications.

The MIND Diet recommends limiting the following five foods:

(1) Red meat. Limit consumption to no more than four servings a week to help protect brain health.

(2) Limit consumption of butter and margarine to no more than four servings a week to help protect brain health.

(3) Eat cheese no more than once a week if you want to reduce your risk of Alzheimer's.

(4) Limit pastries and sweets to no more than five treats per week.

(5) Limit fried foods and fast foods to no more than once a week for optimal brain health.

The MIND Diet Favors the following:

- It emphasizes the *natural foods* that contain vitamins, flavonoids, antioxidants, and omega-3 fatty acids.[6]

- *Olive oil* seems to be better than other cooking oil and fats. People who use olive oil as their primary source at home have greater protection against cognitive decline. Coconut oil could also be used.

- Eating *green leafy vegetables* at least six times a week and other vegetables at least once a day. Leafy vegetables include kale, spinach, collards, and broccoli. They are rich in nutrients that keep the brain healthy, such as vitamin K, lutein, folate, and beta carotene. These nutrients in green, leafy vegetables are linked to slower cognitive decline.

---

[6] https://www.mdlinx.com/internal-medicine/article/3620

Seniors who consume more than two servings of *mushrooms* per week reduce their risk of mild cognitive impairment by 50%. Mushrooms are an essential source of ergothioneine, which may promote cognitive health.

Flatulence could have fantastic health benefits. Human gas may have a foul odor from hydrogen sulfide, but it may prevent dementia, diabetes, and heart disease, according to recent studies.

- Eating nuts at least five times a week. *Nuts are Very Important for The Brain.*

Nuts are rich in vitamins and minerals, low in carbohydrates, and high in fiber, protein, and polyunsaturated fats.

Almonds are native to the Middle-East. They have the highest calcium content of all nuts. They are rich in antioxidants, fiber, vitamin E, phosphorus, and magnesium. They help in lowering LDL cholesterol, blood pressure, and the risks of heart disease and diabetes.

Brazil nuts are native to the Guianas, Venezuela, Brazil, eastern Colombia, eastern Peru, and eastern Bolivia. They are rich in selenium. They help the immune, kidney, and thyroid functions, and increase sperm motility.

Cashews are native to northeastern Brazil. They contain oleic acid, an unsaturated fat, which lowers triglycerides and raises HDL-cholesterol. They are rich in iron, magnesium, zinc, copper, phosphorus, manganese, and copper. They strengthen bones and promote general good health.

Hazelnuts or filberts are native to North America, Europe, and Asia. They are rich in unsaturated fats and contain thiamine, folate, magnesium, calcium, and vitamins B and E. They help in maintaining cognition, healthy skin, hair, nails, and general good health.

Macadamia nuts are native to Australia. They are rich in flavonoids that produce antioxidants. They have anti-inflammation properties and promote heart health.

Peanuts are legumes, not nuts. They are native to tropical South America. They are rich in folate, necessary for proper brain development, and reducing the risk of birth defects. They can also improve memory and decrease depression and the risk of heart disease.

Pecans are native to the southern United States and northern Mexico. They contain polyphenols (act as antioxidants) and beta-sitosterol that help enlarged prostates. They are rich in manganese, which supports bone health and eases the symptoms of premenstrual syndrome.

Walnuts are produced by any tree of the *Juglans* genus. They contain high amounts of antioxidants, phytosterols ("plant cholesterol"), and omega-3 fatty acids (polyunsaturated fats - omega-3 alpha-linolenic acid), which benefit the brain. Walnuts are rich in flavonoids and plant pigment anti-cancer compounds. Eating less than a handful daily improves performance on tests of memory, concentration, information-processing speed, and ameliorates overall brain health. They also help with depression, Alzheimer's, and other age-related diseases.

- Eating beans more than three times every week.

- Eating whole grain at least three servings every day.

- Eating poultry at least twice a week.

- Eating *berries* at least twice a week. *Berries* decrease the production of *amyloid,* which is a marker for Alzheimer's disease. In older women, cognitive decline may be delayed for up to two and a half years, by eating two or more servings of blueberries and strawberries weekly.

- Eat fish at least once a week. *Fatty fish* (salmon, mackerel, herring, lake trout, sardines, and albacore tuna) are rich in omega-3 fatty acids, particularly docosahexaenoic acid (DHA), which humans cannot synthesize. It is important for brain maintenance and function in Alzheimer's.

S. S. SANBAR, MD, PHD, JD

Chapter 21
Exercise and Physical Activity

Physical activity is for all age groups. It is one of the lifestyle interventions that seem to delay or prevent Alzheimer's and improve cognitive function. Physical activity helps the brain by keeping the blood flowing. It increases the chemicals that protect the brain and counters some of the natural reduction in brain connections that occurs with aging.

What Are the Benefits of Exercise for Seniors?

In 2011, the World Health Organization (WHO)[7] noted that the benefits of physically active older adults, as compared to those who are not active, include better cognitive function, higher levels of functional health, a higher level of cardiorespiratory and muscular fitness, a healthier body mass and composition, a lower risk of falling,

---

[7] https://www.who.int/dietphysicalactivity/factsheet_olderadults/en/

and lower rates of coronary heart disease, hypertension, stroke, diabetes, and colon and breast cancer.

The WHO noted that in adults aged 65 years and above, physical activity includes leisure time physical actions (for instance, walking, dancing, gardening, hiking, swimming), transportation (e.g., walking or cycling), occupational (if the individual is still engaged in work), household chores, play, games, sports, or planned exercise, in the context of daily, family, and community activities.

The WHO recommended that irrespective of gender, race, ethnicity, or income level, individuals aged 65 and above engage in 150 minutes of moderate-intensity aerobic exercise every week, or 75 weekly minutes of vigorous-intensity aerobic exercise, to keep this Alzheimer's dementia at bay. However, individuals with specific health conditions, such as cardiovascular disease and diabetes, may need to take extra precautions and seek medical advice before trying to achieve the recommended physical activity levels for older adults.

Is Alzheimer's Preventable Through Lifestyle Changes?

In 2017, scientists from the University of Southern California in Los Angeles reported that as many as 1 in 3 cases of Alzheimer's disease were preventable through lifestyle changes, including increasing physical activity.[8]

In 2018, Gregory Panza, an exercise physiologist in the Department of Cardiology at Hartford Hospital in Hartford, Connecticut, and his co-workers examined the cognitive benefits of exercise in more depth. They found that *aerobic exercise*, such as power walking or jogging, maybe the best form of exercise for preventing Alzheimer's disease.[9]

They conducted a meta-analysis of 1,145 seniors, who were reportedly at risk of Alzheimer's either because one of their parents had been diagnosed with the illness, or because they already had mild cognitive impairment. They found that overall, seniors who did any type of exercise demonstrated better cognitive function than those who did not exercise at all.

---

[8] https://www.thelancet.com/journals/lancet/article/PIIS0140-6736(17)31363-6/fulltext
[9] https://www.medicalnewstoday.com/articles/320770.php

However, *cognitive function* in elderly adults who engaged only in the aerobic exercise was three times better than that of seniors who did a combination of aerobic exercise and muscle-strengthening exercises. And, those who did not exercise had a slight cognitive decline.

What About Exercise Before Symptoms Develop?

In 2019, the Harvard Aging Brain Study at Massachusetts General Hospital (MGH) assessed physical activity in 182 healthy older adults, including those with preclinical Alzheimer's (without symptoms). They found that higher levels of daily physical activity may protect against both cognitive decline and loss of brain tissue (neurodegeneration) from Alzheimer's. The beneficial effects were seen at even modest levels of physical activity but were most prominent at around 8,900 daily steps.

What Exercise Precautions Should Inactive People Take?

Inactive people should start with small amounts of physical activity and gradually increase the duration, frequency, and intensity over time. Inactive adults and those with disease limitations will have added health benefits when they become more active. Exercise should also be conducted in a safe place. Every "public place" where older people gather for various functions, including physical activity, should consider having a defibrillator and individuals trained in using it and performing cardiopulmonary resuscitation (CPR) promptly, while a sudden death victim is waiting for the arrival of 911 responders.

What is Sudden Death?

On June 13, 2008, *Timothy John Russert,* the journalist, lawyer, and moderator of NBC's Meet the Press, collapsed and died from a heart attack. He had coronary heart disease. He was only 58 years of age, but by no means elderly. His sudden cardiac death resulted from a fatal, irregular heart rhythm disturbance. Mr. Russert, who covered several presidential elections, was included in the Time Magazine list as one of the "100 most influential people in the world" in 2008. The nation and the world mourned his death.

*"**Sudden cardiac death**"* means the abrupt, unexpected death which results from heart or lung clots, irregular heart rhythm, hemorrhage in the brain, or the rupture of a major blood vessel. It occurs primarily in older people. The incidence of sudden death is higher for men (2.86 per 100,000 person-years) than for women (1.24 per 100,000 person-years) and increases by age. The most common cause of sudden cardiac arrest is a heart attack resulting in the quivering of the heart's lower chambers (ventricular fibrillation), extraordinarily rapid but ineffective beating of the heart's lower chambers (pulseless ventricular tachycardia), or extreme slowing of the heart (bradycardia).

As a result of this irregular rhythm, the heart suddenly stops pumping blood effectively, leading to collapse, unresponsiveness, and often death within minutes if the victim receives no treatment. The cardiac arrest or the deadly heart rhythm disturbance causes immediate unconsciousness due to a lack of oxygen and a brain shut down. Brain damage can start to occur in just four to six minutes after the heart stops pumping blood effectively. The brain tissue suffers irreversible damage from the lack of oxygen and nutrients.

In contrast, heart tissue deprived of oxygen remains alive for over an hour after a sudden collapse.

Why are Defibrillators Useful for Heart Attack Victims?

Death may be prevented if the sudden cardiac arrest victim receives immediate bystander cardiopulmonary resuscitation (CPR) and defibrillation within a few minutes after collapse. When bystanders perform effective CPR immediately after sudden cardiac arrest, they can double a victim's chance of survival.

The most effective means of treating sudden cardiac arrest is using a defibrillator and administering an electric shock, a process referred to as the defibrillation of the heart. Therefore, the availability of a defibrillator coupled with immediate CPR in a public place is the key to a successful resuscitation, even before the arrival of the emergency medical service in response to a 911 call.

The Lucky Senior Ballroom Dancer

Unlike Mr. Timothy Russert, the following true story involves an elderly ballroom dance club member, who had a more fortunate outcome. On April 28, 2007, Shawn, a member of a ballroom dance club, and his wife arrived at a country club shortly before 7:00 p.m. in hopes of enjoying an evening of dining and ballroom dancing. He was in his early 70's and had prior coronary artery bypass surgery. He had no heart disease symptoms.

He was slim, exercised regularly, and was taking a few medications. Shortly after arrival, he and his wife feasted on a delicious dinner and socialized with friends and club members. There were approximately 90 dancers altogether. After the dessert was served, the band started playing great dance music, which attracted the members to the dance floor.

At approximately 8:45 p.m., after dancing, Shawn was greeting another member, when he suddenly collapsed on the dance floor with a thumping noise, falling on his back and hitting his head. To Shawn's good fortune, two of the club members who were cardiologists happened to be dancing very close to him. They immediately rushed to the fallen dancer. Shawn was totally unconscious, flaccid, and without pulse or respirations. The facility defibrillator was immediately requested, and a 911 call was made for EMSA (Emergency Medical Services Authority). In less than a minute, cardio-pulmonary resuscitation was begun. One of the cardiologists started cardiac chest compression. The second cardiologist placed a handkerchief over Shawn's mouth and began mouth-to-mouth resuscitation.

Fortunately, there were five other physicians at the ballroom dance. A third cardiologist and an anesthesiologist joined the first two cardiologists and assisted by taking turns with chest cardiac compressions and mouth-to-mouth breathing. A nephrologist kept track of the femoral pulse, and two other family physicians kept track of the resuscitation time and the numbers of breaths and chest compressions. All of the other ballroom dancers and wait staff observed in awe the speedy and well-coordinated resuscitation of a clinically dead dance club member and a dear friend.

The Defibrillator

The defibrillator arrived about five minutes after starting the resuscitation. The defibrillator leads were positioned appropriately on the patient, and the device was turned on. It indicated that the patient should receive an electric shock. The rescuing physicians separated themselves from Shawn before he was shocked. Then, resuscitation was promptly resumed.

Following the first electric shock, Shawn remained unconscious. His skin was moist. He had urine incontinence and wetted his pants. He had no palpable pulse and no breathing on his own. His face color was good, but his fingers were bluish (cyanotic). Six minutes after the first electric shock (11 minutes after the cardiac arrest occurred), the defibrillator indicated that the patient should be shocked again, which was done. Immediately after the second defibrillation, his pulse was palpable and strong at a rate of 110 beats per minute. He started breathing on his own. No oxygen or drugs were used during the resuscitation.

Emergency Medical Service (EMS)

The EMS personnel arrived about 15 minutes after the cardiac arrest. The patient was regaining consciousness gradually and moving all four extremities. The electrocardiogram (EKG) tracing revealed regular sinus rhythm. His heart rate was 108. His blood pressure (BP) was significantly elevated to 186/118. He was placed on oxygen, administered via nasal prongs, and an intravenous was started in case he needed treatment.

Because Shawn was still not conscious enough to swallow, he was not given aspirin or other medications by mouth. Because of severe hypertension, one of the physicians requested that a nitroglycerin tablet be placed under Shawn's tongue to lower the BP. The EMS personnel are highly trained individuals who receive orders from their supervising medical director, and no one else. They had been instructed to administer nitroglycerin only to a patient with chest pain. Thus, they could not honor the Good Samaritan physician's request.

The physician asked to talk directly by telephone to the EMSA medical director, who happened to be the ER physician at the receiving hospital. He was allowed to do so. He informed the medical director about the dancer's sudden collapse and resuscitation, and what his condition was. The ER physician instructed the EMSA personnel to place a nitroglycerin tablet under the tongue. Then, the patient was safely transported to the hospital ER. At the ER, the patient was fully conscious, in no distress, without rib fractures from chest compression, and his vital signs were stable. His electrocardiogram and blood tests showed no evidence of heart muscle damage.

Coronary Angioplasty and Defibrillator Implantation

The next day the dancer underwent heart catheterization. He was found to have significant narrowing of the right coronary artery, which required a stent (angioplasty). The dancer did well, and the procedure was successful.

Four days later, a defibrillator was implanted to prevent a recurrence of the deadly rhythm problem. The following day, Shawn "danced" his way out of the hospital.

The seven physicians were honored for being 'Good Samaritans.' They received expressions of thanks and gratitude from the dance club members for successfully resuscitating the grateful ballroom dancer. The physicians' efforts were the true labors of love to a fellow dancer. They deserved congratulations for demonstrating their superb qualities like caring and compassionate.

The "public place," country club, where the dance function occurred, was also congratulated for having a defibrillator for such emergencies. When someone collapses suddenly due to cardiac arrest in a public place, as did Shawn, the availability of a defibrillator coupled with immediate cardiopulmonary resuscitation (CPR) was key to successful resuscitation. The EMS personnel were also congratulated for stabilizing and transporting Shawn to the hospital.

As to Shawn and his wife, they resumed their dancing within a month. The couple truly enjoyed being among their dance club members. But two years later, Shawn succumbed to his heart condition and died of another heart attack.

Are 'Good Samaritans' Liable for their Help?

None of the physicians had a legal duty to render aid to Shawn; he was not their patient. However, physicians are encouraged to rescue injured and sudden death victims in emergency situations without fear of malpractice. In doing so, they are well protected from claims of *ordinary negligence* by rescued individuals in emergency situations.

The State, *Good Samaritan Act*, encourages medical providers to risk helping 'strangers' in need of assistance and support in times of hardship and distress. Shawn had no prior established physician-patient relationship with any of the rescuing physicians. When Shawn collapsed suddenly, he needed emergency medical aid right there and then on the dance floor of the country club. The physicians rescued Shawn in good faith, voluntarily, and without compensation.

The physicians knew that emergency rescue triggered a *duty of care*. Once the rescuing Good Samaritan physicians started the emergency medical aid, a "rescuer-injured" relationship was created. Additionally, a duty of care arose, an obligation owed by the physicians to act so as not to harm Shawn.

The physicians knew that by rendering emergency care to restore breathing or heart-beat, they were not liable for ordinary negligence. They would only be liable for injury caused by *grossly negligent or willful and wanton conduct* in rendering the emergency care. The physicians were provided immunity by law from civil liability for medical care or treatment by using the automated external defibrillator. The physicians did a successful resuscitation and had an opportunity to communicate directly with the receiving physician. The dancer and his wife were incredibly grateful to the angels who surrounded and protected the elderly dancer, Shawn.

Chapter 22

The Senior Driver

On several occasions, patients and their family members annually ask their doctors for advice on how to diagnose impaired older drivers, how to balance the older patient's desire to continue to drive with public safety, who reports impaired older drivers to state agencies, and how to ensure that the impaired elderly or Alzheimer's patient has indeed stopped driving.

Health care providers learn a great deal during practice on handling personal and difficult problems that concern the elderly and Alzheimer's patients, including driving. The approach to elderly patients and their families is that of kindness, sincerity, courteousness, and empathy. Providers appreciate the need to spend extra time educating and evaluating the elderly, especially when family members are concerned about driving vehicles.

Evaluation of Senior Drivers by Doctors

Doctors first focus on the elderly's physical health, then mental health. Driving safely requires three things. The ability to (1) move, (2) think, and (3) see, all at the same time. Elderly patients often have multiple medical problems, including vision, hearing, reflexes, and physical coordination. They may have difficulty identifying hazards, road signs, warnings, and obstacles while driving. Their reaction time is usually unreliable. Their physical strength may be diminished. They may have advanced arthritis with a restricted range of motion or diminished physical strength. They may be slow to respond to the unpredictable demands of the road, which require quick decisions and movements necessary for operating a vehicle.

Older patients have challenging care with diagnostic and follow up problems. They may have glaucoma, dementia, Alzheimer's disease, Parkinson's, cataracts, seizures, hypertension, diabetes, heart disease, and other chronic conditions. They are prone to falls, aspiration, malnutrition, dehydration, and skin tears. They suffer more adverse drug interactions and are subject to abuse and neglect.

Effects of Medications on Senior Drivers

Elderly patients may be taking multiple medications that may affect them mentally and physically. They may accidentally overdose. Some medications can cause side effects, which may, in turn, affect driving.

The doctor always obtains a list of all medications that the elderly patient is taking. When treating older patients, the doctor determines whether the patient understands the risks and benefits of, and alternatives to, those treatments, and the consequences of stopping or refusing treatment.

Evaluation of Mental Capacity

The doctor tracks the elderly patient's mental capacity over time with repeated annual mental testing. Elderly patients infrequently undergo a complete psychiatric or psychological evaluation, together with a Mini-Mental State Examination. More often, elderly patients undergo simple mental capacity tests by their primary care physicians, for example:

- *Clock-Drawing Test* – It is a standard geriatric test. The patient is asked to draw a clock with hour and minute hands to indicate a specific time.

- *Make-a-Dollar Test* – The patient is given three quarters, three dimes, and three nickels and is asked to make a dollar.

- *Three-in-One in Two Minutes Test* – This involves naming three unrelated objects, then asking the patient to repeat them right away, one minute later, and again, two minutes later.

- *Fact test* – Here, the patient is asked to name five of each of the following: foods, animals, cities in a state, and things that can be purchased at the mall. A perfect score is 20 out of 20. This test is objective, as it can track a patient's mental status over time. Its results can be shown to the patient's family members, alerting them to cognitive deterioration, and the data collected is transferable from physician to physician.

Communication Between Seniors and Doctors

Doctors communicate openly and honestly when caring for seniors, who often require extra time for evaluation and treatment. Elderly patients with waning cognitive function or significant hearing loss are encouraged to bring a family member, a representative, or friend to the office.

Advising elderly patients to stop driving is challenging for the patient, the doctor, and the family or caregivers. Communication is the key to a proper medical evaluation of patients with dementia and requires determination of whether the elderly patient may be a hazard to himself or others.

Most laws and legal guidance about older adult drivers refer specifically to physicians. Some states have regulations that apply to nurse practitioners, physician assistants, chiropractors, and optometrists. The physician may be held liable for injuries to the patient and others involved in an auto accident if it can be established that the physician knew the patient had a condition that made driving risky.

Mistreated or Self-Neglected Seniors

The physician evaluates the elderly patient for mistreatment, which may be:

- Physical, such as assault, forced sexual contact, overmedication, inappropriate physical restraints;
- Psychological or emotional, such as threats;
- Denial of basic human needs by the caregiver, such as withholding indicated medical care or food;
- Deprivation of civil rights, for example, freedom of movement and communication;
- Financial exploitation; and
- Self-neglect. It may be suspected in the presence of dehydration, malnourishment, skin decubitus ulcers, poor personal hygiene, or the lack of compliance with basic medical recommendations.

Federal regulations, state institutional licensing statutes, and common law tort standards condemn the mistreatment of elderly people by the staff of long-term care institutions. That includes restrictions on using involuntary mechanical and chemical restraints. If an elderly person is being abused or neglected, the physician has a duty to report the findings to adult protective services.

When Should the Senior Stop Driving?

Many older people continue to drive safely for years. To convince your elderly loved ones to surrender their driver's license is not easy.[10] The decision to surrender the license can potentially feel like a punitive and debilitating loss of personal freedom by the elderly. Keep in mind that driving cessation can lead to depression, reduced quality of life, and social isolation. Non-drivers are likelier than those who drive to get institutionalized in long-term care facilities. Also, caregivers are negatively affected if a patient stops driving because they are expected to arrange or provide alternative transportation.

The family member should present the elderly with valuable information about the risks of driving, compassion, and available solutions. Such an approach may be helpful to the loved one to understand the right decision to make. For instance, the following statistical information may be helpful:

About 40 million American older drivers are licensed to drive.

Between 2007 and 2016, the number of older drivers increased

---

[10] https://www.aginginplace.org/when-should-a-senior-stop-driving/

by 34 percent.

In 2017, there were almost 44 million licensed drivers aged 65 and older in the United States.

The total traffic fatalities among the older population, 65 and above, increased by 13 percent, 20 percent in males, and 4 percent in females. Males have substantially higher death rates than females.

Older drivers, particularly those over 75, have higher crash death rates than younger drivers, mainly due to increased vulnerability to injury in a car accident, decline in vision, and lower cognitive functioning.

Most crashes involving older adults occur during the daytime and on weekdays and involve other vehicles.

On average, driver involvement in fatal crashes increases significantly after 75 for women and after 80 for men.

Unsafe Driving

The family should also look for warning signs that driving is no longer safe, for instance:

- Forgetting to signal when turning or switching lanes;
- Inability to keep track of speed limits;
- Failure to recognize the right of way;

- Failure to yield or stop when prompted by signs or traffic lights;
- Becoming lost repeatedly while driving;
- Road rage, anxiety, and stress;
- Erratic control of speeds and inconsistent acceleration;
- Difficulty with recognizing distance between vehicles and objects;
- Difficulty in merging and changing lanes;
- Frequent "near-misses" of accidents; and
- The most concerning are traffic violations and collisions.

The safety issue is the most crucial aspect because it involves not only the elderly loved one but also the public.

Alternatives to Driving

Giving up driving entails the redistribution of expenses. Instead of paying for gas, car maintenance, and insurance, the 'savings' should be used for public transportation, carpool services, Uber, and Lyft. There are volunteer programs like churches that help the elderly with transportation. The family should offer assistance, as well.

After the elderly hands over the driver's license, cancels the insurance, sells the car, and obtains a different state-issued identification card, their options to traveling become limited.

Reporting Unsafe Driver

Professionals are obligated by federal (Health Insurance Portability and Accountability Act of 1996 (HIPAA)) and state law to keep every patient's medical information private, secure, and confidential. This means that the physician may not disclose the elderly patient's medical information to anyone, including spouse and family members, without specific permission by the patient to do so.

On the other hand, the physician may be legally obliged to report to the state's licensing agency evidence of driver impairment and the recommendation to stop driving because of public safety concerns or reduce or restrict driving rather than stopping altogether.

The physician's legal obligations may include:

1. Failure to report according to regulatory requirements due to laws governing driver's licenses; and

2. Malpractice lawsuits by injured parties, including third parties. In some states, clinicians are obligated to warn third parties that they may be at risk because of the patient's potentially risky behavior.

Physicians should use their best judgment in determining when to report impairments that could limit a patient's ability to drive safely. All patient discussions, testing, and referrals should be documented in the health record. Older people should stop driving when the risks of continued driving outweigh the benefits to the patient, family, and the public.

Reporting Statutes for Unsafe Drivers

The American Automobile Association (AAA), *Driver Licensing Policies and Practices*, has a comprehensive online source of information about driving regulations in each state. California, Delaware, New Jersey, Nevada, Oregon, and Pennsylvania mandate that physicians report medically at-risk drivers to the licensing agency. California requires reporting patients with a diagnosis of dementia.

In other states, reporting of at-risk drivers is voluntary, but physicians may still have legal obligations to report the impaired drivers. Some states provide civil immunity against lawsuits for clinicians who report an at-risk driver in good faith. Physicians should inform their patients before filing a report with the state, so the patients are aware that they will be reported and know what to expect next. Physicians should also provide patients with as much information as possible, possibly including a copy of the state licensing agency report.

Chapter 23
Gambling in Elderly People

Do You Have a Gambling Disorder?

One way to screen for a gambling disorder is to use the NORC Diagnostic Screen[11] and honestly answer the following ten questions. If a person responds in affirmative to one or more of these questions, he/she should seek professional help.

1. Have there ever been periods lasting two weeks or longer when you spent a lot of time thinking about your gambling experiences, planning out future gambling ventures or bets, or thinking about ways of getting money to gamble with?

2. Have there ever been periods when you needed to gamble with increasing amounts of money or with larger bets than before to get the same feeling of excitement?

3. Have you ever felt restless or irritable when trying to stop, cut down, or control your gambling?

---

[11] NORC DIAGNOSTIC SCREEN FOR GAMBLING PROBLEMS-SELF ADMINISTERED (NODS-SA), based on the APA's DSM-IV criteria for pathological gambling. http://www.npgaw.org/tools/screeningtools.asp

4. Have you tried and not succeeded in stopping, cutting down, or managing your gambling three or more times in your life?

5. Have you ever gambled to escape from personal problems, or to relieve uncomfortable feelings such as guilt, anxiety, helplessness, or depression?

6. Has there ever been a period when, if you lost money gambling one day, you would often return another day to get even?

7. Have you lied to family members, friends, or others about how much you gamble, and/or about how much money you lost on gambling, on at least three occasions?

8. Have you ever written a bad cheque or taken money that didn't belong to you from family members, friends, or anyone else in order to pay for your gambling?

9. Has your gambling ever caused serious or repeated problems in your relationships with any of your family members or friends? Or, has your gambling ever caused you problems at work or your studies?

10. Have you ever needed to ask family members, friends, a lending institution, or anyone else to loan you money or otherwise bail you out of a desperate money situation that was largely caused by your gambling?

What is Compulsive Gambling?

It is a behavioral, impulse control disorder, similar to hair pulling, kleptomania, or chronic fire setting but can also be likened to a substance use disorder like nicotine, alcohol, marijuana, or opioids. Compulsive gamblers may, among other criteria, have a preoccupation with gambling. They may need to gamble with increasing amounts of money to achieve the desired excitement, lie to others to conceal the extent of the involvement with gambling, and commit illegal acts, such as forgery, theft, or embezzlement to finance gambling.

Gambling becomes problematic when it disrupts, damages, or limits a person's life. Gamblers may feel bad, sad, guilty, anxious, or depressed about addiction. They may not have sufficient money for food, utility bills, rent, or credit card debts.

How is a Gambling Disorder Diagnosed?[12]

In 1980, the *Diagnostic and Statistical Manual of Mental Disorders* (DSM) first included gambling as a disorder. It is a psychological impulse control behavioral problem. It is also referred to as "gambling addiction," "problem gambling," "pathological gambling," and "compulsive gambling".

In 2013, the American Psychiatric Association (APA) recognized the severity of the gambling problem in its latest DSM-5 by placing it into a new category called "Addictions and Related Disorders," along with more commonly known substance-related addictions. Presently, individuals suffering from this affliction, and other impulse-related disorders require treatment for their addictions.

Who are the Elderly Gamblers?

They are often unnoticed because of diminished contact with relatives and friends. They are generally unwilling to seek professional help and treatment.

---

[12] From the Diagnostic and Statistical Manual of Mental Disorders, 5th Edition (section 312.31).

Gambling alone does not draw the elderly to the casinos. They are motivated by the entertainment, being around other people, a distraction from everyday problems, such as loneliness and boredom, escaping feelings of grief and loss associated with the death of a loved spouse, relative, or close friend, winning money, and supplementing income.

The elderly are more likely to develop a gambling problem when they are coping with major life changes or losses. Those who continuously talk about gambling wins but rarely mention losses may be at risk. Family members should be concerned when gambling starts to replace long-cherished activities.

Some seniors have an addictive relationship with gambling. Others gamble in senior centers and retirement homes during bingo nights, as a social experience. And they do not have to hide their gambling problem. During gambling, some seniors become so preoccupied that they forget their aches and pains.

What are the Risks of Compulsive Gambling?

About 3 to 5 percent of all gamblers, regardless of age, become compulsive. For the elderly, the risks of problem gambling for the elderly include the loss of financial security and possible legal problems. Often, their income is fixed, and their savings are limited. Should they lose all their money, they may not become eligible for Medicaid for several years after becoming desolate.

Elderly people with mild cognitive impairment due to dementia have difficulty making sound decisions. Some may develop suicidal ideas and ban themselves from casinos because of their fear of suicide.

Gambling has a significant impact on the health and welfare of all citizens, including the elderly. It has become a substantial source of revenue for states that endeavor to plug gaping budget holes. Some 200 million people bet more than $10 billion on the Super Bowl alone. It is arguably the biggest one-day betting event in the world.

Older people are the lifeblood of the gambling industry. Casinos are the second favorite activity after bingo. Many older people use gambling as an escape.

About 6 million Americans suffer from compulsive gambling (gambling addiction). This can lead to financial ruin, destroyed relationships, physical and mental health problems, suicide, lying, stealing, and other criminal activity. The number of patients struggling with gambling problems is growing. The ubiquitous nature of gambling is a major force driving the increase. In 2014, forty-three states, the District of Columbia, Puerto Rico, and the US Virgin Islands had lotteries, and 39 states allowed some form of legalized electronic gaming, including traditional slot machines, video poker, and bingo, at Indian casinos, commercial casinos, racetracks, or other establishments.

In 2013, people placed 313,000 calls for help to the National Center for Responsible Gaming (NCRG) hotline (1-800-522-4700). This number has been steadily increasing at a rate of 10% per year for the past decade. The NCPG estimated that in 2018, 100 million people will have a gambling account on their mobile phones.

Is Compulsive Gambling a Brain Disorder?

Yes. Gambling is no longer regarded as merely a financial or moral problem. It is an addiction, a chronic brain disorder that can contribute to depression, coronary heart disease, hypertension, disrupted sleep patterns, ulcers, and drug abuse.

Gambling triggers a reward stimulus in the brains of problem gamblers, similar to that experienced by individuals addicted to substances, such as nicotine, marijuana, and opioids. Patients with gambling addiction must gamble with more money to achieve the desired excitement. They exhibit restlessness or irritability when attempting to cut down or stop gambling. They have repeated unsuccessful attempts to control or stop gambling.

About one out of 5 gambling addicts attempt suicide; a small number succeed

What is the Treatment for Compulsive Gambling?

Many gambling addicts can curb their addiction without professional help. Friends, family, and loved ones can be quite helpful, as are Gamblers Anonymous meetings, though not as readily available as Alcoholics Anonymous meetings.[13] States provide less treatment money for gambling addiction than for substance abuse.

Cognitive behavioral therapy is often helpful. Providers must show empathy and be nonthreatening and nonjudgmental. Any treatment for older adults should involve the attention to the quality of life, relief of pain, grief, loss, hopelessness, and a sense of meaning. Gambling addicts feel abandoned, most often by their own children, especially those who have been placed in nursing homes or assisted living facilities; that provokes problem gambling.

Primary care physicians can be instrumental in helping patients with gambling problems access treatment. They should hang an educational poster about problem gambling in the waiting area or the examination room to prompt a conversation. They should screen for gambling addiction, just as they do for substance abuse by asking their patients if they gamble. If so, ask if they have ever lied about how much they gamble. And also ask if they ever felt the need to bet more and more money. If so, the doctor should refer the

---

[13] For information on gambling problems and for a list of support groups, visit Gambler's Anonymous at http://www.gamblersanonymous.org/ga/node/1

patient to a gambling problem therapist and/or provide the patient with the NCPG hotline (1-800-522-4700) to inquire about self-help resources and local counselors.

The US Food and Drug Administration has to-date not approved any pharmacologic treatments for gambling addiction. However, it is possible that some drugs used to treat substance abuse, such as selective serotonin reuptake inhibitors and opioid receptor antagonists, which target reward pathways in the brain, may benefit some patients with gambling addiction.

The addiction treatment helps people develop a coping mechanism and refusal skills and address the underlying issues that lead them to gamble. The treatment often includes cognitive-behavioral therapy and participation in a 12-step group therapy program offered by Gamblers Anonymous.

Chapter 24
Alcohol Use by Elderly

Prudent Drinking is Advisable

Wine or other alcoholic beverages are recommended by the MIND diet (See Chapter 20). A daily drink appears to be beneficial.

Healthy adults over 65 should have no more than seven drinks in a week, and no more than three drinks in a day. The recommended limit is based on the following amounts of alcohol in a drink.[14] The standard one-drink serving for some alcoholic beverages are:

- Brandy, liqueur, or aperitif – 4 oz.;
- Wine – 5 oz.;
- Beer – 12 oz.;
- Liquor – 1.5 oz. of 80 proof.

---

[14]https://wa.kaiserpermanente.org/healthAndWellness/index.jhtml?item=%2Fc
ommon%2FhealthAndWellness%2FhealthyLiving%2Flifestyle%2Falcohol-
seniors.html

Binge Drinking

Heavy alcohol drinking on five or more days in the past month is called 'binge drinking.' It is highly detrimental to general health, particularly to the cardiovascular, gastrointestinal, and nervous systems. The blood alcohol concentration levels rise to 0.08 g/dL, usually after four drinks for women and five drinks for men, consumed in about two hours.

Avoid Supersized Drinks

Super-sized flavored alcoholic beverages can increase the risk of binge drinking and alcohol-related injuries. The National Institute on Alcohol Abuse and Alcoholism (NIAAA)[15] noted in 2008 that about 40 percent of adults aged 65 and older drink alcohol. Some elderly people drink heavily, and many take medications for health problems.

Aging and Alcohol Effects

The elderly people have a lower tolerance for alcohol. It takes longer for the body to break down alcohol. Vital

---

[15] https://www.niaaa.nih.gov/older-adults

organs, such as the brain and heart, are more susceptible to the toxic effects of alcohol. These factors increase the risks of car accidents, falls, and other injuries.

Mixing Alcohol and Medications

When the elderly are already taking herbal remedies, prescription, or over-the-counter medications, the addition of alcohol can be dangerous or even lethal, for instance, like pain medications, marijuana, sleeping pills, antidepressant, and anxiety drugs, as well as Acetaminophen, Aspirin, cold, and allergy medications.

- Some sleeping pills, pain pills, or antidepressant medicine taken with alcohol may be lethal.
- Large amounts of acetaminophen (Tylenol) taken with Alcohol can cause liver damage.
- Aspirin taken with alcohol increases the risk of stomach or intestinal bleeding.
- Cold and allergy medicines, some of which already have a high alcohol content, taken with alcohol can make a person feel drowsy or confused.

Alcohol Abuse Red Flags

- Repeatedly neglecting one's responsibilities at home due to drinking alcohol;
- Using alcohol in situations where it's physically dangerous;
- Consuming alcohol to cope with difficulties or avoid feeling bad;
- Experiencing repeated legal problems on account of your drinking;
- When alcohol use is causing problems in one's relationships.

Alcoholism

This is considered the severest form of problem drinking because of physical dependence on alcohol. The body first develops a tolerance to alcohol, which is an early sign of alcoholism. This means that one has to drink a lot more than usual to feel the pleasant effects of alcohol, such as being relaxed. Second, when someone drinks heavily, their body gets used to the alcohol and experience withdrawal symptoms if it is taken away. These include anxiety, depression, irritability, agitation, trembling, shakiness, sweating, loss of appetite, nausea, vomiting, inability to sleep, and headaches.

Long Term Effects of Alcohol

The long-term effects of drinking excessive amounts of alcohol on the body include:

1. Worsening health conditions, such as diabetes, high blood pressure, and ulcers;

2. Damaging the brain, liver, reproductive organs, nerves and heart;

3. Problems with the immune system, and may lead to some kinds of cancer; and

4. Becoming forgetful and confused, mimicking the signs of Alzheimer's.

The Perils

- Death of a loved one, moving to a new home, or health issues may cause drinking.
- Loneliness, boredom, anxiety, or depression may aggravate drinking.
- A loved one cannot be forced to stop abusing alcohol.

- An alcoholic cannot stop drinking and stay sober without help.

- Recovery from alcoholism is a bumpy, slow, and an ongoing process.

- Alcoholics benefit significantly if they talk to a family member, friend, caregiver, or doctor.

- A 12-step program, like *Alcoholics Anonymous (AA)*, can offer support to people who want to stop drinking.

The Noble Experiment: Alcohol Prohibition in America

In 1851[16], the Maine legislature was the first to pass a statewide statute prohibiting alcohol sale. Neal Dow, then the mayor of Portland, Maine, was known as the Napoleon of Temperance. Liquor prohibition laws were similarly enacted in about 12 other states, including Delaware, Massachusetts, Rhode Island. Vermont, Connecticut, Indiana, Texas, Ohio, Pennsylvania, Iowa, and Kansas. The challenges of early prohibition laws were ruled unconstitutional by a few State Supreme Courts. However,

---

[16] https://www.history.com/news/10-things-you-should-know-about-prohibition

there was widespread opposition to alcohol prohibition. Many working-class people and immigrants rioted and demanded the repeal of those laws.

On June 2, 1855, during the Portland Rum Riot, about 200-300 opponents of the Maine Law stormed Portland City Hall because they thought Mayor Dow was keeping liquor in the basement. Newspapers reported that Dow ordered rioters to be fired upon, killing one and wounding seven. In 1856, the riot was a contributing factor to the law being repealed.

Despite the repeal, the alcohol prohibition law was re-enacted in various forms in Maine. In 1885, it was written into the Maine state constitution.[17] Groups including the American Temperance Society, the Anti-Saloon League, and the Women's Christian Temperance Union called for a "dry" America.

World War I and the Anti-alcohol Crusaders

In 1917, President Woodrow Wilson announced before Congress, a break in official relations with Germany. Two

---

[17] https://en.wikipedia.org/wiki/Maine_law#cite_note-Bouchard-2

months later, the U.S. joined its allies, Britain, France, and Russia, to fight in World War I. More than two million U.S. soldiers fought on battlefields in France.

The anti-alcohol crusaders argued that barley should not be used to brew. Instead, it could be made into bread to feed American soldiers and war-ravaged Europeans. The anti-alcohol crusaders also painted America's mainly German brewing industry as a threat. They stated that "… the worst of all our German enemies, the most treacherous, the most menacing, are Pabst, Schlitz, Blatz and Miller."

Amendment XVIII of the U.S. Constitution

In 1919, the prohibition of "intoxicating liquors" in the U.S. was established by the Eighteenth Amendment. The 18th Amendment was ratified by the states. It only forbade the "manufacture, sale and transportation of intoxicating liquors" but not their consumption.

By law, any wine, beer, or spirits that Americans had was theirs to keep and enjoy in the privacy of their homes. The 18th Amendment banned the sale of liquor with an alcohol content greater than 2.75%. However, sacramental wine was still permitted for religious purposes. It remained legal to drink alcohol during the Prohibition. The "Noble Experiment" lasted 14 years.

Drug stores continued to sell alcohol as "medicine." They were allowed to sell *"medicinal whiskey"* to treat everything from toothaches to the flu. Physicians could prescribe to "patients" who, in turn, could legally buy a pint of hard liquor, *"medicinal whiskey"* every ten days.

The Volstead Act (1919)

The rules enforcing the alcohol ban were set down under the Volstead Act. Andrew Volstead, then Chairman of the Judiciary, was known as 'The Father of Prohibition.' He wrote the National Prohibition Act named after him. The Act stipulated that, along with creating an army of federal agents, individual states should enforce Prohibition within their own borders. City police officers were confiscating alcohol and dumping it. Alcohol consumption fell by approximately 70 percent during the early years of the "noble experiment."

Some states refused to enforce the Prohibition.

- Governors resented the added state financial strain. Many neglected to appropriate any money toward policing the alcohol ban.

- Maryland never even enacted an enforcement code.

- New York repealed its measures in 1923.

- Other states gradually became more lackadaisical.

- Many speakeasies, illicit liquor stores, or nightclubs eventually operated under the guise of being pharmacies, and legitimate chains flourished.

- During the 1920s, windfalls from legal alcohol sales helped the drug store chain Walgreens to grow from around 20 locations to more than 500.

- Winemakers and brewers found creative ways to stay afloat during the Prohibition.

Some small distilleries and breweries remained open but continued to operate in secret. Other factories who were creative, such as Yuengling and Anheuser Busch, refitted their breweries to make ice cream. Coors produced pottery and ceramics. Still, others produced "near beer," a legal brew that contained less than 0.5 percent alcohol.

Many brewers peddled malt syrup, a legal extract that could be easily made into beer by adding water and yeast and allowing time for fermentation. Similarly, winemakers sold chunks of grape concentrate called "wine bricks," which could be used to make wine at home.

Rise of The Mafia

The Prohibition of Alcohol under the 18th Amendment of the U.S. Constitution did not anticipate the rise of the Mafia, which involved illegal and coordinated bootlegging activities. Interestingly, in the 1880s, the word 'bootlegger' arose in the Midwest. Bootleggers concealed flasks of liquor in their boot tops when they traded with Native Americans.

In the 1920s, bootleggers smuggled brews from Canada and Mexico. Al Capone, Lucky Luciano, Alphonse Kerkhoff, and Bugs Moran became notorious. Later, they distilled their own liquor in hidden places. Some residents in Iowa chose to become outlaws and produced a high caliber whiskey – so-called TEMPLETON RYE, or "THE GOOD STUFF," which became Al Capone's whiskey of choice.

Every year on January 17, the National Bootlegger's Day is observed, commemorating the birthday of Templeton Rye Whiskey bootleggers, Al Capone and Meryl Kerkhoff.

During the Alcohol Prohibition era, some bootleggers produced "bathtub gin" and rotgut moonshine. It consisted of grain alcohol, juniper berries, and other flavorings with water. However, it had a foul taste, and drinking it could result in blindness and even death. To mask the awful flavor of homemade hooch and bathtub gin, cocktails were invented. Thousands of Americans died from drinking tainted liquor.

"Blind pig" dive bars opened, which had a floor show or just an animal on display. To circumvent the law, customers paid an entry fee for the floor show or to view the animal displayed and received a complimentary drink per entry.

Prohibition Loophole

The most crucial prohibition loophole was the ability to legally drink alcohol at home. President Warren G. Harding moved his entire inventory of alcohol to the White House just before prohibition.

By 1930, alcohol prohibition resulted in Americans spending a lot of money on black market booze. New York City boasted more than 30,000 speakeasies. Detroit's alcohol trade ranked second to the auto industry.

The 21st Amendment to the U.S. Constitution

The Great Depression helped anti-Prohibition activists to repeal the 18th Amendment. They argued that the potential savings and tax revenue from alcohol should not be ignored.

In 1932, during his presidential campaign, President Franklin D. Roosevelt called for a repeal of Prohibition. In 1933, the 21st Amendment was approved and ratified by the states. It repealed the 18th Amendment, thereby terminating the Alcohol Prohibition in the U.S. Kansas and Oklahoma remained dry until 1948 and 1959, respectively. Mississippi remained dry until 1966. And some counties in 10 states still prohibit alcohol sales.

Chapter 25
Marijuana Use by Elderly

Medical cannabis is a safe and effective alternative medicine. People do not die from cannabis overdoses, in contrast to opioids. In 2018, the Farm Act legalizing the cultivation of hemp in the U.S. was signed into law. Since then, many CBD (Hemp) based products have entered the market. THC (Marijuana) use is also on the rise. CBD and Marijuana products have been shown to provide some relief in chronic pain, muscle spasms, and poor sleep. They stimulate appetite and can result in a higher intake of nutrients.

CBD Use

According to a 2019 Gallup poll:

- Almost one in five Americans over 50 now uses some kind of CBD product.
- 14% of Americans say they use CBD products.
- 8% of those aged 65 and older say they use CBD.

- 50% do not use them, and 35% are not at all familiar with them.
- 40% of users utilize CBD products for pain, 20% for anxiety, and 11% for sleep.
- 21% of those in the Western U.S. use CBD products, compared with 13% in the South, and 11% in both the East and Midwest.
- CBD users in the U.S. cite relief from pain (40%), anxiety (20%), insomnia (11%), and arthritis (8%) as the top reasons for use.

Elderly Evaluation to Use CBD and THC

In some states, elderly patients may have access to recreational marijuana or may purchase CBD without consulting with a physician. However, it is advisable that the elderly and Alzheimer's patients should first be thoroughly evaluated medically to determine whether medical marijuana may be beneficial.

People seeking marijuana may have a variety of complaints, for instance, pain, muscle soreness or spasticity, arthritis, nausea, diminished appetite, insomnia, PTSD,

AIDS, Alzheimer's, Parkinson's disease, or seizure disorder.

Patients must keep in mind that some physicians are neither knowledgeable enough nor comfortable in managing medical marijuana issues. Marijuana handling was not taught in medical school during the marijuana prohibition period. Ethically, if a physician is not comfortable recommending marijuana, a referral to another healthcare provider who is experienced with cannabis may be appropriate.

Dosage of THC and CBD for the Elderly

After completing the medical evaluation, physicians will try to determine and recommend three things:

- The dose of marijuana and/or CBD,
- The route of administration (smoking, sublingual, ingestion, transdermal, or intravaginal), and
- The ratio of THC to CBD in the product.

In general, a one-to-one ratio of THC to CBD is the ideal cannabinoid proportion. It allows the medicine to be effective while limiting the unwanted side effects.

Start at the Lowest Dose

The elderly patients or their caregivers should be fully informed about the potential side effects of CBD and marijuana. Those who have never used cannabis must start slow with a dose of 1, 2.5, and then no more than 5 mg THC or CBD orally; *always start at the lowest possible dose*.

Tiny doses of THC, balanced with CBD to moderate the effects of the THC, are sufficient to meet most patients' symptomatic needs without causing intoxication.

- For example, elderly patients should start at a low dose of 2.5 mg CBD. The dose is gradually increased in 2.5 mg increments between two days and a week. Then, physicians must wait to see how the patient feels.

- The majority of senior patients will respond to somewhere between 40 and 100 mg of CBD per day.

Elderly patients should expect a period of exploration to find the right formulation that works for them. Underreporting of drug use is common in the older population. Many cannabis candies are created with the cannabis-savvy consumer in mind. These people can comfortably tolerate high doses of THC. The provider should develop a chart for all patients, particularly those who are marijuana naïve (have not used cannabis recently) to document the day, time, type of product, how it was used, amount, time to feel effects, level of symptom relief, and unwanted side effects.

Risks of Using Cannabis

Most marijuana users are somewhat experienced and at low risk of harming themselves or others after use. Elderly patients who have used marijuana in the past may know how CBD and THC affect their bodies. However, they may need help to determine the best type, product, and dose of cannabis.

Past marijuana users should be informed or reminded that the potency of THC has steadily increased from 3.8% in the early 90s, to 12.2% in 2014, and to 25% THC and higher in 2020. Marijuana use has been associated with numerous side effects, including:

- Falls, injury, mental health problems, cardiovascular disease, respiratory problems, metabolic syndrome, cancer, unhealthy diet, and drug-drug interactions.

- Increased use of emergency departments;
- Anxiety, nausea, vomiting, hallucinations, and impaired memory and learning;
- Vaping cannabis may cause short-term anxiety, distraction, memory loss, and paranoia;
- Marijuana use disorder is often associated with dependence. Those who quit may experience irritability, mood and sleep difficulties, decreased appetite, marijuana cravings, restlessness, and/or various forms of physical discomfort for up to two weeks;
- Driving while under the influence of marijuana can slow cognitive processing speed and visual skills, slow reaction time and coordination, cause sedation, and lower blood pressure (hypotension), thereby making it harder for older drivers to react to unexpected situations and increasing the risk of vehicular accidents.

Chronic marijuana use has been associated with an increased likelihood of motor vehicle accidents. Elderly patients should be advised to avoid driving or make critical decisions for a few hours after taking a dose of marijuana.

- Elderly patients should cut back or refrain from taking opioids, benzodiazepines, sleeping pills, and alcohol concomitantly. The provider should only introduce or remove one medication at a time.

- Marijuana may also interact with the patients' other prescription drugs, by compromising the metabolism and excretion functions in elderly patients and potentially causing toxicity. For instance, cannabis can increase the blood-thinning effect of warfarin (Coumadin) and the antihypertensive effects of blood pressure medications.

- Patients on anti-HIV medications may need to titrate their THC dosage.

- Patients should stay well-hydrated to help reduce the risks of dizziness and falling.

Follow Up of Cannabis Users

Elderly patients should be followed up and periodically assessed by their providers to determine if they are deriving the relief of symptoms both subjectively and objectively, and whether to continue taking the same dose of CBD or THC.

- Subjective assessments involve the use of a consistent scale and asking the same questions during each assessment. For example, the use of the 10-point pain scale is easily replicated. If the patient shows no improvement, consider adjusting the marijuana dosage, type, or ratio of THC to CBD to achieve the best outcome. Otherwise, marijuana should be discontinued gradually and replaced with a different option.

- Objective assessments of improvement are more desirable and easier to implement. For example, measuring weight, blood sugar level, heart rate, and blood pressure. These can also be performed by the patient.

- Some elderly patients may benefit from a combination of different marijuana products. For instance,

o A patient may smoke a joint for an immediate effect or use a lotion infused with marijuana for muscle soreness.

o At other times, that same patient might use edibles, such as gummy bears or cookies, for a mild effect.

o   Elderly people typically prefer a tincture containing marijuana to place under the tongue.

Cannabis 'Pearls'

1.   *THC is federally illegal*. Medical marijuana is still considered illegal by the U.S. federal government as of 2020, despite being legalized in 33 states. Currently, only two prescription medical marijuana pills are available. Some providers are fearful of the possible legal implications of medical marijuana. Therefore, they do not discuss it with their patients.

2.   *Medical cannabis cards do not protect patients on federal property*, such as federal checkpoints like borders, national parks, airports, or reservations, including casinos, private homes, or a workplace that has a drug-free policy. This can affect those traveling to national parks and campgrounds, and Native American lands.

3.   *Patients and providers may encounter societal stigma* and other significant barriers when trying to access and experiment with medical marijuana.

4.   *Sharing a marijuana product with other people who do not have a medical marijuana card may be a problem.*

5. *Only hemp-derived CBD candies are available* in most states at retail outlets and through the internet. This may change in the future, though.

6. *Younger people prefer THC in candies*. In contrast, more than one-third of older adult cannabis candy consumers regularly use a CBD-only product.

7. *Any product containing THC, particularly candies, should always be stored out of reach of children.*

8. *Less than a third of CBD products purchased online are accurately labeled by standardized testing*. The burden of due diligence is on the consumer/patient.

Cannabis (THC and CBD) Products

Cannabis Seeds and Plant Clippings: These are available to purchase and grow according to the state and federal law.

Cannabis Plant Flowers: These may be obtained from the Sativa, Indica, Hybrid, and CBD plant species. They are sold in grams (or ounces) and contain specified percentages of THC and/or CBD content. Some are highly potent.

Cannabis Cigarettes, Pre-Rolls: They include regular cone, slim cone, super cone, filtered, and palm blunt cigarettes. They may be purchased as singles or packs. They contain from 0.4 to 2.5 grams of ground plant flowers.

Oral Tinctures: These are liquid cannabis concentrates applied under the tongue. It is best to use a coconut/MCT oil-based tincture to dissolve the THC or CBD oil and improve absorption.

- It is best to hold the tincture under the tongue to allow faster, direct absorption into the blood, which takes seconds.

- If the tincture is swallowed, it will take about one hour to be processed through the gastrointestinal (GI) tract. They are effective for four to six hours.

Gel Caps: They look like regular capsules that are easy to swallow. The contents are similar to oral tinctures. The Gel Caps contain THC or CBD extract dissolved in an organic MCT coconut oil carrier. It takes gel caps about an hour to act, and their effects last four to six hours.

Isolates: These are pure cannabis crystals pulverized into a powder. They are vaporized to obtain instantaneous effects and fast relief. Their effects last from 1.5 to about 3 hours.

Topicals: These skin products may be used for skin lesions, but others penetrate into the muscle and joints underneath the skin. Usually, the effects of CBD topicals can be felt within 15-20 minutes and may last for up to six hours. Topicals are known to be the longest-lasting form of CBD administration.

CBD Salves/Creams/Rubs: These are CBD infused topical creams that are rubbed directly on the skin for localized relief of pain and inflammation, making them perfect for treating muscle, joint, and surface-oriented pain. Their effect is felt within 15 minutes and lasts for several hours. They are re-applied as necessary. For instance:

- *Lip balm moisturizer* contains 50mg THC:10mg CBD, (5:1 ratio).

- *Creams* contain 25mg THC:25mg CBD, (1:1 ratio) for relief of muscle, joint, and skin irritation.

- *Muscle Balm* contains 100mg THC:100mg CBD, (1:1 ratio).

- *Extra strength* salves contain 250mg THC:50mg CBD (5:1 ratio). They are used for headaches and joint relief.

- ***CBD Sprays*** are similar to salves or rubs, but in spray form, making them gentle and less oily. They have been used for eczema, burns, rashes, skin irritation, and rejuvenation of the skin.

- ***CBD Soaks*** are bath salts, which are CBD infused and may also be infused with aromatic essential oils. They induce a calming and relaxing effect on the body and soothe the skin. They contain 25mg THC:25mg CBD (1:1 ratio).

Vaginal Lubricants contain 15mg THC. They are used to enhance sexual arousal and pleasure.

Vaginal Suppositories contain 60mg THC:10mg CBD, (6:1 ratio). They are used mostly for menstrual pain relief.

Medicinal Transdermal Patches: These are single-use and time-release, 2x2-inch square patches. They should adhere to a venous part of the skin. Their effects begin in 15 to 30 minutes and last between 8 and 12 hours of time-released relief. They include:

- THC-CBD 5mg:5mg (1:1 ratio) Transdermal Patch;

- CBD 10mg Transdermal Patch;

- Sativa THC 20mg Transdermal Patch;

- Indica THC 20mg Transdermal Patch;

- Transdermal Compound 100mg Blend of THC, CBD, and CBC. It is used for all-round relief.

Edibles: In general, 2.5 to 5 mg. of THC is considered a low dose for an edible. The onset of effects from eating cannabis sometimes takes up to two hours. Examples of edibles include, Satori Milk Chocolate Blueberries, Stillwater gummies, Goodship pastilles, Grön Pearls/gummies, and Petra Mints.

- THC/CBD-infused edibles include sugar drops, icicles, caramels, confectionaries like brownies, cookies, shortcake, cream bars, and peanut butter.

- Gummies with all flavors and each gummy contains 10mg of THC, with four gummies per package.

- Chocolates of all kinds with varying amounts of THC and CBD.

- Pills containing different ratios of THC and CBD.

- Butter – THC and CBD are easily infused into butter, which can be used for baking confections. However, baked goods can be quite challenging for micro-dosing, which may result in side effects that can be uncomfortably intoxicating.

Drinks can include:

- 5mg THC, Dealcoholized Belgian-style Wheat Ale Cannabis Beer;

- 10mg Hybrid, Orange Crush Cola, Blue Raspberry Cola, Root Beer Soda, Cherry Soda, and Ginger Ale Soda;

- 100mg THC, Hybrid Dissolvable Powder;

- 100mg CBD: 5mg THC, Hybrid (20:1 ratio) Dissolvable Powder

- 100mg THC, Hybrid, Tropical Beverage and Watermelon Drink;

- 100mg CBD: 5mg THC, Hybrid (20:1 ratio) Green Tea.

Accessories and Apparels: These are used for cleaning, concentrate tools, grinders, hand pipes, novelty items such as cookbooks, greeting cards to games, shot glasses, sunglasses, pins, bandannas, footbags, and pet accessories.

Apparels include all imaginable wearable items, from clothes to belts and shoes.

Religious (Sacramental or Spiritual) Entheogen Marijuana

For thousands of years, marijuana (cannabis) and other psychoactive drugs[18] were used to induce religious, sacred, and spiritual experiences. Religious Marijuana is regarded as an *'entheogen'*, and not *'medicinal'* or *'recreational'* marijuana, all of which contain THC. Regardless of the name, THC affects brain function and alters perception, mood, consciousness, cognition, or behavior.

Incense in the Middle East

Marijuana, as a type of incense, was used in the temples of Assyria and Babylon because its aroma was pleasing to the Gods. The Assyrians, Egyptians, and Hebrews, among other Semitic cultures of the Middle East, acquired cannabis

---

[18] Peyote (mescaline), psilocybin and *Amanita muscaria* mushroom, opioids, uncured pipe tobacco, bupropion, cannabis and hashish, ayahuasca, *Salvia divinorum*, iboga, and Mexican morning glory, cocaine, crack cocaine, methylphenidate, ephedrine, MDMA (ecstasy), LSD blotter, among other psychoactive drugs.

from Aryan cultures and have burned it as incense for 3,000 years. In Exodus 30:23 of the Bible, God directed Moses to make a holy oil, composed of "myrrh, sweet cinnamon, kaneh bosm and kassia". The root *kan* has two meanings in many ancient languages, hemp, and reed. In the original Hebrew Bible, *kaneh bosm* meant hemp (cannabis plant).

Shamans in Northeast Asia

Shamans were medicine men who were practicing magicians. They transmitted the medical and spiritual uses of cannabis to the ancient Chinese. In ancient China, as in most early cultures, medicine has its origin in magic.

In northeastern Asia, shamanism was widespread from the Neolithic down to recent times. Shamans were known in China as '*wu.*' This vocation was quite common. In the far north, among the nomadic tribes of Mongolia and Siberia, shamanism was widespread and common until quite recently. In China and Japan, the ingestion of cannabis resin was used for psychoactive, ritualistic purification. After Confucianism, around 500 BC, the rituals were suppressed in both countries.

From 2000 to 1400 BC, cannabis was regarded in India as one of the five sacred plants, which relieved anxiety and had a guardian angel residing in its leaves. According to the Atharva Veda, the knowledge storehouse of *atharvāṇas*, Cannabis was a source of happiness, a joy-giver, and a liberator.

In the Indian subcontinent, *bhang* is the most commonly consumed beverage form of cannabis in religious festivals.

- *Ganja* is a smoked form of cannabis, consisting of the leaves and the plant tops.
- *Charas* or *hashish*, consists of the resinous buds and/or extracted resin from the leaves of the marijuana plant. It is quite potent.

Cannabis in India, Himalaya, and in Tantric Buddhism

In 1008 BC, the Indian king, *Vallabha-raja*, believed that the gods sent hemp to the human race so that they might attain delight, lose fear, and have sexual desires.

Cannabis brought down from the Himalayas was often consumed in devotional meetings, weddings, or festivals honoring Shiva (Mahadeva – the great god), a supreme being within Shaivism, one of the major traditions within contemporary Hinduism. In Tantric Buddhism, a large oral dosage of cannabis is taken to facilitate meditation and heighten awareness of all aspects of their rituals and ceremony.

Greece and Central Asia

Both early Greek history and modern archeology show that Central Asian peoples were utilizing cannabis 2,500 years ago.

Mexicans, Mayans, and Aztecs

Mexican, Mayan, and Aztec cultures used cannabis, along with magic mushrooms (psilocybin), peyote (mescaline), and other psychoactive plants in cultural, shamanic, and religious rituals. Some Mexicans leave bundles of cannabis on church altars in religious ceremonies to be consumed by the attendees.

Cannabis Use in Churches

Some Protestant churches and Jewish factions in America have supported the use of medicinal cannabis. However, many religions prohibit the use of 'intoxicants,' including Christianity, Islam, Buddhism, Baha'i, Latter-day Saints (Mormons), Scientology, Sikhism, and others.

According to the catechism of the Catholic Church, "The *use of drugs* inflicts very grave damage on human health and life. Their use, except on strictly therapeutic grounds, is a grave offense. Clandestine production of and trafficking in drugs is scandalous practices. They constitute direct co-operation in evil, since they encourage people to practices gravely contrary to the moral law."[19]

Sunni Islam considers cannabis to be permissible by Bukhari laws. The Quran does not directly forbid cannabis. Some modern Islamic leaders state that medical cannabis, but not recreational, is permissible in Islam.

Many churches and ministries founded in North America during the past century treat cannabis as a sacrament, including the Church of Cognizance, the Church of the Universe, the Church of Cognitive Therapy (COCT Ministry), the Santo Daime church, the THC Ministry,

---

[19]
http://www.vatican.va/archive/ccc_css/archive/catechism/p3s2c2a5.htm #2291

Cantheism, the Cannabis Assembly, Temple 420, Green Faith Ministries, the Free Marijuana Church of Honolulu, the First Cannabis Church of Florida World Wide, the Free Life Ministry Church, the Church of Higher Consciousness, the Informer Ministry Collective of Palms Springs, CA, the Temple of the True Inner Light, the First Church of Cannabis Inc. in Indiana, and the International Church of Cannabis in Denver.

The Rastafari religion is an Abrahamic religion that developed in Jamaica during the 1930s. It uses cannabis as a sacred herb. It brings the users closer to God (Jah) and allows them to penetrate the truth of things more clearly.

In Mexico, followers of the growing cult of Santa Muerte regularly use marijuana smoke in purification ceremonies, with it often taking the place of incense used in mainstream Catholic rituals.

In California, organizations holding religious services claim they should be able to sell pot as "sacrament" and be exempt from paying taxes. Others say it is an excuse to run unlicensed dispensaries.[20] For instance, Hundred

---

[20] https://en.wikipedia.org/wiki/Cannabis_and_religion

Harmonies' Protestant church has a fully-stocked, unlicensed marijuana dispensary, with strawberry pot gummies, glass jars of Versace OG buds, and $30 mega-blunts in a display case labeled "Sacrament." The Los Angeles County Sheriff's Department seized $30,000 worth of weed in a 2017 raid on Hundred Harmonies. The church's parent organization, the Association of Sacramental Ministries, sued the county, claiming religious discrimination. In 2019, the movement for religious marijuana continues to grow in size and fervor.

Marijuana Prohibition in America

In 1492, Christopher Columbus sailed across the Atlantic Ocean from Spain in the Santa Maria, with the Pinta and the Niña ships alongside, in search of a new route to India. He made a total of four voyages to the Caribbean and South America between 1492 and 1504. He opened up the Americas to European colonization. Spain claimed a good part of the territory discovered in the Western hemisphere, including Texas, New Mexico, California, Caribbean islands, and South America.

In 1545, the Spaniards imported marijuana to the Western hemisphere

Chile made use of the plant as fiber. In North America, the cannabis plant, called *Indian hemp*, was grown on many plantations for use as food, oil, rope, clothing, and paper, among other products. Farmers preferred to grow hemp instead of cotton.

In 1606, the Jamestown Colony Settlers also brought Marijuana

Three ships, *Susan Constant*, the *Godspeed*, and the *Discovery*, brought 104 English people to Virginia. In 1607, the passengers started the first permanent English settlement and named it Jamestown, Virginia, after their king, James I.

The Jamestown Settlers grew the cannabis (hemp) plant

The hemp fiber from the cannabis plant was a significant export throughout the colonial period. In 1762, Virginia imposed penalties on those who did not produce hemp and

313

awarded bounties for hemp culture and manufacture.

President George Washington grew Indian hemp

From 1745 to 1775, President Washington grew Indian Hemp at Mount Vernon. He had a particular interest in the medicinal use of cannabis, and he grew it with a highly psychoactive content of marijuana.

Betsy Ross sewed the *first United States of America flag* from hemp cloth. And the *first draft of the Declaration of Independence* was written on hemp paper.

President Thomas Jefferson also grew hemp

From 1774 to 1824, President Thomas Jefferson grew hemp at Monticello. He made reference in his Farm Book to separate male and female hemp plants, suggesting that he was cultivating hemp for recreational smoking.

Dr. William O'Shaughnessy

In 1838, Dr. William O'Shaughnessy, an Irish

physician, working in India, found that cannabis was not lethal. Animals always recovered from cannabis ingestion, regardless of the dose. He used cannabis to treat cholera, tetanus, rheumatism, and convulsions. In 1856, he was knighted by Queen Victoria. By the 20th Century, over 100 papers about cannabis (marijuana) were published in Western medical journals. Cannabis preparations were available at most local pharmacies.

Pharmaceutical Companies

Cannabis tinctures were manufactured and sold around 1900 by:

- Eli Lilly, founded in 1876 in Indianapolis, Indiana;
- Parke Davis, founded in 1866 in Detroit, Michigan; and
- Merck & Co., founded in 1891 in New York, NY.

In 1851, Cannabis (marijuana) was listed as a medication effective in treating many illnesses in the *United States Pharmacopeia*. Marijuana was removed from the U.S. Pharmacopeia after 91 years in **1942**.

Hashish (Hasheesh) was smoked freely and legally in America.

In 1862, hasheesh (hashish) was advertised in America as candy in an issue of *Vanity Fair*, as a treatment for nervousness and melancholy.[21]

"Vanity Fair (magazine) Aug 16, 1862 pp74., **HASHEESH CANDY**. A most wonderful Medicinal Agent for the cure of Nervousness, Weakness, Melancholy, confusion of thoughts, etc. A pleasurable and harmless stimulant. Under its influence all classes seem to gather new inspiration and energy. Price, 25c. and 8. per box, Beware of imitations. Imported only by the Gunjah-Wallah Company 476 Broadway. On sale by druggists generally."

After 1910, marijuana was referred to as the 'M-word'

Two significant factors contributed to the racist "M" word after 1910:

---

[21] http://antiquecannabisbook.com/chap15/QCandy.htm

1.   Political: The territorial conflicts among Spanish, Mexican, and American people that lasted over two centuries.

2.   Ideological: The well-meaning prohibitionist movement in America against drugs, including alcohol, marijuana, cocaine, and opioids.

Politically, the U.S. negotiated on April 30, 1803, an agreement with France to purchase the Louisiana territory, including New Orleans, for $15 million. The acquisition of approximately 827,000 square miles would double the size of the United States. However, Spain owned the Louisiana territory. Because Spain had no military power to block the sale, it formally returned Louisiana to France on November 30, 1803. France officially transferred the territory to the Americans on December 20, and the United States took formal possession on December 30, 1803. The Louisiana territory was named after King Louis XIV of France.

In 1803, the *American Louisiana Purchase* from Napoleon Bonaparte of France gave the United States and Spain an undefined Southern border with Mexico, another Spanish territory.

In 1821, after a decade of bloody civil conflict, Mexico obtained independence from the Spanish Empire. Texas, New Mexico, and California were Mexican territories, among others.

Mexican–American War

From 1846 to 1848, the U.S. and Mexico entered into an armed conflict, which followed the 1845 U.S. annexation of Texas. The U.S. won the *Mexican-American War* and annexed Texas, New Mexico, and California. The relations between Mexicans and Americans were quite strained. Many Mexican citizens left the newly annexed U.S. territories and resettled in Mexico.

Mexican Revolution

Between 1910-1920, the *Mexican Revolution* caused Mexican civil war refugees and political exiles to flee to the United States to escape the violence and search for employment and stability. The number of *legal* migrants grew from around 20,000 migrants per year during the 1910s to about 50,000–100,000 migrants per year during the 1920s. Between 1910 and 1920, approximately 900,000 Mexicans and other people from South America immigrated legally into the United States.

American Xenophobia

Because of the long-standing wars between the U.S. and Mexico, *American xenophobia* against Mexicans became evident, exemplified by fear, hatred, dislike, and prejudice.

Mexican immigrants smoked marijuana recreationally

The practice of *smoking marijuana* leaf in cigarettes or pipes was largely unknown in the United States until it was introduced by the Mexican immigrants. Americans quickly picked up the marijuana smoking habit.

Ideologically, the introduction of marijuana smoking fueled a negative reaction in the U.S., which was tinged with anti-Mexican xenophobia. The Mexican and Black immigrants and their jazz musicians who consumed marijuana were targeted by many white Americans for using the drug to corrupt the minds and bodies of low-class individuals.

Pure Food and Drug Act

In 1906, Congress enacted federal legislation of the Pure Food and Drug Act. The Act imposed labeling regulations on narcotics, including opioids and marijuana, and prohibited the manufacture or shipment of any adulterated or misbranded drug traveling in interstate commerce.[22] The federal law regulated the labeling of patent medicines that contained "cannabis indica." The marijuana prohibitionists were determined to criminalize marijuana.

Criminalization of Marijuana

In 1913, California was one of the first States to prohibit the sale and possession of marijuana, because it was a Killer Drug - a powerful narcotic in which lurked 'Murder,' 'Insanity,' and 'Death.'[23] *California criminalized the cultivation of "locoweed."* That 1913 law was not racially motivated.

---

[22] Pure Food and Drug Act of 1906, Ch. 3915, 34 Stat. 768, repealed by Act of June 25, 1938, Ch. 675, §902(a), 52 Stat. 1059.
[23] 1913, Cal. Stats. Ch. 324, §8a; see also Gieringer, The Origins of Cannabis Prohibition in California, Contemporary Drug Problems, 21-23 (rev. 2005).

The Harrison Narcotics Tax Act

In 1914, the *Harrison Narcotics Tax Act* was passed. It controlled the possession and sale of narcotics, specifically cocaine, opiates, and marijuana.

Between 1914 and 1925, twenty-six states passed laws prohibiting the cannabis (marijuana) plant. Subsequently, other laws were enacted, dealing with the medical and pharmacy professions.

The 18th Amendment to the U.S. Constitution and its Repeal

Meantime, alcohol consumption was being targeted by the American prohibitionists. In 1919, the 18th Amendment to the U.S. Constitution passed, which established the prohibition of alcohol and "intoxicating liquors" all over the United States. Marijuana was not included as intoxicating liquor. In 1933, the 21st Amendment to the U.S. Constitution repealed the 18th Amendment and ended the nationwide prohibition on alcohol.

The prohibitionist's focus turned to marijuana

In 1925, the United States supported the regulation of "Indian hemp" at the International Opium Convention. That helped develop the Uniform State Narcotic Act between 1925 and 1932.

In 1930, **Harry Anslinger** was appointed the first Director of the Federal Bureau of Narcotics. He launched a vigilant campaign against marijuana, which lasted 32 years. He was an outspoken man who used the movie theater to spread messages that racialized the marijuana plant for white audiences. Anslinger testified before Congress and stated:

"Marijuana is the most violence-causing drug in the history of mankind... Most marijuana smokers are Negroes, Hispanics, Filipinos and entertainers. Their satanic music, jazz and swing, result from marijuana usage."

"Reefer makes darkies think they're as good as white men...the primary reason to outlaw marijuana is its effect on the degenerate races."

The Marihuana Stamp Tax Act

In 1937, Congress passed the *Marihuana Stamp Tax Act*. Doctors could prescribe marijuana for medical purposes but had to register and pay prohibitive taxes. Consequently, prescribing marijuana was curtailed.

The Marihuana Stamp Tax Act was the first step to an all-out marijuana prohibition. That was, in part, the culmination of Anslinger's work. The 1937 U.S. federal law criminalized the cannabis plant in every state.

Supreme Court Decisions
Linder v. United States

In 1925, the U.S. Supreme Court decided the case of *Linder v. United States,*[24] in which an Oklahoma Physician gave Ida Casey one tablet of morphine and three tablets of cocaine for her addiction. She took the drugs alone in divided doses over a period to satisfy her cravings. The Trial Court ruled that the treating physician violated the *Harrison Narcotic Law.*[25] However, the U.S. Supreme Court reversed

---

[24]268 U.S. 5 (1925)
[25]1914, c. 1, 38 Stat. 785

the case and held that the direct control of medical practice in the states is beyond Congress's power.

Robinson v. California

In 1962, the case of ***Robinson v. California***[26] was the first landmark decision of the U.S Supreme Court involving the Eighth Amendment of the U.S. Constitution, which deals with cruel and unusual punishment. At issue was a California statute that made narcotic 'addiction' a punishable misdemeanor offense.

The Amendment was interpreted by the Supreme Court to prohibit criminalization of particular acts or conduct, as contrasted with prohibiting the use of a particular form of punishment for a crime. The U.S. Supreme Court ruled that California could not imprison a person solely for being addicted to narcotics. In general, a law that punishes a 'status' like addiction will not be upheld. However, a law that criminalizes 'behavior against the public interest' is likely to be upheld.

---

[26]370 U.S. 660 (1962)

Leary v. United States

In 1969, the U.S. Supreme Court held in *Leary v. United States,*[27] that some provisions of the Marihuana (Marijuana) Tax Act and other narcotics legislation were unconstitutional.

Dr. Timothy Leary was a clinical professor of psychology at Harvard University. He was a prolific author and known for experimenting with psychedelic drugs. Leary was arrested in the early 1960's at the Texas-Mexico border for possession of marijuana, which was in violation of the Marihuana (Marijuana) Tax Act. He was sentenced to 30 years in prison. The U.S. Supreme Court ruled in his favor.

The Controlled Substances Act (CSA)

In 1970, President Richard Nixon declared a national *war on drugs* and signed DAPCA, the comprehensive Drug Abuse Prevention and Control Act.

Title II of DAPCA is the **Controlled Substances Act** (CSA). And Marijuana was placed on Schedule I. Doctors were not permitted to prescribe it. In 1973, the DEA

---

[27] 395 U. S. 6 (1969)

(Drug Enforcement Agency) was the federal agency established to implement the CSA regulations.

The Shafer Commission

In 1972, the Shafer Commission (or the National Commission on Marijuana and Drug Abuse) wrote a report recommending the partial prohibition of the drug, as well as lowering the penalties for people found in possession of small marijuana amounts. However, the findings of the report were largely ignored by President Nixon and the establishment at the time.

The California Compassionate Use Act

In 1996, California passed the Compassionate Use Act (Proposition 215) and became the first U.S. state to officially legalize the medicinal use of marijuana by people with chronic or severe illnesses. Today, 29 states, Washington, DC, and the territories of Puerto Rico and Guam, allow the limited medical use of cannabis.

U.S. v. Randall

In 1999, the U.S. Supreme Court decided the case of Bob Randall, who had glaucoma that could not be treated with medications or surgery. To alleviate his eye symptoms, he grew his own marijuana plants and began smoking it. He was arrested with possession of marijuana, a schedule I controlled substance. Medical experts indicated that the inhalation of marijuana was actually beneficial to his glaucoma. Defendant Randall asserted a '*necessity defense*' to his prosecution. The issue before the U.S. Supreme Court was: Whether Randall is barred from asserting the 'necessity defense.' The Court held that he was not barred from asserting the '*necessity defense*' to his charge of possession of marijuana.

Gonzales v. Oregon

In 2006, the U.S. Supreme Court ruled in *Gonzales v. Oregon*[28] that the U.S. Attorney General cannot enforce the federal Controlled Substances Act against physicians who prescribed drugs, in compliance with Oregon State assisted suicide law, to terminally ill patients seeking to end their

---

[28] 546 U.S. 243 (2006)

lives, often referred to as medical aid in dying. Medical practice is controlled by states and not the federal government.

The Agriculture Improvement Act

In December 2018, the **FARM Bill**, called the **Agriculture Improvement Act**, became law. The bill de-scheduled **hemp** products from the Controlled Substances Act. It was defined as cannabis and its derivatives with very low concentrations of THC, no more than 0.3% on a dry weight basis.

The MORE Act

On November 19, 2019, the Marijuana Opportunity Reinvestment and Expungement Act (MORE Act) cleared the congressional House Judiciary Committee. If enacted, the MORE Act would remove criminal penalties for marijuana, take the drug off the federal controlled substances list, and expunge conviction records.

On November 25, 2019, the FDA noted that despite removing hemp from the definition of marijuana in the Controlled Substances Act, CBD products are still subject to the same laws and requirements as FDA-regulated products that contain any other substance.

In 2020, Federal cannabis law has made almost a full circle from 1906, triggered by cannabis state laws.

State Marijuana Laws

As of 2020, 33 states, and the District of Columbia, Guam, and Puerto Rico have approved a comprehensive public medical marijuana-cannabis program. 12 states allow recreational use. While 13 states allow the use of "low THC, high cannabidiol (CBD)" products for medical reasons in limited situations or as a legal defense. Only four states have no public cannabis access programs.[29]

---

[29] http://www.ncsl.org/research/health/state-medical-marijuana-laws.aspx

Chapter 26
Opium Use by Elderly

In the 21st Century, the use of opioids remains plagued with significant problems. The drugs have too many side effects, dependency, addiction, and overdose deaths. Newer opioids are incredibly potent, such as Fentanyl and Carfentanyl, which can be lethal even with a tiny dose.

More than 702,000 people have died from a drug overdose between 1999 to 2017. Over 70,000 people died from drug overdoses in 2017. This makes drug overdose a leading cause of injury-related death in the United States. Of these deaths, over 47,600 involved a prescription or illicit opioid. On average, 130 Americans die daily from an opioid overdose.

Sherry's newspaper editor had asked her to research timely and cover the hot topic of the use of opioids by seniors for the newspaper. Sherry and Annie had also talked about this topic a couple of times. They decided to get together at the end of April 2019 to talk about the opioid crisis in America and the pain management in elderly and

Alzheimer's patients.

They met on a Wednesday at Sherry's home for lunch. Annie brought with her a bouquet of roses that she picked up from her backyard. They were freshly cut, half of them were yellow, and the rest were pink. Annie handed the flowers to Sherry, and they greeted and hugged each other. They were so happy and glad to see each other. They were smiling and giggling.

Sherry had prepared an assortment of small bite-sized sandwiches with vegetables, walnuts, almonds, and fruits. They sat in the living room. There were thick, disposable plates that were triangular designed with a picture of a poppy plant. The drinks were champagne and half-sweetened iced tea, mango flavor. Soft music was soothingly audible in the background. They gossiped a little and talked about the current movies at the theaters and on television. About halfway through lunch, they delved into the opioid topic for the day. Both of them had prepared notes.

Plant of Joy, 'Hul Gil'

Annie looked at the poppy plant design on her plate and began talking about the medical use of the poppy plant. She said, "Around 4,000 BC, The Sumerians, who lived in Mesopotamia (now Iraq), grew the opium poppy flower and named it Hul Gil, meaning the plant of joy. Over the past centuries, various physicians were so impressed with the medical benefits of the opium poppy that they called it, The Sacred Anchor of Life, Milk of Paradise, Hand of God, and Destroyer of Grief. Some people believed that opium had magical powers. The Eber papyrus discovered in 1300 BC documented the Egyptian's advice to use condensed juice of the unripe seedpod "to prevent the excessive crying of children."

The Peoples of the Sea – Philistines

Just north of Egypt in the Mediterranean Sea, the political states of Crete and Cyprus were invaded around 1200 BC by migrants called the "Peoples of the Sea." On the island of Cyprus, these invaders crafted surgical-quality culling knives to harvest opium, which they would cultivate, trade, and smoke before the battle.

The "Peoples of the Sea" invaded next the Egyptian Empire from the north by sea and brought with them the opium needed for battle injured soldiers. The Pharaoh's armies stopped the invasion, but the Pharaoh allowed the invaders to settle in the peripheral territories of Egypt, in "Canaan." They grew the poppy plant. These settlers were the Philistines of the Bible. And as you can tell, the name Palestine was derived from the name Philistine.

Sherry interrupted, "I did not know about the "Peoples of the Sea" using so much opium to ease the pain of battle injuries.

Hippocrates

Annie sipped some tea while listening and continued: "About 400 BC, Hippocrates, considered "The father of medicine," dismissed opium's magical attributes of opium. He acknowledged its usefulness to stop bleeding (styptic), as a narcotic and a beneficial drug to treat a variety of internal diseases, women's diseases, and epidemics.

Sherry said, "When my husband and I visited Greece a few years ago, we bought a souvenir with the picture of Hippocrates on it. We may still have it in our house hidden somewhere."

Alexander the Great

Annie continued, "Another impressive person was Alexander the Great. At age 20, he became the king of the ancient Greek kingdom of Macedon. He was a military campaigner who was undefeated in battle. By the age of thirty, he had created one of the largest empires of the ancient world, stretching from Greece to India. He used opium to kill his army's pain as they marched and battled. Around 330 BC, he introduced opium to Persia and India, as he fought in these countries. Subsequently, during the Roman empire, the Roman soldiers used opium for pain relief and create a battle fervor, which dulled soldiers' awareness of the risks and pain of battle."

Sherry commented, "Wars are horrible. But I am glad those poor soldiers had opium to relieve their suffering in battle."

Galen

Annie continued, "Around 300 AD, Galen was as great a Greek physician as Hippocrates. He listed the medical indications for opium. He wrote that opium "... resists poison and venomous bites, cures chronic headache, vertigo, deafness, epilepsy, apoplexy, dimness of sight, loss of voice, asthma, coughs of all kinds, spitting of blood, tightness of breath, colic, the lilac poison, jaundice, hardness of the spleen stone, urinary complaints, fever, dropsies, leprosies, the trouble to which women are subject, melancholy and all pestilences."

Sherry said, "Wow, you have covered an interesting background of the 'Hul Gil – the Plant of Joy,' and the great people that used opium in battle and for treating various medical conditions. Please enjoy more snacks. Would you like some more champagne?"

"No, thank you. I am enjoying the tea," said Annie.

Opium in America

Sherry began reading from her prepared text. She said, "In the 19th and early 20th Centuries, narcotics were widely available in the United States, and they were not regulated. Drug addiction was mostly accidental. Opiates were as readily available in drug stores and grocery stores as aspirin, serving many of the same functions that alcohol, tranquilizers, and antidepressants serve today.

Morphine was the most popular drug, although highly addictive at the time. But the public was ignorant of its habit-forming properties. It was used for medical operations, convalescence, every day potions, and elixirs.

Morphine was commonly regarded as a universal panacea. It was used to treat about fifty-four diseases, including insanity, diarrhea, dysentery, menstrual and menopausal pain, and even nymphomania. That perception was drastically altered after the use of opium was criminalized in the U.S. in 1914.

Annie commented, "That is just a little over a hundred years ago that opium was criminalized in our country."

The Harrison Narcotics Act

Sherry said, "That is right. It was in 1914 that the federal Harrison Narcotics Act was signed into law.

The Act outlawed the nonmedical use of opium, morphine, and cocaine, and made it illegal for any physician or druggist (pharmacist) to prescribe narcotics to an addict.

It was the first federal law to criminalize the nonmedical use of narcotic drugs. Upon its passage, the Harrison Act adversely affected one-quarter of a million drug-addicted citizens and their doctors as potential criminals. The Act was supported by advocates of Prohibition.

By 1916, that's only two years after the Harrison Narcotics Act was passed, 124,000 physicians, 47,000 druggists, 37,000 dentists, 11,000 veterinarians, and 1,600 manufacturers, wholesalers, and importers had registered with the Treasury Department, as required by the Act.

Between 1914 and 1970, the U.S. government pursued both physicians and addicted patients. Hundreds of doctors were arrested and prosecuted for prescribing narcotics to so-called "addicted" patients.

Prosecutions

Between 1914 and 1938, U.S. attorneys prosecuted more than 77,000 people. They included approximately 25,000 doctors arrested under the terms of the Harrison Act for giving narcotic prescriptions to addicts. Many doctors were eventually put on trial, and most of them lost their reputations, careers, or life savings.

By 1928, the average sentence for violation of the Harrison Act was one year and ten months in prison. During that period, Rufus King noted in his book entitled, "The Drug Hang-Up: America's Fifty-Year Folly" that more than 19 percent of all federal prisoners were incarcerated for narcotics offenses.[30] Clinics closed down, and physicians had little choice but to abandon thousands of so-called "addicted" patients. Some of them were probably pain patients who were not addicted but instead might have been physically dependent on the opiates. And as a consequence of abandoning the allegedly "addicted" patients, a black market for narcotics arose.

Annie said, "What a shame. The way they treated addicts and doctors was horrible. Compounding was the rise in the black market, and the distribution and sale of illicit drugs that kill people. So, what happened next?"

---

[30] King, Rufus. 1972. The Drug Hang-Up: America's Fifty-Year Folly. 2d ed. Springfield, Ill.: Charles C. Thomas.

Drug Abuse Prevention and Control Act [31]

Annie continued, "Well, after 56 years, in 1970, the Harrison Act was repealed. But it was replaced by the Comprehensive Drug Abuse Prevention and Control Act of 1970 (DAPCA). This new Act was quite stringent on doctors. It also required the pharmaceutical industry to maintain physical security and strict record-keeping for certain types of drugs. And that brings me to the Controlled Substances Act (CSA).

Title II of DAPCA is called the federal Controlled Substances Act (CSA). It is the legal foundation of the government's fight against the abuse of drugs and other substances. Actually, the CSA is a consolidation of numerous laws regulating the manufacture and distribution of narcotics, stimulants, depressants, hallucinogens, anabolic steroids, and chemicals used in the illicit production of controlled substances.

---

[31] Pub. L. No. 91-513, 84 Stat. 1236 (Oct. 27, 1970).

Annie said, "Wasn't President Richard Nixon, the one who signed the Comprehensive Drug Abuse Prevention and Control Act with the Controlled Substances Act?"

Drug Enforcement Administration (DEA)

Sherry said, "Yes, President Nixon did sign DAPCA. Three years later, in 1973, he also established the Drug Enforcement Administration (DEA) as part of the Justice Department.

The DEA is the Federal Regulatory agency that administers federal laws, maintains opioid records, registers health professionals, sets quotas, and enforces violations of the Controlled Substances Act (CSA).

Annie said, "So, every physician who prescribes drugs listed in the CSA, such as opioids, must be registered and have a federal DEA license. This is separate from the state license to practice medicine. Is the doctor liable under both the state and federal laws for narcotic violations?"

U.S. v. Moore (1975)

Sherry answered, "The answer is yes. In 1975, two years after the DEA was established, the U.S. Supreme Court decided the case of U.S. v. Moore[32]. The issue was, *can a State-licensed physician be federally prosecuted under § 841 of the CSA under his status as a DEA-registrant?*

Dr. Moore was a licensed physician who was registered under the Controlled Substances Act (CSA). He was convicted of unlawful distribution and dispensation of methadone (a controlled substance or addictive drug used in the treatment of heroin addicts) in violation of § 841 of the CSA.

The evidence showed that the physician prescribed large quantities of methadone for patients without giving them adequate physical examinations or specific instructions for its use and charged fees according to the prescribed amount of methadone, rather than for medical services rendered.

The U.S. Supreme Court reversed the Court of Appeals and held that *DEA-r*egistered physicians can be prosecuted when their activities fall outside the usual course of

---

[32] U.S. v. Moore, 423 U.S.122 (1975)

professional practice. Also, a doctor may be criminally charged with unlawfully prescribing (or "diverting") highly addictive narcotic drugs that the Drug Enforcement Agency (DEA) classifies as Schedule II "controlled substances."

Annie asked, "What happens to the doctor at the state level?"

Sherry answered, "At the State level, the Attorney General may prosecute criminal activity of physician offenders, and the State Medical Board and the State Health Care Authority may impose severe civil sanctions."

Annie said, "Great, Sherry. Let's take a short break."

Sherry agreed.

Pain Medicines

A few minutes later, Annie started talking, "The elderly and Alzheimer's patients seem to take too many prescription drugs (called polypharmacy) and over the counter medications. Most of them are on some kind of pain medicine for several chronic conditions. I was surprised at how many of them were taking opioids."

Sherry said, "When pain is not relieved with non-opioid drugs, such as aspirin, acetaminophen, and ibuprofen, or other NSAIDs (Nonsteroidal anti-inflammatory drugs), the next step is to try other drugs, including marijuana or opioids."

Annie said, "But opioids have numerous side effects. They are addictive. And elderly people may inadvertently take an overdose and end up dead."

Sherry said, "You are right about that.

Pearls for Seniors Using Opioids

Annie continued, "I found Online what are the 'pearls' or some vital recommendations for elderly and Alzheimer's patients who are being treated with opioids:

1. Never take a prescription painkiller unless it is prescribed to you. Everyone responds differently to pain medications. What is safe for one person may not be safe for another.

2. Do not take pain medicine with alcohol and never mix the two. It is a dangerous combination that can be deadly. Alcohol increases the toxicity of pain medication.

3. Do not take more doses than prescribed. Even after the effects of pain medicine seem to have worn off, it is still depressing the respiratory system. The body must develop a tolerance to the respiratory depressant effects before the dose can be increased.

4. Use of other sedative or anti-anxiety medications can be dangerous. Combining pain medicines with other sedative drugs, such as valium, can increase the toxicity of pain medication. Only take other medications, if directed by the prescribing doctor.

5. Avoid using prescription painkillers to facilitate sleep. Prescription pain medications can suppress respiration during sleep. Speak to your physician about safe methods to manage pain during sleep.

6. Lock up prescription painkillers. If consumed by children or other family members, or stolen and sold on the street, prescription pain medicine can kill.

7. Finally, an addict is *any individual who habitually uses any narcotic drug so as to endanger the public morals, health, safety, or welfare, or who is so far addicted to the* *use of narcotic drugs as to have lost the power of self-control with reference to his addiction."*

Sherry said, "These are excellent pearls recommendations. Let me read to you what I learned about pain."

Pain

Sherry said, "For centuries, blood pressure, pulse, respiration, and temperature have been regarded as the basic four "vital signs." They provide a simple baseline compass to determine if a patient is ill. Recently, pain has been added to the list and is often regarded as the 5th vital sign.

Pain may last a short time, such as after an injury or surgery. If the pain persists for weeks or months, it is considered chronic. The pain may be mild, moderate, or severe. It may be due to tissue or nerve injury.

Intolerable pain can also affect mood, activity, appetite, sleep, hygiene, and the ability to focus and concentrate, all of which impact the quality of life."

Pain Scales

Annie said, "But you know that pain is quite subjective and difficult to assess objectively. The pain scales that doctors and nurses use to diagnose and treat patients vary with the patient's age and consciousness.

- In unconscious patients or those requiring respirators, who are unable to speak, pain is determined by closely monitoring the patient's four vital signs, and behaviors, such as their level of agitation, irritation, and restlessness.

- For infants and children, there is a pediatric pain scale, with six pictures with facial expressions, the 1st being a happy expression and the 6th describing a grimacing face, suffering from intolerable pain.

- In conscious adult patients, the subjective pain level may be measured by using a scale of 0 to 10, with the number 0 meaning no pain and a score of 10 representing the worst pain imaginable."

Once pain is assessed, what kind of treatments are available before using opioids? An opioid drug should be used only when less dangerous non-opioid medications are ineffective in relieving pain. What have you found out?"

Before Starting Opioids

Sherry said, "You are right. Many elderly people do not use any drugs at first. Some try herbal treatments, acupuncture, manipulative and physical therapy, biofeedback, counseling, or a TENS unit (Transcutaneous electrical nerve stimulation). The next step is to use over-the-counter medications or non-opioid prescription drugs.

Doctors prescribe opioids carefully. They have to follow stringent guidelines to:

1. Evaluate the patient properly;

2. Tailor the treatment to the patient's medical condition;

3. Make sure to fully inform the patient about the opioids;

4. Follow the patients to see if the treatment is beneficial;

5. Consult with pain specialist when needed; and

6. Document everything done in the medical records."

Annie asked, "How does a patient know that the treatment is appropriate?"

Appropriate v. Inappropriate Management

Sherry answered, *"Appropriate pain management* is the physician's responsibility. It is based on trust. The patient expects to receive the right medication and the correct dose that is effective and safe for the medical condition. Based on my reading, I found four main categories where pain management may be inappropriate*:*

1. The pain medicine is needed, but the patient may not receive it;

2. The patient may receive pain medications, but maybe under-treated;

3. The patient may be over-treated; or

4. The patient continues to receive pain medicine despite being ineffective.

We all expect quality medical care. If the pain management is inappropriate, patients may complain to the State licensing boards, which will investigate the doctor, and if necessary, sanction that doctor. Doctors always check for tolerance, dependence, or addiction to the drugs, and address them appropriately."

Office Clinic Policy

Annie said, "Also, medical offices or facilities which use controlled substances for pain management adopt a *"Clinic Policy"* to improve the quality of and access to appropriate pain care. They avoid under- or over-treatment and address concerns about abuse, addiction, and diversion of controlled substances."

21st Century Opioid Crises in America

Sherry said, "Let's finish our discussion with the Opioid Crisis in our country. Deaths from drug overdose have resulted in opioid actions against manufacturers, distributors, and healthcare providers, aimed at reducing the death toll.

Hundreds of lawsuits have been filed across the U.S. against opioid makers and distributors. For instance, in 2007, Purdue Pharma paid a penalty of more than $630 million for misleading marketing.

In 2017, McKesson agreed to pay a $150 million settlement to the Department of Justice for failing to report suspicious orders of pharmaceutical drugs, particularly opioids. In 2008, McKesson paid over $13 million in fines for similar violations.

Kentucky settled with Purdue (for $24 million) and Janssen (for nearly $16 million) in cases alleging misleading marketing.

Mississippi, Oklahoma, Missouri, New Hampshire, Ohio, Nevada, Texas, Florida, North Carolina, North Dakota, Tennessee, and other states, as well as local jurisdictions, filed lawsuits.

Physicians and pharmacists were also sued or disciplined. Those who *under-prescribe* pain medications may confront monetary, licensure, and hospital privileges risks. Those who *overprescribe* faced criminal liability."

Annie commented, "The war on drugs has no end in sight. I shall make every effort to stay away from taking opioids."

Sherry said, "Me too."

With that, Annie and Sherry ended their discussion, chatted about their next get-together, and said goodbye.

Chapter 27
COVID-19 Impact on the Elderly

The day was April 25, 2020. It was a beautiful sunny day with the temperature in the 70s. The lawns were green, and the flowers were simply gorgeous with fresh flowers all around. Sherry had arranged a video call on Skype with Annie just before noon to talk about the horrible new coronavirus.

The two ladies were seated at their computers. They talked from their homes where they have been sheltered in place, as ordered by the Governor at the end of January 2020. They had not seen each other in person since. They were both dressed nicely, though.

They greeted each other enthusiastically. They both looked great. They were rested, though anxious to get back to some kind of normal life. But they knew that there will be a new normal with social distancing, schools teaching online, many employees working from home, and business will be different in the next couple of years.

Sherry said, "I have been trying to keep up with the deluge of information about the new coronavirus."

Annie said, "Me too. But I can't keep up. What have you found out about this deadly coronavirus infection?"

Sherry said, "I have written an article and submitted it for review to my newspaper editor. Most of what I shall tell you is from that article."

Annie said, "That is great."

Sherry said, "Here is how I started my article."

Since 2002, there have been three major **coronavirus** illnesses. The most recent has occurred in 2019-2020. It is a pandemic. The outbreak of that disease occurred over a wide geographic area and affected an exceptionally high population proportion. It will be remembered as a dark moment in history. It was caused by a novel **CO**rona**VI**rus**D**isease 20**19** (**COVID-19**); it was a viral tsunami with global scope. No country was spared. People were immunologically defenseless to the new virus.

Annie said, "Yeah, I have seen pictures of this new coronavirus. Its surface looks like a crown under an electron microscope. It has some kind of projections sticking out."

Sherry said, "That's why it was called 'corona,' which, as you know, is Latin for a crown. It is extremely contagious and deadly. You probably have been checking the news."

Annie said, "Oh, have I!"

Sherry said, "As of this morning, April 25, there were 2,910,298 coronavirus cases documented worldwide and 202,671 deaths. And in the United States, there were 953,918 coronavirus cases documented with 53,858 deaths.

And that is just a little more than a quarter of the fatalities worldwide, said Annie. I read a few days ago that the U.S. fatalities could exceed 100,000 later this year."

Acute Respiratory Distress Syndrome

Sherry added, "Fortunately, less than 5% of the COVID-19 cases develop severe inflammation of the lungs (pneumonia). Here is what I wrote in my article about what happens to these people.

The virus infection damages their air sacs (alveoli) and floods them with inflammatory cells to counter the infection. Additionally, fluid seeps into the air sacs from nearby blood vessels and floods them (pulmonary edema). This fluid affects the regular gas exchange in the lungs. The buildup of fluid compromises the ability of the lungs to diffuse oxygen across the air sacs to nearby small blood vessels (pulmonary capillaries)."

Annie said, "So they cannot get any oxygen. That reminds me of when I used to climb high mountains, I would not be able to get enough oxygen. I would get dizzy and short of breath. What happens to these people?"

Sherry continued reading from her article and said:

"As a result of the diminished supply, the oxygen level in the blood drops (hypoxemia), and less oxygen is transported to body organs, causing a state of low oxygen in the entire body (hypoxia). In severe cases, they have marked difficulty breathing, a condition called 'Acute Respiratory Distress Syndrome' (ARDS)."

"Wow! That sounds terrible," Annie remarked.

Sherry continued and said, "When the lack of oxygen to the body organs (hypoxemia) becomes severe and prolonged, many complications develop. The blood pressure drops to critical levels, referred to as a 'shock.' The functions of various body organs begin to fail, such as heart failure, brain confusion, liver damage, kidney failure, clotting problems, and other complications. These patients are treated in an intensive care setting with oxygen, ventilators, and supportive measures."

Causes of Deaths from COVID-19

Annie commented, "I just read recently that the patients who are placed on a ventilator generally die from drowning in their own fluids."

Sherry said, "Here is what I wrote about the drowning issue:

The severely inflamed air sacs in the lungs become flooded with fluid containing the virus and inflammatory cells. The illness resembles drowning, where the lungs are too full of fluid, making breathing impossible. This happens in a subset of patients who first improve during the first week of their illness, but they get worse in the second week. In fact, the levels of virus in their body tends to fall. But their immune system shifts to overdrive and floods the lungs with inflammatory cells and additional fluid.

It is their body's immune response, rather than the virus, that is lethal. The patients struggle to breathe. Even placing them on the ventilators may not always help. In fact, the majority of individuals placed on ventilators do not get off alive.

The only way to help patients in such dire situations is to place them on a heart-lung machine that delivers oxygen directly to the blood. This rescue therapy machine is called ECMO, which stands for Extracorporeal Membrane Oxygenation (ECMO)."

Annie asked, "Okay, the lungs get flooded and cannot deliver oxygen to the blood, which causes an oxygen shortage. What is the effect of the lack of oxygen on the body organs?" Sherry said,

1. Some patients develop heart failure due to the lack of oxygen (hypoxic cardiomyopathy) and subsequent heart attack (type 2 myocardial infarction). The damage to the heart muscle is due to oxygen deprivation and not due to a typical heart attack (type 1 myocardial infarction). Irregular and rapid heart rhythm may also develop (cardiac arrhythmia).

2. In patients who already have chronic pre-existing cardiovascular or lung problems, obesity, or diabetes, COVID-19 exposes them to oxygen deprivation and the risk of sudden death.

3. Kidney failure, liver, and skeletal muscle injury, as well as clots forming in the leg veins (thrombophlebitis), may also develop due to the lack of oxygen supply, all of which may contribute to the patient's demise."

COVID-19 Targeted the Elderly

Annie said, "I feel sorry for these people. I would hate to be in their situation. We are surely old. I have read that the elderly are targeted at a greater rate than younger people. We must be very careful."

"You are right. Here's what I wrote," said Sherry.

"The impact of COVD-19 on people aged 65 years and older was overwhelming, especially those who lived in a nursing home or long-term care facility.

In Europe, over 90% of people who died of coronavirus were over 60. Among these, half were over

80. In the U.S., the majority of deaths were also elderly. Many nursing homes' residents died from the coronavirus with no family members near them.

American Indians and Black people were also at an elevated risk, especially those with underlying medical conditions, such as chronic lung disease, asthma, heart conditions, severe obesity, diabetes, liver and advanced kidney disease, and those with the compromised immune system due to treatment for cancer or HIV (human immunodeficiency virus)."

The First Coronaviral Illness

Annie asked, "Tell me about the first coronaviral illness, which occurred about two decades ago."

Sherry said, "In **November 2002**, that first severe coronavirus illness emerged in Southern China. The patients had a high fever, sometimes with chills, headache, a general feeling of discomfort, body aches, diarrhea, a dry, nonproductive cough, and low oxygen levels in the blood (hypoxia). Most patients develop pneumonia, and 10-20% of them required mechanical ventilation.

In **March 2003**, the respiratory illness was recognized as a global threat and was called **Severe Acute Respiratory Syndrome (SARS-CoV)**.

By **July 2003**, the World Health Organization (WHO) reported that a total of 8,098 people worldwide became sick with **SARS-CoV**, and 774 (9.6%) patients died due to either pneumonia or respiratory distress syndrome."

"And what about the second coronaviral illness?" Asked Annie.

The Second Coronaviral Illness

"In **September 2012**," Sherry said, "a second outbreak of severe coronavirus illness, with symptoms like **SARS**, was reported in Saudi Arabia and called the **Middle East Respiratory Syndrome (MERS)**.

As of January 16, 2020, 2,521 cases had been reported worldwide, including 919 deaths (crude case fatality of 36%). Most cases have been reported from the Arabian Peninsula."

Ebola

Sherry continued and said, "Interestingly, in 2012, there was also an **Ebola** infectious viral disease; **it was not a coronavirus**. It was first identified in Zaire (modern-day, Democratic Republic of the Congo) in 1976. It got its name from the nearby Ebola River, a tributary of the Congo River.

The Ebola virus originated in fruit bats. It circulated in nonhuman primates, including gorillas, fruit bats, monkeys, antelopes, and porcupines, then in humans. Over 3,000 people died; the death rate was 50%."

The Third Coronaviral Illness

Annie said, "And now, we have the worst coronavirus illness. This is fascinating what you have written. Please continue, Sherry."

"In **December of 2019**, **Dr. Li Wenliang**, 34 years of age, an ophthalmologist, witnessed a new virus outbreak, causing pneumonia, acute respiratory distress, and death in Wuhan, China. Wuhan is the capital of the Hubei Province with a population of 11 million people."

Warning by Dr. Li Wenliang

Sherry continued, "On **December 30, 2019**, Dr. Li posted an online alert in a chat to fellow doctors about the emergence of a Severe Acute Respiratory Syndrome (SARS)-like viral illness and warned them to wear protective clothing to avoid infection. He noted into a chat group that,

'A new coronavirus infection has been confirmed, and its type is being identified. Inform all family and relatives to be on guard.'

Dr. Li was promptly arrested by the local security police, along with seven others in Wuhan, Hubei province, China, on charges of spreading rumors and "severely disturbing the social order." He was forced to sign a document disavowing his statements and agreeing to quit speaking out.

On **December 30, 2019**, however, on the same day when Dr. Li posted notice, the Chinese authorities alerted the **World Health Organization** of an outbreak of a novel strain of coronavirus causing severe illness. And the Chinese started to identify what the virus looked like, study its genetic makeup (genome), and then develop testing for that virus."

Death of Dr. Li Wenliang

Sherry said sadly, "In early February, **Dr. Li**, most unfortunately, contracted the novel coronavirus from a patient. He was hospitalized at Wuhan Central Hospital. On **February 6, 2020, Dr. Li Wenliang died**. His death caused national anger, which triggered a national backlash over freedom of speech and censorship in China."

Annie said, "This is so tragic. I am very sad. I need to get a glass of water. Let's take a break." Annie returned after a few minutes.

The Genome of the Novel Virus

Sherry continued, "On **January 7, 2020,** China reported that the cases in Wuhan were caused by a new coronavirus.

On January 10, 2020, which remarkably was 11 days after Dr. Li's post, the Shanghai Public Health Clinical Center & School of Public Health, along with other collaborators, published the **complete genome** for the new, severe acute respiratory syndrome (SARS) coronavirus 2 (COVID-19 – the abbreviation for coronavirus disease 2019) which was isolated in Wuhan-Hu-1. The genome strongly suggested that **COVID-19 originated in bats**. The virus is the product of natural evolution and selection and not the product of genetic engineering.[33] Researchers at both the Scripps Research Institute and at ETH Zurich reported that COVID-19 naturally arose in humans through interspecies transfer. They put its origin in late November or early December of 2019."

Origin of COVID-19 Virus

Annie asked, "Where did the coronavirus originate from?"

Sherry answered, "COVID-19 probably originated in a 'wet market,' or live animal market, selling seafood and meat in Wuhan, China. Alternatively, it could possibly have been brought to the market by an already infected person. Regardless, someone bought contaminated meat at the market, ate it, got sick, and infected others, creating a ripple effect around the world.

---

[33] Scientists found that the RBD portion of the SARS-CoV-2 spike proteins had evolved to effectively target a molecular feature on the outside of human cells called ACE2, a receptor involved in regulating blood pressure.

On **February 7, 2020,** Chinese researchers at South China Agricultural University reported that the coronavirus was probably transferred to humans through the intermediary species, the pangolin (scaly anteater). The research team tested more than 1,000 samples from wild animals and found a 99% match between the genome sequences of viruses found in pangolins and those in human patients.[34]

Pangolins, scaly anteaters, are the only scaly mammals. They eat ants and termites with their incredibly long, sticky tongue. When threatened, they curl up into a ball. They are valued for their meat and are viewed as a delicacy in some Asian countries. Their scales are used for traditional medicine."

Annie said, "You sure have done a tremendous amount of research on this subject. I would love to hear more."

They chatted a little bit. Sherry was very grateful, then she continued.

---

[34] https://www.nature.com/articles/d41586-020-00364-2

Symptoms of COVID-19 Infection

"Some people with documented COVID-19 infection never develop symptoms (asymptomatic). These individuals unknowingly transmit the virus to other people. Similarly, patients who have not yet developed symptoms (pre-symptomatic) can transmit this highly contagious disease.

The transmission of COVID-19 results from coughing, breathing, or sneezing from an infected person, or touching contaminated objects. The virus can linger in the air and on objects for about 2-3 hours after the patient leaves the room. An average of 1.5-3 people are infected by one patient, thereby spreading the disease rapidly.

Most patients will have the following symptoms between 2-14 days after exposure to COVID-19:

1. Fever (83-99%) and chills, at times, repeated shaking with chills;

2. Cough (59-82%)

3. Fatigue (44-70%)

4. Lack of appetite (Anorexia) (40-84%)

5. Shortness of breath or difficulty breathing (31-40%)

6. Sputum production (28-33%)

7. Muscle pain (Myalgias) (11-35%)

8. Headache, sore throat, a new loss of taste or smell, confusion, runny nose (rhinorrhea), sore throat, coughing up of blood or blood-stained mucus (hemoptysis), nausea, vomiting, and diarrhea have been reported but are less common (<10%)."

Annie said, "Many people get infected but do not have symptoms. Are there different types of COVID-19 infections?"

Types of COVID-19 Infections

Sherry said, "Based on a 2020 study in China of over 44,000 people diagnosed with COVID-19 infection,[35] patients can be classified in the following manner:

(1) 81% had mild to moderate infection (mild symptoms up to mild pneumonia; no hypoxia); they generally do not require hospitalization.

---

[35] The diagnosis of COVID-19 requires the detection of SARS-CoV-2 RNA by reverse transcription-polymerase chain reaction (RT-PCR).

(2)   14% had severe infections (dyspnea, hypoxia, or >50% lung involvement on imaging), which may require hospitalization for management. The chest x-ray shows a nonspecific pattern in the lungs that looks like ground-glass opacities.

(3)   5% were critical (respiratory failure, shock, or multi-organ system dysfunction). Shortness of breath developed after 5 to 8 days from the onset. Acute respiratory distress syndrome (ARDS) developed in 8 to 12 days after the start. The average stay in the ICU ranged from 10 to 12 days. The majority of those who end up on mechanical ventilators become coronavirus fatalities."

COVID-19 Treatment

Annie said, "As of this month, April 2020, it is my understanding that there are no medications or vaccines for COVID-19 that are currently approved by the Food and Drug Administration. How are these patients treated?"

Sherry answered, "The treatment is aimed at relieving the symptoms of COVID-19 infection and providing adequate oxygen, which is the most important.

You remember what I said earlier that patients with acute respiratory distress syndrome (ARDS) may require ventilators. Those who that do not improve with mechanical ventilation and those who develop multiple organ failures, such as heart failure, heart attacks, blood clotting, kidney failure or liver, and muscle injury due to the lack of oxygen supply may benefit from Extracorporeal Membrane Oxygenation (ECMO); it is one of the extracorporeal lung assist (ECLA) technologies."

Annie said, "It's all about oxygen, oxygen, and oxygen!"

First Patient Treated with ECMO

Sherry said[36], "This is interesting. I want to tell you about the first patient, who was placed on an ECMO machine.

On **January 13, 2020**, a 54-year-old man in Wuhan City, China, had chills and fever of 38.1°C. He received no treatment. On January 19, 2020, he returned home from Wuhan City.

On **January 23, 2020**, the disease deteriorated; he had a body temperature of 39°C, muscle pain (myalgia), chest

---

[36] Eur Rev Med Pharmacol Sci 2020; 24 (6): 3385-3389

tightness, and pain. He was treated with antipyretics to lower his temperature and an antibiotic (cephalosporin).

On **January 26, 2020**, he was admitted to Xinyang Central Hospital, still with fever for 13 days as the main complaint. His body temperature was 39.1°C, and he had some fluid (moist rale) in both lungs. His admission blood routine examination was normal, as was the blood oxygen level (pO2 91 mmHg). The chest CT showed an infectious lesion in the right lower lung and chronic inflammation of both lower lungs.

He was given oxygen inhalation (5 L/ minute) by nasal catheter, and antiviral drugs, antibiotics, and steroids (IV Lopinavir/ritonavir, ribavirin, moxifloxacin, cefoperazone/sulbactam, and methylprednisolone). However, patient's conditions became worse, and chest tightness and shortness of breath occurred after activity.

On **January 30, 2020**, his blood oxygen level dropped to pO2 58 mmHg. He was immediately placed on a mechanical ventilator after intubation (orotracheal tube). His chest X-ray showed patchier shadows in both lungs than before.

On **February 3, 2020**, his condition did not improve. He

was deeply sedated and placed on Extracorporeal membrane oxygenation (ECMO) rescue therapy. During ECMO treatment, the patient was daily awakened to assess his consciousness and brain function. After his chest x-ray improved, he was taken off ECMO and subsequently discharged from the hospital in good condition."

Annie commented, "This is truly a fantastic success story. It seems to me that what the body needs most is old fashioned oxygen."

"That's right," said Sherry. "Other COVID-19 cases have received ECMO treatment; they were unresponsive to conventional care. EMCO provides prolonged extracorporeal life support."

Annie asked, "How do these ECMO machines work?"

Sherry answered, "There are two types of machines:

1. The VV ECMO machine provides lung support only, where the blood circulation is adequate and stable. It is used for patients with acute respiratory failure. Instead of the lungs providing oxygen, the patient's blood is taken outside the body through a tube and is enriched with oxygen by the machine. Then, the machine pumps the oxygen-enriched

blood back into the patient, circulating and supplying the body organs with the needed oxygen.

2. Another machine, the VA ECMO or VVA ECMO, provides both lung (respiratory) and blood circulation (hemodynamic) support. It is used in patients with cardiac shock or cardiac arrest and Acute Respiratory Distress Syndrome (ARDS). This machine bypasses the patient's heart and lungs. It does the work of both. It pumps the blood like the heart would, maintains adequate blood pressure, and enriches the blood that passes through the machine with oxygen. Basically, it does double duty until the functions of the heart and lungs recover."

Annie commented, "Tell me more about these ECMO machines, and where have they been used!"

Sherry continued, "EMCO is an accepted treatment option for patients with severe respiratory distress, who are suffering from a lack of oxygen. But the use of ECMO machines is associated with potentially severe side effects, such as the increased risk of hospital infections and poor mental outcomes.

In 2009, during the H1N1 influenza A pandemic, almost a third of the patients admitted to intensive care units (ICUs) were supported by ECMO. In 2015, during the Middle East respiratory syndrome (MERS), caused by a coronavirus (MERS-CoV), ECMO was used on some critical patients.

There are several reports about COVID-19 patients receiving ECMO treatment.[37] However, ECMO is a challenging, resource-intensive, and expensive form of life support that can only be used as a rescue therapy in critical patients."

Annie said, "I can understand why these machines mean life and death for many patients. However, I understand also why it would not be feasible to have enough machines available for use. We have to consider the availability of doctors, nurses, and specialized personnel to operate those complicated and highly sophisticated machines. Can you tell me how this virus spread so quickly from China to the rest of the world?"

---

[37] https://www.futuremedicine.com/doi/10.2217/fca-2020-0040#B1

Spread of COVID-19 to Other Countries

Sherry took a couple of deep breaths, then said, "The same day that Dr. Li posted his notice about Wuhan pneumonia on **December 30, 2019**, a Toronto-based startup (BlueDot) picked up the information and alerted its private sector and Canadian government clients about a cluster of 'unusual pneumonia' cases happening around a market in Wuhan, China.

BlueDot uses a platform built around artificial intelligence, machine learning, and big data to track and predict the outbreak and spread of infectious diseases worldwide. Basically, BlueDot is an automated infectious disease surveillance platform, an early warning system that can provide a time-critical heads-up to health professionals around the world and potentially save thousands of lives. The system flagged articles in Chinese that reported 27 pneumonia cases associated with a market with seafood and live animals in Wuhan.

The next day, **December 31, 2019**, BlueDot identified the cities that were highly connected to Wuhan using things like global airline ticketing data to anticipate where the infected might be traveling. The international destinations that BlueDot anticipated would have the highest volume of travelers from Wuhan were Bangkok, Hong Kong, Tokyo, Taipei, Phuket, Seoul, and Singapore. In the end, 11 of the cities at the top of their list were the first places to see COVID-19 cases.

The 2019-20 timeline for the coronavirus pandemic is detailed on a day-to-day basis online.[38]

On **January 6, 2020**, the US Centers for Disease Control and Prevention got the word out about the new viral infection.

On **January 9, 2020**, the World Health Organization notified the public of a flu-like outbreak in China and stated that a cluster of pneumonia cases had been reported in Wuhan, possibly from vendors' exposure to live animals at the Huanan Seafood Market.

On **January 13 and 16, 2020**, the first cases of COVID-19 appeared in Thailand and Japan, respectively.

On **January 23, 2020**, the Chinese government placed

---

[38]https://en.wikipedia.org/wiki/Timeline_of_the_2019%E2%80%9320_coronavirus_pandemic_in_January_2020

the City of Wuhan and other cities on lockdown, and the WHO warned that 'all countries should be prepared for containment [of the virus], including active surveillance, early detection, isolation and case management, contact tracing and prevention of onward spread.'

On **January 24, 2020**, the first five cases who were tested and confirmed to have COVID-19infections were reported in France. They were published in The Lancet on March 27, 2020.[39]

The patients were three men (aged 31 years, 48 years, and 80 years) and two women (aged 30 years and 46 years), all of Chinese origin. They had traveled to France from China around mid-January, 2020.

Testing was done at the National Reference Center for Respiratory Viruses (The Institute Pasteur, Paris, and Hospices Civils de Lyon, Lyon, France). They all tested positive for COVID-19. The two women had mild symptoms diagnosed within a day of exhibiting symptoms. They recovered well.

---

[39] https://www.thelancet.com/journals/laninf/article/PIIS1473-3099(20)30200-0/fulltext

The two young men first improved but had worsening of their infection around 10 days after the onset, despite a decreasing viral load in nasopharyngeal samples.

All four patients recovered and were discharged by February 19, 2020. The 80-year-old man had a rapid evolution and developed multiple organ failures with a persistent high viral load in the lower and upper respiratory tract. The virus spread to his body and was detected in his plasma. On February 14, 2020, he died on day 14 of his illness."

Annie interrupted, "Based on what you said, the United States knew about the new viral infection in Wuhan, China, since January 6. What did our government officials do about it?"

COVID-19 in America

Sherry answered, "On **January 17, 2020,** the U.S. started screening for symptoms of coronavirus at certain airports. The next day, **January 18**, the U.S. Health and Human Services Secretary, Alex Azar, briefed President Donald Trump on the dangers of the virus.

On **January 21, 2020,** the first U.S. case of coronavirus infection was confirmed in Washington state. By **January 24,** there were two confirmed cases of the disease in the United States.

On **January 27, 2020**, the Centers for Disease Control and Prevention (CDC) issued a Level 3 warning to avoid nonessential travel to China.

On **January 29, 2020**, U.S. White House Aide, Peter Navarro, wrote a memo warning that the coronavirus was likely far more contagious than the flu, more like the bubonic plague or smallpox, and that it could kill up to half a million Americans.

On **January 30, 2020**, the WHO declared the coronavirus infection a global public health emergency.

On **January 31, 2020,** the U.S. stated that it would deny entry to foreign nationals who had traveled in China in the last 14 days. However, during January, many people had already traveled from China to the United States. Thus, by the end of January, the viral infection was well established in the United States.

On **February 6, 2020**, the first known coronavirus-related fatality in the U.S. was a 57-year-old Northern California woman, Patricia Dowd, from the Bay Area who suddenly died. She was always active, in good health, worked as a manager, exercised routinely, watched her diet, did not smoke, and took no medications. She had flu-like symptoms for a few days, then appeared to recover. Santa Clara County in California announced on **April 21, 2020**, that, at postmortem, tissue samples confirmed that she tested positive for coronavirus.

On **February 17, 2020**, the County also reported a second fatality, a 69-year-old man who developed flu-like symptoms a few days before he died; he tested positive postmortem for coronavirus.

Neither of the two victims who died in February had been tested for the virus at the time of their deaths because testing capacity was limited. Testing for COVID-19 was only available through the U.S. Centers for Disease Control and Prevention (CDC). Testing was restricted to people who had a known travel history and showed certain symptoms.

The medical examiner suspected that the first two deaths were caused by Covid-19. He sent autopsy tissue from the

379

deceased to the CDC for definitive testing. They had COVID-19. These two coronavirus-related deaths presumably represented community transmission because neither of them had a recent travel history that would have exposed them to the virus.

On **February 26, 2020**, the CDC announces what was then thought to be the first possible U.S. case of community spread in California.

On **February 29, 2020**, the third coronavirus-related death occurred in Washington state.

On **March 11, 2020**, the World Health Organization declared the rapidly spreading coronavirus outbreak a **pandemic**, and that the virus would likely spread to all countries on the globe.

On **April 2, 2020**, the head of the World Health Organization's office in Europe stated that more than 95% of people who have died of coronavirus on the continent have been aged over 60, with more than half aged over 80.[40] There were then 30,098 coronavirus deaths reported in Europe, mostly in Italy, France, and

---

[40] https://time.com/5814330/who-europe-over-60/

Spain. More than four in five of the people who died had at least one other underlying chronic medical disorder, as noted earlier."

Annie asked, "Well, what does the future hold for us? When might we expect some kind of treatment for this virus? I have been reading about experiments with medications, vaccines, antibodies, and testing techniques for the whole virus and some of its parts. What have you written about that?"

Future Treatment of COVID-19

Sherry answered, "Coronaviruses represent a threat to human health and the global economy. In 2020, the first consideration is to focus on novel countermeasures to control the COVID-19 pandemic. Secondly, attention must be paid to the vast array of high-threat animal viruses poised for human emergence in the future. As for COVD-19, several things are being investigated.

1.   The most effective ways to treat coronaviruses are vaccines. With COVID-19, success will be achieved by preventing the virus from attaching to the human body cells. But the development and testing of new vaccines take one or

more years. Furthermore, the virus may mutate, and another novel virus may emerge. So, other approaches are necessary in the meantime.

2.   Researchers are looking for effective and safe broad-spectrum antivirals, which mimic the genome structure of the virus and stall the replication process. However, most antiviral drugs do not work well with this virus. For instance, Remdesivir has not been successful in treating COVID-19. Hydroxychloroquine and Chloroquine seem to be harmful, and the FDA has warned about their use.

3.   Another approach is the use of convalescent blood plasma from recovered patients. The blood contains antibodies against the virus. This approach is slower to develop but is preferable because there are antibodies in the plasma that can be harvested and mass-produced through biotechnology. These can also be used to give "passive immunization" and short-term immunity to certain individuals that may be at high risk of becoming infected.

4.   Finally, there is one other attractive method for treating COVID-19, and that is using gene therapy. The treatment is delivered to the upper human airways through another virus [adeno-associated virus (AAV)]. This virus

has been proven to be safe and effective for human use. Gene therapy would entail a fast, targeted delivery of antibodies to the upper airways to give short-term protection. Such tools can be developed, adapted, and tested quickly. It is likely that a single dose could mount a protective response within a week and last for more than a year."

Annie said, "I sincerely hope that some treatment will become available this year. In the meantime, we have to listen to our Public Health Care officials. Don't we?"

Message from the U.S. Public Health Officials

Sherry answered, "Yes, older people like us should:

- Stay home if possible;
- Wash hands often;
- Avoid close contact (six feet, which is about two arm lengths) with sick people;
- Clean and disinfect frequently touched surfaces;
- Avoid all cruise and nonessential air travel; and
- Call a healthcare professional if one gets sick.

Social isolation or distancing is absolutely necessary for the elderly. It is expected that 40-60% of the total U.S. population may become infected with COVID-19 by the end of 2020."

Annie and Sherry chatted a little longer. Annie was so pleased to listen to Sherry and learn about the 2020 COVID-19 pandemic. Then, they bid each other farewell until they meet in person again.

9 7 8 1 9 5 2 2 6 3 5 7 6